"For over four decades, Chip Berlet has tirelessly exposed the reactionary forces that threaten our democratic foundations. With this book he assembles prescient contributions from a diverse array of scholar-activists committed to confronting anti-democratic threats both within and outside of political parties. The authors lay bare the roots of current political challenges; and offer progressive paths forward. Anyone seeking astute analysis of the forces that drive right-wing populism in the 21st century should look no further than this volume."

Professor David Cunningham, *Author of* Klansville, USA: The Rise and
Fall of the Civil Rights-Era Ku Klux Klan

"This book will help you to understand how authentic movements harmonize individual freedom and aspirations with community ones. Communities raise up authentic leaders rather than leaders raising themselves up above their communities because of their empire credentials. Movements for liberation start with a common vision that the collective agrees to struggle and risk together to achieve."

Ruby Sales, *Civil Rights and Human Rights Activist, founder,*
Spirit House Project

"We can build a world based on friendship or fear. The authors in this volume document what happens when political strategists choose to mobilize our fears and unilateralism that are elements of de-civilization."

Professor Mohammad Jafar Mahallati, *Presidential Scholar in Islamic Studies and*
Chair in Middle East and North African Studies at Oberlin College

"If you want to know about right-wing populism you should read Chip Berlet."

Professor Noam Chomsky, *Emeritus, Massachusetts Institute of Technology.*
Linguistics department, University of Arizona in Tucson. Author of Global Discontents:
Conversations on the Rising Threats to Democracy

"Chip Berlet continues to courageously and brilliantly expose the dangers of white supremacy and Christian nationalism. This book is a fascinating and indispensable roadmap of the US political right … arriving just in time!"

Penny Rosenwasser, *PhD. Founding Board Member: Jewish Voice for Peace.*
Author of Hope into practice: Jewish women choosing justice despite our fears

"For scholars seeking a better understand events which led to the Trump Presidency, this is a must read. For interested readers, shocked by the rise of the American right, this is the history you need. For Americans who genuinely desire for our country to live up to ideals of our Constitution - ideas of justice and equality—this is where you start."

Professor Angelia Wilson, *University of Manchester, England; Chair of the Political*
Studies Association of the United Kingdom. Author of The Politics of Intersectionality:
Politics, Policy, and Power

TRUMPING DEMOCRACY

Since 2014, over 80 people have been killed in the United States of America by Right-wing terrorists. In 2016 Donald Trump was elected President of the United States and received substantial support from White nationalists.

This book explains the increase in violent White nationalism and Trump's ascendancy in the context of the backlash against the presidency of Barack Obama. It demonstrates how there is a dynamic relationship between the Republican Party, various Right-wing populist movements, and the Right. Far Right social movements, political campaigns and the online presence of the so-called 'Alt-Right' are all discussed. The book argues that unfair hierarchies of race, gender, and class are not aberrational tremors in America, but the fracturing bedrock of a nation in which being White, male, Christian, or straight no longer ensures a stable floor for power, status, or privilege.

This is vital reading for students, researchers, and activists interested in American politics and the dangers of Right-wing movements and political parties.

John Foster "Chip" Berlet is an American investigative journalist, research analyst, photojournalist, scholar, and activist specializing in the study of Right-wing movements in the United States.

ROUTLEDGE STUDIES IN FASCISM AND THE FAR RIGHT

Series editors: Nigel Copsey, *Teesside University*, and **Graham Macklin,** *Center for Research on Extremism (C-REX), University of Oslo.*

This new book series focuses upon fascist, far right and right-wing politics primarily within a historical context but also drawing on insights from other disciplinary perspectives. Its scope also includes radical-right populism, cultural manifestations of the far right and points of convergence and exchange with the mainstream and traditional right.

Titles include:

The Far Right and the Environment
Politics, Discourse and Communication
Edited by Bernhard Forchtner

Vigilantism against Migrant and Minorities
Edited by Tore Bjørgo and Miroslav Mareš

Trumping Democracy
From Reagan to the Alt-Right
Edited by Chip Berlet

A.K. Chesterton and the Evolution of Britain's Extreme Right, 1933–1973
Luke LeCras

Cumulative Extremism
A Comparative Historical Analysis
Alexander J. Carter

CasaPound Italia
Contemporary extreme-right politics
Caterina Froio, Pietro Castelli Gattinara, Giorgia Bulli and Matteo Albanese

The International Alt-Right
Fascism for the 21st Century?
Patrik Hermansson, David Lawrence, Joe Mulhall and Simon Murdoch

For more information about this series, please visit: https://www.routledge.com/Routledge-Studies-in-Fascism-and-the-Far-Right/book-series/FFR

TRUMPING DEMOCRACY

From Reagan to the Alt-Right

Edited by Chip Berlet

Routledge
Taylor & Francis Group

LONDON AND NEW YORK

First published 2020
by Routledge
2 Park Square, Milton Park, Abingdon, Oxon OX14 4RN

and by Routledge
52 Vanderbilt Avenue, New York, NY 10017

Routledge is an imprint of the Taylor & Francis Group, an informa business

Visit https://doi.org/10.6084/m9.figshare.c.4493693

British Library Cataloguing-in-Publication Data
A catalogue record for this book is available from the British Library

Library of Congress Cataloging-in-Publication Data
A catalog record has been requested for this book

ISBN: 978-1-138-21248-0 (hbk)
ISBN: 978-1-138-21249-7 (pbk)
ISBN: 978-1-315-43841-2 (ebk)

Typeset in Bembo
by Taylor & Francis Books

CONTENTS

FOREWORD

What we know is that history is written by those privileged enough to have an education and own a pen. In many ways, this moving collection documents an American history rarely told in school curriculum, on national monuments, or shared in the wider media political discourse. If you understand the world in binary terms, this is definitely a partisan narrative—so are those traditional stories celebrating American history. Histories that challenge the hegemonic, easy, narrative must be written by those with evidence, confidence, and the audacity to use their voice.

The history found in these pages tells of the struggle to understand the meaning of American values of freedom, equality, and justice in a world where very few with privilege and audacity live those values. Political Research Associates is a leading voice in American politics because it challenges leaders and citizens to see the injustice and inequalities. The PRA researchers write through a lens of concern and worry about the gaps between who America could be and who it sometimes, and all too vividly, has become.

At least since the deaths of John F. Kennedy and Martin Luther King, polite political society has understood the importance of keeping the articulation of hatred in the private sphere. In addition, the Vietnam War, Nixon, Iran-Contra taught us to question the politics of private dealings, the lack of government transparency and to let go of naïve assumptions that statesman are concerned for the interests of all citizens. For the last 40 years in politics, those with more far-Right intentions have worked behind the scenes through campaign finance, personal networks and, often, through the language of culture wars. Strategy, as the military experts define it, is about using all the relevant instruments of power and to that end the Right has had significant moments of success. Many of those are documented here.

The passion-fueled tsunami unleashed first by the Tea Party and then by the Trump campaign, clearly marked a change in temper and tone of American political discourse. When US Presidential candidates do not reject a discourse of hate, we cannot be surprised that becomes an invitation for many to turn up the volume of hate in our public square.

However, academic scholars, researchers and commentators alike must not dismiss this passion as uneducated, irrational political outbursts. As Walzer (2002) argues, "it's a common mistake to associate passionate intensity with ignorance". A zero-sum political strategy requires one to make use of all instruments at one's disposal to gain power. Those desiring political leadership have made a rational, logical judgment to fan flames of populism. Many on the Right have benefitted tremendously from this strategy and now sit by the White House fireside glowing in their accomplishments.

In this collection, researchers document American political events in real time. They offer analysis which places these events in the context of American history and what many in the mainstream would assume are values at the heart of our republic. In doing so, they draw upon leading academic research and a range of theoretical frames found in sociology and politics. Their analysis is intelligent, thoughtful and reflects years of first-hand evidence-gathering from interviews, participant observation, and poring over reams of documents produced by Right-wing political leaders. The result is a profound eye-witness account of an American history not taught in classrooms but lived by thousands of Americans on the margins, as well as those now agog in the remnants of the American political middle.

For scholars seeking a better understand events which led to the Trump Presidency, this is a must read. For interested readers, shocked by the rise of the American Right, this is the history you need. For Americans who genuinely desire for our country to live up to ideals of our Constitution—ideas of justice and equality—this is where you start. And then you roll up your sleeves.

Angelia R. Wilson, Ph.D.
Professor, University of Manchester, England; Chair of the
Political Studies Association of the United Kingdom

PREFACE

For justice-minded people, the unfolding drama of the 2016 presidential contest was disorienting and frightening. The usual jockeying for control of the Republican Party among Christian Nationalists, neoconservatives, and Chamber of Commerce types quickly gave way to primaries—and then a general election—dominated by stridently bigoted exclusionary populism. As the United States under the Presidency of Donald Trump was gearing up for the 2020 midterm election the nation was already unstable and in crisis mode.

We've all witnessed ugly rhetoric in presidential campaigns before, but this campaign descended into a different kind of threat. Donald J. Trump launched his presidential candidacy with a speech vilifying Latino immigrants as sexual predators. Trump closed his campaign with an advertisement built around classic antisemitic themes; lambasting "establishment" elites on Wall Street and in Washington, DC "that have bled our country dry." He singled out for punishment or outright expulsion African Americans, immigrants, Muslims, and others. Trump's misogynist attacks on women were astonishing.

Through a consistent, racially coded narrative of "makers" versus "takers", Trump promised to deliver "real" Americans—defined in exclusionary racial and cultural terms—from the parasites threatening them from above and below. He courted White nationalists and adopted a rhetoric of economic nationalism that implicitly blamed the financial and social insecurity of many White Americans on people of color and liberal elites (sometimes coded as Jews). Political commentators Left, Right, and Center considered the obvious parallels to the presidential campaigns of segregationist George Wallace, and to mid-20th-Century fascism. The media circus around the primaries pulled the national conversation to the Right, opening space for liberal politicians to soften commitments to immigrant justice and other progressive demands while appearing to be champions of inclusion.

In the general election, Trump continued to mobilize racism, xenophobia, misogyny, and economic resentment. In a context of historic levels of income and wealth inequality, and a global crisis of legitimacy for liberal democracies, he also distinguished himself as the only major party candidate on the November 2016 ballot to reject the existing political and economic order as an abject failure. In the end, Trump forged a cross-class, cross-gender coalition of White voters sufficient to win an electoral college victory.

Many people wonder, how could this possibly have come to pass? How could open-throated bigotry and fake news win a national election?

From the mid-1970s forward, progressive activists, along with serious journalists, scholars, (and a handful of political analysts in both the Republican and Democratic party) warned of the takeover of the Republican Party by a bourgeoning alliance of hard Right forces seeking to roll back the political and economic system of the United States to the Gilded Age of unregulated capitalism.

These observers were witness to efforts on the part of Right-wing apologists for racial, gender, and economic inequality to advance an elitist policy agenda that was unpopular then—and remains so now—by inciting a popular insurgency against government and the social sector. They targeted progressive movements fighting for inclusion and equity for women, LGBTQ people, religious minorities, and people of color. By waging "culture wars" on divisive issues such as school integration, LGBTQ inclusion, abortion, and affirmative action, among others, this New Right divided and conquered the coalitions built to support Roosevelt's New Deal and Great Society reforms. The Rightists launched attacks on civil rights, feminist, sexual liberation, and other movements that sought to open society to a more expansive view of citizenship. The New Right's goal was minority rule; how to push their unpopular ideas into public policy against the interests of a deeply divided majority.

To defeat the upsurge in nationalism and forestall the specter of authoritarianism, progressives will need to disrupt, defuse, and—critically—compete for portions of the constituency mobilized by the Right since the election campaign of Ronald Reagan, with his appeal to a backward-looking nationalism in the slogan he used in his 1980 presidential campaign (and recycled by Trump): "Let's Make America Great Again."

Nations are founded on territory, managed through institutions, and bounded by physical borders, but nationalism is about belief. It is not about who we are in fact, but about who we aspire to be. Nationalism is the realm of believing in what we should stand for, what those beliefs mean for us, who gets to belong, and how we will relate to one another. It is within nationalism that these beliefs are contested.

Nationalism is the currency of nation-building in the modern world. It has always been at the heart of American politics. Every fight over race, gender, sexuality, disability inclusion, workers' rights, taxes, religious freedom, education, and immigrant rights has been a fight over the meaning of citizenship.

Do we live in a patriarchal state or a gender equal one? Are we a Christian theocratic state or one in which there is genuine religious freedom? Which will rule, White racial nationalism, or multicultural civic nationalism? How will we balance the need for strong communities and healthy, prosperous workers with the profit interests of business? Are migrant workers entitled to the same rights as citizen workers? Just who gets to be "American?" These are the questions that have been and are now at the heart of American politics.

One thing we desperately need is a compelling story about race and the economy to upend the false but increasingly dominant Right-wing populist explanation: that liberal elites have usurped the wealth and social standing of "real Americans" and doled it out as patronage to communities of color and other undeserving masses of "takers."

Race was an idea created originally to justify the enslavement of a people and has displayed pernicious staying power in the centuries since the racism that once helped to build the White middle class has in recent decades been strategically redeployed by the Right to undermine public support for democratic institutions and antipoverty programs. The result: falling real wages and accelerated income and wealth inequality even among Whites. Simply put, White racism is destroying the American middle and working classes.

But that story is not told clearly, loudly, or often enough. As during the 2016 presidential contest, most liberal and even progressive discussion of the economy addresses race, if at all, only in terms of disproportionate economic hardship. Seldom does it address the ways that our economic opportunities are deeply structured around race and gender. Much of the recent national discussion about racism has centered on critical realities of deadly state violence while sidelining on the one hand powerful critiques of the structural economic exclusion and exploitation of people of color; and on the other hand, the gendered violence disproportionately visited upon women of color and transgender women.

What we need is a synthesis of our racial, economic, and gender justice movements that offers an alternative to neoliberal austerity economics. Let's make it clear that racism and sexism are now acceptable vehicles for economic advancement for the growing White precariat. Only a multi-racial, multi-gender equality movement of and for the 99 percent can accomplish that. We can start by flipping the script on race, and gender, and the economy. We need to reach out to those being drawn to snake oil solutions to their suffering. This edited collection is part of that project.

The authors are among the most knowledgeable and thoughtful researchers and analysts of Right wing and authoritarian movements in the US. Collectively, they trace the rise of the Right in the United States from the Right-wing backlash against President Roosevelt, through the presidential campaign of Ronald Reagan in 1980, to the first year of the presidency of Donald Trump.

What all the authors have in common is a relationship with Political Research Associates, a national watchdog and think tank challenging exclusionary Right-wing ideology founded in the early years of Reagan's first term as president. PRA uses an analytical lens that considers the issues of race, gender, and class as inextricably linked. This is the model established by the gentle yet fierce academic Jean

V. Hardisty, PhD when she founded Political Research Associates in 1981. Jean died in 2015.

This collection of studies traces the rise of the Right in the United States from the presidential election campaign for Ronald Reagan in 1980 through to the first years of the Presidency of Donald Trump.

As these chapters demonstrate, contrary to the corporate media narrative, *we did see it coming.*

Tarso Luís Ramos and Scot Nakagawa

CONTRIBUTORS

Nikhil Aziz came to work at Political Research with a PhD and an analysis of the global systems of oppression weaving together injustice based on race, gender, and class. He rose to the position of associate director at PRA. Aziz is currently director of Land, Water and Climate Justice at the American Jewish World Service. Before joining AJWS, he was executive director of Grassroots International, which funded social movements for resource rights in the Global South and did advocacy in the United States. Aziz has served on the boards of Africa Today Associates, Massachusetts Asians & Pacific Islanders for Health, MASALA (Massachusetts Area South Asian Lambda Association), Resist, the Jessie Smith Noyes Foundation, the Human Rights Funders Network, and the Engaged Donors for Global Equity (EDGE Funders). More details about Aziz and his industrious career are at https://ajws.org/author/naziz/.

Chip Berlet describes himself as an investigative journalist abducted by progressive sociologists. Dropping out of the University of Denver in 1973 to work in the College Press Service (CPS) collective in Denver. Berlet continued to be active in the antiwar and civil rights movements in that city, while also writing for several underground and alternative publications. CPS sent him to Washington, DC to cover education and other campus-related issues. He moved on to be editor of the National Student Association magazine, and then worked at the National Student Education Fund as a researcher and publications editor. His website is https://www.researchforprogress.us/topic/.

Berlet was Washington correspondent for *High Times* magazine when in 1977 he and his partner moved to Chicago and spent ten years in labor and anti-racism projects. His photographs and articles about anti-Black racial unrest spurred on by neo-Nazis and Klansmen were carried nationwide in the alternative press. Berlet helped establish a legal newsletter on suing police for abuse and other misconduct and became editor of *The Public Eye Magazine*. This led in 1981 to his employment at what became Political Research Associates.

In 1998 he was invited to present: "Mad as Hell: Right-wing Populism, Fascism, and Apocalyptic Millennialism," a paper presented at the 14th World Congress of Sociology. Repeated abductions followed. Berlet is co-author (with Matthew N. Lyons) of *Right-wing Populism in America: Too Close for Comfort* (2000). Berlet's byline has appeared in numerous alternative, mainstream, and scholarly publications. Berlet was a co-coordinator of the national emergency strategy retreat for Defending Democracy and Pluralism at the Blue Mountain Center in 1993. https://www.progressive-movements.us/commons/statements/.

Pam Chamberlain is a former senior researcher at Political Research Associates, with an expertise in gender justice, education, and campus issues. She holds degrees from Smith College and the University of Chicago. Chamberlain has championed the needs of LGBTQ youth since the 1970s as a feminist teacher, administrator, government agency manager, and social science researcher. She was a founding member of the groundbreaking Massachusetts Safe Schools Program for Gay and Lesbian Students, the first public project of its kind in the country. Chamberlain has worked on dozens of social justice projects including the Resist Foundation, Women's Pentagon Action, and PFLAG. She has designed attitudinal and behavior change campaigns for schools and community groups. Chamberlain is the author of the PRA study *Deliberate Differences: Progressive and Conservative Campus Activism in the United States* (2004). https://www.politicalresearch.org/2005/09/05/conservative-campus-organizing-growing-pains-or-arrested-development.

Frederick Clarkson was among the first wave of serious progressive journalists to study the roots and branches of the interlocking Right-wing movements in the United States. He is surprised that he has now been writing about religion and politics generally, and the Christian Right in particular, for about 40 years. His work has appeared in a wide range of publications, from *Mother Jones, Ms*, and *Church & State* magazines to *The Christian Science Monitor, Religion Dispatches*, and *Salon.com*. He is the author of *Eternal Hostility: The Struggle Between Theocracy and Democracy* and editor of *Dispatches from the Religious Left: The Future of Faith and Politics in America*. All of which landed him at Political Research Associates where he is a Senior Research Analyst. His work and views are often featured in national and international media, large and small, including recently *The New York Times, The Guardian, Religion News Service* and the *BBC*. The late author and Southern raconteur Joe Bageant, wrote, "Fred Clarkson, a New England Yankee with a streak of liberty a mile wide, has been thinking and writing about this longer than anybody I know." Clarkson participated in the national emergency strategy retreat for Defending Democracy and Pluralism at the Blue Mountain Center in 1993. Follow him on *Twitter* @FredClarkson. His website is at https://www.frederickclarkson.org/.

Alex DiBranco began challenging the Right-wing backlash while she was at Dartmouth College where Right-wing funders had planted a conservative newspaper. As this book goes to press, DiBranco is a Sociology PhD student at Yale University, and is working on her dissertation. She has been studying the US Christian Right, reproductive justice, and sexual violence movements for several decades. She was previously the Communications Director at Political Research Associates. During her tenure as a Change.org editor and senior organizer specializing in women's and immigrant rights, she helped the company grow from six people to more than a hundred employees globally. DiBranco researched torture and human intelligence in Iraq and Afghanistan for the book *None of Us Were Like This Before*, and her writing has appeared in progressive outlets including *RH Reality Check, The Nation, Alternet,* and the *Public Eye Magazine*. DiBranco is the director of the Institute for Research on Male Supremacism online at: https://www.malesupremacism.org/.

Frederick Douglass, a legendary abolitionist, was an orator who in the mid-1800s drew crowds as he painted a picture of a United States freed from the sin of slavery. His quote in this book is from a speech on the abolition of slavery in the British West Indies, which includes Haiti and other islands in the Caribbean. The British Parliament had passed the Slavery Abolition Act in 1833 and it took effect in most British colonies on August 1, 1834. Douglass was speaking in Canandaigua, New York, August 3, 1857 (near Rochester, NY) urging the end of the slavocracy in the South in the United States. His goal of the abolition of slavery was carried out only through the US Civil War (1861–1865) in which over 600,000 soldiers died as well as a large number of civilians. https://rbscp.lib.rochester.edu/4398/.

Michelle Fawcett, PhD, is a graduate of the University of California, Berkeley (BA), the London School of Economics and Political Science (MSc) and New York University's Tisch School of the Arts (PhD), where she taught media and communications. While there she also co-founded the New York City Grassroots Media Conference and organized as a shop steward with UAW Local 2110, which won the first graduate student labor union at a private university in the country. Fawcett's dissertation on the neoliberalization of culture in public-private partnerships at UNESCO won the Cinema Studies department's best dissertation award in 2009 and was a Graduate School of Arts and Science Dean's Outstanding Dissertation Award nominee. In 2011, Fawcett founded the Occupy USA media project, a series of articles and videos covering 40 occupations in 27 states, with journalist Arun Gupta, with whom she wrote "Inside the Occupy Movement," *The Progressive* magazine, 2012. With Gupta she visited nearly 30 occupations in 20 states in two months, filing dispatches along the way. Michelle currently lives in the Northwest and is involved in documentary films and their distribution. She was seriously injured by a police grenade while at a protest against neofascist groups in Portland, Oregon. https://www.oregonlive.com/portland/2018/09/portland_woman_says_she_was_ma.html/.

Bill Fletcher, Jr. is a former president of TransAfrica Forum, writer, and trade unionist. He is a Senior Scholar with the Institute for Policy Studies; an editorial board member of BlackCommentator.com; and in the leadership of several other projects. An activist since his teen years, after graduating from college he went to work as a welder in a shipyard. Over the years he has been active in workplace and community struggles as well as electoral campaigns. He has worked for several labor unions in addition to serving as a senior staff-person in the national AFL-CIO. Fletcher is the co-author (with Peter Agard) of *The Indispensable Ally: Black Workers and the Formation of the Congress of Industrial Organizations, 1934–1941* (W.G. Fletcher: 1987); the co-author (with Dr Fernando Gapasin) of *Solidarity Divided: The Crisis in Organized Labor and a New Path Toward Social Justice* (2008); and the author of *"They're Bankrupting Us" – And Twenty Other Myths About Unions* (2012). Fletcher is a syndicated columnist and a regular media commentator on television, radio and the Web. https://www.billfletcherjr.com/.

Arun Gupta is a journalist who has written for the *Washington Post, The Nation, Raw Story, The Guardian*, and *Jacobin*. Gupta co-founded the *Indypendent* in September 2000 and built it into an award-winning newspaper. In 2011, he co-founded the *Occupied Wall Street Journal* and covered the Occupy movement across the United States for outlets including the *Guardian, the Nation*, and *Salon*. During that time, he helped found other Occupy newspapers across the country. Gupta is a Lannan Foundation writing fellow and a recipient of a Wallace Global Fund grant for his reporting. A graduate of the French Culinary Institute in New York City, he is co-author, with Michelle Fawcett, of "Inside the Occupy Movement," *The Progressive* magazine, 2012. https://www.patreon.com/arunguptareporter/.

Jean V. Hardisty, PhD, was the founder of the progressive think-tank Political Research Associates, which began as Midwest Research in Chicago. In the late 1970s Hardisty was studying the anti-feminist movement for the American Civil Liberties Union of Illinois. The ideological and political leader of that movement was Phyllis Schlafly (who lived in midstate Illinois near St. Louis, Missouri) from where Schlafly ran "Stop ERA;" the successful national Right-wing campaign to block passage of the "Equal Rights Amendment."

When Hardisty was unable to convince feminist and liberal political organizations "Inside the Beltway" that Right-wing activists were skilled strategists and social movement organizers, she raised the funds to start a think tank in Chicago that began with her learning the research model of the union-supported investigative outfit Group Research Report in Washington, DC.

Back in Chicago in 1981, with a tiny office and computer system the size of a stove, Hardisty founded a progressive think tank named "Midwest Research." and began subscribing to hundreds of Right-wing periodicals and developing a model of the different sectors of Right-wing organizing which is still used today. Moving the offices to the Boston area, the name was changed to Political Research Associates. There Hardisty authored *Mobilizing Resentment: Conservative Resurgence from the John Birch Society to the Promise Keepers* (1999). Hardisty was a co-coordinator of the national emergency strategy retreat for Defending Democracy and Pluralism at the Blue Mountain Center in 1993.

Hardisty described herself as a political scientist and lesbian feminist activist. She died in 2015 after a long struggle against cancer. In a memorial tribute Gloria Steinem called Hardisty a "prophet." Her friends and allies called her both gentle and fierce—an accomplished scholar, strategist, mentor, activist, writer, and public speaker. Hardisty was all that and more. https://www.politicalresearch.org/a-tribute-to-jean-v-hardisty/. Hardisty's work is collected at: https://jeanhardisty.com/booksandessays.html/.

Matthew N. Lyons has been writing about Right-wing politics for more than 25 years. His work focuses on the interplay between Right-wing movements and systems of oppression, and the responses to these movements by Leftists, liberals and the state. He writes regularly for Three Way Fight, a radical anti-fascist blog. His work has also appeared in the *Guardian, New Politics, Socialism and Democracy, Upping the Anti*, and other publications and outlets. His most recent book is *Insurgent Supremacists: The U.S. Far Right's Challenge to State and Empire*. Lyons is co-author (with Chip Berlet) of *Right-wing Populism in America: Too Close for Comfort* (2000). https://matthewnlyons.net/.

Carol Mason, PhD, began using the library at Political Research Associates while on a postdoctoral fellowship at the Bunting Institute at Radcliffe College. Harvard University funded the research for her first book, *Killing for Life: The Apocalyptic Narrative of Pro-life Politics* published in 2002. She is currently professor of Gender and Women's Studies at University of Kentucky. Among other writings that address different aspects of the rise of the Right since the 1960s, she is co-author with Chip Berlet of "Swastikas in Cyberspace: How Hate Went Online," in *Digital Media Strategies of the Far Right in Europe and the United States*, edited by Patricia Ann Simpson and Helga Druxes. (2015). Mason is also known for a wicked sense of droll humor that endears her to her students and friends. https://gws.as.uky.edu/users/cama239/.

Scot Nakagawa has been a leader in fighting Right-wing movements and initiatives since 1988 when he became the principal staffperson of the Coalition for Human Dignity, an Oregon statewide organization dedicated to monitoring, exposing and building opposition to violent white nationalist and neo-Nazi groups. In subsequent years, Scot served as Director of Statewide Development of the 1992 No on 9 Campaign for a Hate-Free Oregon which successfully opposed a proposed amendment to the Oregon state constitution to exclude LGBTQ people from civil rights protection, and as Fight the Right Organizer and Field Director of the National Gay and Lesbian Task Force (now the National LGBTQ Task Force). In the decades since then, Scot has worked in a variety of issues and sectors, serving as the Associate Director of the Partnership for Safety and Justice, a progressive criminal justice reform organization, as Education Coordinator of the Highlander Center, a rural, Southeast based residential popular education school, and as an executive in social change philanthropy. Currently, Scot is a Senior Partner in ChangeLab, a national racial equity think/act lab; and collaborates with the Center for Racial Justice Innovation. His writings on race have been published in *The Nation, The Washington Post: The Root, ColorLines*, and numerous other publications and have been included in two recent anthologies: *Killing Trayvons: An Anthology of American Violence, and Race, Class,* and *Gender in the U.S: An Integrated Study.* Scot is an Open Society Foundations Soros Equality Fellow, a program through which he is developing resources for understanding and organizing against the far-Right. He participated in the national emergency strategy retreat for Defending Democracy and Pluralism at the Blue Mountain Center in 1993. More information about Scot can be found at: https://www.changelabinfo.com/about/.

Margaret Quigley walked into our offices at Political Research Associates in Cambridge, Massachusetts while a student at Harvard University. She announced that she was destined to work for PRA. She was correct. An energetic and cheerful addition to the staff, Margaret was a relentless force of nature as a researcher and analyst. Her major achievement at PRA was unraveling of the strands of thought in the new European Right's influence on the New Right in the United States. Margaret was a punctilious editor who could deface your work with notes and comments and then tell you it was "really good, just a few tweaks." Sadly, Margaret and her partner Susie Chancey O'Quinn were killed in 1993 by a drunk driver. Some of her work can be found at https://www.politicalresearch.org/bio/margaret-quigley/.

Tarso Luís Ramos is the executive director of Political Research Associates. Tarso emerged as one of the leading theorists and journalists exposing the anti-environmentalist "Wise Use" movement in the mid-1980s. As director of the Wise Use Public Exposure Project, he monitored the Right's anti-union and anti-environmental campaigns. Ramos served as founding director of the Western States Center's racial justice program, which resists racist public policy initiatives and supports the base-building work of progressive people of color-led organizations. Ramos has a busy schedule as a public speaker and his work has been featured in *The Guardian, The New York Times*, and *Time Magazine*, among other outlets. He has served as an activist in residence at the Barnard Center for the Study of Women and a Rockwood Leadership Institute National Yearlong Fellow for 2017–2018. Ramos participated in the national emergency strategy retreat for Defending Democracy and Pluralism at the Blue Mountain Center in 1993. Tarso can be reached through Political Research Associates: https://www.politicalresearch.org/bio/tarso-luis-ramos.

Abby Scher uses her PhD to explore systems of oppression from a perspective that examines civil rights, civil liberties, and the political economy of gender in the United States. Her dissertation was *Cold War on the Home Front: Middle Class Women's Politics in the 1950s* (New School for Social Research, 1995). Scher was a driving force in helping build the Independent Press Association and in 2002 published "Many voices, one city: the IPA guide to the ethnic press of New York City. She is co-author with Chip Berlet of several articles including "Political Profiling: Police Spying on Peaceful Activists." Amnesty Now, Amnesty International USA, 2003; and was lead author of "The Tea Party Moment," in Nella van Dyke and David S. Meyer, eds., *Understanding the Tea Party Movement* (2014).

Spencer Sunshine has a PhD in sociology and has written extensively about organized racist, fascist, and antisemitic movements and organizations. He is the author of the guide *40 Ways to Fight Nazis: Forty Community-Based Actions You Can Take to Resist White Nationalist Organizing* published by Showing Up for Racial Justice (SURJ) http://www.showingupforracialjustice.org/disrupting-white-na tionalists.html/. His columns appear regularly on the online Truthout news service https://truthout.org/authors/spencer-sunshine/. Sunshine and Jessica Campbell (with Daniel HoSang; Steven Beda; and Chip Berlet) wrote *Up in Arms: A Guide to Oregon's Patriot Movement* published by the Rural Organizing Project and Political Research Associates, online at http://www.rop.org/up-in-arms/. Sunshine is also the executive director of Action Against Fascism and Xenophobia (AAFX), with alerts at https://www.facebook.com/ActionAgainstFascismAndXenophobia/. Sunshine is co-author with Chip Berlet of the study "Rural rage: the roots of right-wing populism in the United States" in *The Journal of Peasant Studies* (May 2019). Sunshine has written numerous studies for Political Research Associates. His personal website is at https://spencersunshine.com/.

Angelia R. Wilson is a professor at the University of Manchester, England where she is the Internationalisation Lead for the School of Social Sciences. As this book goes to press, she is Chair of the Political Studies Association of the UK. She is a former Council member of the American Political Science Association, and the author of several path-blazing books, including: *A Simple Matter of Justice?: Theorizing Lesbian and Gay Politics* (1995); *Below the Belt: Religion, Sexuality and Politics in the Rural South* (1999); *The Politics of Intersectionality: Politics, Policy, and Power* (2013); *Why Europe Is Lesbian and Gay Friendly (and Why America Never Will Be)* (2014). As a colleague and friend, she has encouraged my research and writing for over a decade. https://www.research.manchester.ac.uk/portal/angelia.r.wilson.html.

HOW THIS BOOK IS ARRANGED

This book is an unusual edited collection in several ways:

- Every author considers themselves to be a scholar and an activist assisting the progressive struggle for collective human rights.
- Many of the chapters are co-written, representing the progressive concept that collective research and writing can be a value-added practice for authors.
- There is an intentional inclusive range of author identities based on their race, gender, and class.
- The chapters after the Introduction represent the views of the various authors on the date on which the text was originally published.
- Some chapters cover current events at the time the text was originally published. Others review a specific narrow or broad period of history. There are only careful and modest editing tweaks for consistency.
- Since some chapters were originally written for journalistic outlets and others for scholarly publishing, the inclusion of citations varies. As the Internet expands the online presence of older texts some textual citations appear online as if by magic. These additional cites are collected at https://doi.org/10.6084/m9.figshare.9730337.

Chip Berlet

DEFINITIONS, EXPLANATIONS, RESOURCES, AND ACKNOWLEDGMENTS

A compendium of additional information and resource links for this edited collection are available online at this permanent research repositiory at Figshare: https://doi.org/10.6084/m9.figshare.7582004.

Terminology and conceptual schemes

Much of the terminology and conceptual schema in this edited collection was developed over more than 30 years at Political Research Associates. Links to the most popular resources are here: https://doi.org/10.6084/m9.figshare.9994967.

Expanded online topical resources

A collection of expanded resources on various topics can be found at the permanent Figshare website: https://doi.org/10.6084/m9.figshare.9994949.

Gender and identities

Over the time periods in which these chapters were written there were developments in which different gender identities were claimed and referred to using a variety of terms. All the authors tried to be respectful of the terminology that was current in various progressive movements in the United States at the time the chapter was written.

White nationalism and White supremacy

Over many decades the terms "White supremacy" and "White nationalism" have been defined in a variety of ways by different authors. Biologists reject the popular concept of "race." The perception of biological racial differences, however, plays a central role in historic and current power relationships in our nation.

The term "White supremacy" is often used by scholars and activists to describe a constellation of racist ideologies and practices. There is no consensus on the use of different terms by scholars and activists who study racist and Right-wing politics. For this edited collection I offer the following guide, for which I am solely responsible.

- **White nationalism** claims that the essence of the United States as a nation is carried exclusively in the social, cultural, economic, and political practices of early European settlers.
- **White superiority** is the specious idea that White people are a uniquely talented 'race.'
- **White supremacist system** refers to the systems, structures, and institutions of a nation that give White people special privileges and powers, whether or not they want these privileges or harbor a dislike of people from other races.
- **Organized White supremacist groups** are social and political organizations with the goal of ensuring White people exercise power over people of color. These may work through legal means inside of the democratic system as it exists now to maintain or increase the "White supremacist system"; advocate forming an all-White state; or seek to exterminate or expel people of color. These groups almost always rely on anti-Semitic conspiracy theories for a theoretical core, and often display intense misogyny.

A lively debate on terminology sparked by this book's early draft language resulted in a collection of definitions used by progressive researcher and activists in the United States. Thanks to Scot Nakagawa, Loretta Ross, Ruby Sales, Steven Gardiner, and Devin Burghart for their commentaries.

For more information on these progressive researchers and activists, and additional acknowledgments, visit: https://doi.org/10.6084/m9.figshare.8304731.

Patriot and militia movements

While inside this network there are overlaps, there are also distinctions and complicated relationships with more militant and ultra-Right formations such as neo-Nazis. This is discussed in detail at the beginning of the chapter by Spencer Sunshine and Chip Berlet, in the study published by Political Research Associates and the Rural Organizing Project, "Up in Arms: A Guide to Oregon's Patriot Movement," and in a major report for the *Journal of Peasant Studies*, Forum on Authoritarian Populism and the Rural World, "Rural rage: the roots of right-wing populism in the United States," by Chip Berlet and Spencer Sunshine. Find more information at: https://doi.org/10.1080/03066150.2019.1572603.

What is Christian dominionism?

While some conservatives dismiss the concept, and a few misrepresent the information in critical published research, Christian dominionism is a tendency to promote exclusionary forms of Christian nationalism. Observers debate whether it represents a move toward theocracy, theonomy, religious triumphalism, or some other concept. This is an ongoing debate in the corporate press but in the progressive media environment and among many serious scholar of religion there are numerous serious studies of Christian dominionism.

An extensive set of additional research material is online at the book's Figshare compendium. This includes a set of over 25 thematic classroom discussion themes and the full bibliography: https://doi.org/10.6084/m9.figshare.c.4493693.

Acknowledgments

My thanks to the small army of editors and editorial assistants at Routledge, Taylor & Francis Group. All the authors in this collection are colleagues and friends who were generous with their time. Thanks to the various publishers who gave their permissions. Among the many colleagues from Political Research Associates who gave me support and research advice over several decades I highlight Nikhil Aziz, Pam Chamberlain, Alex DiBranco, Kapya Kaoma, Abby Scher, Peggy Shinner, and Spencer Sunshine. Dozens of members of the American Sociological Association terrorized me into scholarly writing, with exceptional support from Lauren Langman and Kathleen Blee. My long-suffering partner of over 35 years, Karen Moyer, deserves a medal for meritorious patience as does our son.

INTERLUDE A

What is democracy?

Chip Berlet

Democracy is not a specific set of institutions, but a process that assumes the majority of a free and equal people, over time:

- are given an education that inspires curiosity,
- have access to accurate information,
- can take part in free, open, public debates, and
- can vote without intimidation.

Democratic institutions should reach constructive decisions that benefit the whole of society, and:

- preserve liberty,
- protect our freedoms,
- extend equality,

and thus defend democracy itself.

INTRODUCTION[1]

The roots of reaction

Chip Berlet

How did the United States of America get yanked from progressive President Franklin D. Roosevelt in 1933 to conservative President Ronald Reagan in 1981 to reactionary President Donald Trump in 2017? How did we end up with Trump's racist White Nationalist xenophobia, vulgar misogyny, ignorant antisemitism, alarming Islamophobia, and open support from the neofascists in Alt-Right? The goal of this book is to explain this Right-wing trajectory from a progressive political perspective, factoring in struggles over power involving race, gender, and class that extend back many decades.

The political Right has always mobilized people and resources to sway the electoral and social scene in the United States, but as John B. Judis observes, "in the early twentieth century, there was no such thing in American politics as a conservative movement. The right was an unwieldy collection of anti-Semites, libertarians, fascists, racists, anti-New Dealers, isolationists, and Southern agrarians who were incapable of agreeing on anything" (Judis 2001, 142). So, we must start at the roots of reaction.

Ungodly collectivism versus Christian ethics

This analysis begins after the US Civil War with a large railway strike in 1877. The Rev Henry Ward Beecher, a popular and widely-known preacher, suggested that

---

1   This chapter is based in part on research first compiled for my edited collection *Eyes Right! Challenging the Right-Wing Backlash*: South End Press, 1995; my chapter "Following the Threads: A Work in Progress," in Amy Elizabeth Ansell, ed., *Unraveling the Right: The New Conservatism in American Thought and Politics*, New York: Westview, 2001; my chapter "The New Political Right in the United States: Reaction, Rollback, and Resentment," in Michael J Thompson, ed., *Confronting the New Conservatism: The Rise of the Right in America*. New York: New York Univ. Press, 2007; and my online collection "Derailing Organized Wealth & the 1%," at https://www.organizedwealth.us/.

alien ideas from Europe were being imported into the United States. As M. J. Heale notes, Beecher "thought 'un-American' the idea that government should provide for the welfare of its citizens, described collectivist theories as destructive of that 'individuality of the person' that alone preserved liberty, and unabashedly insisted that 'God has intended the great to be great and the little to be little'" (Heale 1990, 28; citing Beecher).

To meet this challenge of ungodly collectivism, Right-wing industrial and business interests organized a series of national networks and institutions between the late 1800s and Roosevelt's New Deal in the 1930s.

In 1895, the National Association of Manufacturers (NAM) was founded with a special interest in stopping labor organizing in the South. No coincidence that the "influential Southern newspaper, *the Dixie*" rallied support for the group (National Association of Manufacturers n.d. circa 2006). NAM "tended to represent small businessmen, was fiercely antiunion and strongly endorsed the 'open shop' crusade to ban union influence in industrial plants" (Heale 1990, 44).

NAM swam in the common currents of White racial supremacy and solidarity prevalent in the 1930s. The *New York Times*, for example, editorialized on August 10, 1930 about "Labor in the South" in a typical White racial frame. According to the *Times*, one boost to NAM president John E. Edgerton and his associates "in their effort to maintain the open shop [was] the racial and language unity of [employees] and employers in the South, and the pressure of long custom."

Edgerton proclaimed that southern wage earners "are almost wholly of one blood, one God, and one language... No people on earth love individual liberty, or will make greater sacrifices for it, than ... those proud Anglo-Saxon elements who constitute the working army of this homogeneous section of the nation" (Edgerton 1930).

To oppose President Franklin Roosevelt's New Deal proposals, in 1934, NAM launched a huge 13-year $15 million public relations campaign "for the dissemination of sound American doctrines to the public." These doctrines included blasting labor unions while calling for reductions in the size of government and the number of government regulations. NAM still brags about how it distributed "leaflets, movie shorts, radio speeches, films for schools, reprints of articles by economists, and other public relations efforts. A daily NAM column appeared in 260 newspapers with a circulation of more than 4.5 million persons in 1936. The NAM's movie shorts were seen by six million persons in 1937" (National Association of Manufacturers n.d. circa 2005).

NAM saw labor unions as a threat to American democracy and the free enterprise system. In 1955 one steel company official warned NAM that employers needed to show some solidarity of their own and organize to defend the free enterprise system against a powerful attack from the AFL-CIO and other unions (Gall 1988, 73). "Red scare tactics were frequently employed in attempts to halt the surge of unionization," with NAM issuing one pamphlet titled "Join the CIO and Help Build a Soviet America" (Heale 1990, 117).

NAM claims credit for having "helped launch the National Council of Commerce in 1907" (National Association of Manufacturers n.d. circa 2005). This predecessor group became the United States Chamber of Commerce in 1912 (National Association of Manufacturers n.d. circa 2005; U.S. Chamber of Commerce 2006). The Chamber of Commerce primarily represented small business interests, although a few big businesses were also members; and the Chamber reflected these sectors in its "periodic imprecations against the New Deal, labor unions, and anything resembling socialism," according to Heale (1990, 139).

The United States Business and Industry Council (USBIC) was even further to the political Right than NAM and the Chamber. John E. Edgerton, the former president of NAM, became the first president of the Council. Originally established in 1933 as the Southern States Industrial Council, the organizing conference attracted "presidents and secretaries of Southern state manufacturers' associations." (Wynn, Sweeney, Georgine, and Barry 1988).

Council founders sought to undermine the New Deal approach to the Depression, "as well as to the political challenges posed to business by the Roosevelt Administration" (USBIC Educational Foundation 2006).

This was unremarkable, since up until the New Deal, laissez–faire economic policies were the "convention wisdom" taught at major universities and business schools (Heale 1990, 27–28). Therefore, Heale notes, it was a widely held belief across much of America in the late 1800s and early 1900s that "workers benefited from the free enterprise of the capitalist, that trade unions were potential monopolies that disrupted the free market, and that labor actions like strikes were offenses against society" (Heale 1990, 28).

Rolling back the New Deal

Many activists on the political Right, especially secular and religious libertarians, see the way Roosevelt pushed through the National Labor Relations Act during the New Deal as greasing the slippery slope toward tyrannical collectivism (von Hayek 1935, 1944; Flynn 1944; von Mises 1944, 1947, 1956).

To this day these opponents of Roosevelt argue that labor disputes were pulled out of the court system and handed over to faceless bureaucrats in a federal agency, the National Labor Relations Board (NLRB). In 1975, these actions by Roosevelt still angered Rightists, including Hans F. Sennholz, who claimed the NLRB "became prosecutor, judge, and jury, all in one. Labor union sympathizers on the Board further perverted this law, which already afforded legal immunities and privileges to labor unions. The U. S. thereby abandoned a great achievement of Western civilization, equality under the law" (Sennholz 1975 quoted in Reed 2006).

As soon as the National Labor Relations Act was passed, According to Gilbert J. Gall, conservatives began writing legislation to gut key sections of the law with a big push between 1938 and the start of World War II (Gall 1988, 14).

The National Association of Manufacturers and the U.S. Chamber of Commerce lobbied Congress to add a clause about "coercion" that Gall argues was essentially designed to allow employers to undermine union organizing drives (Gall 1988, 14–15).

Fanning fears of subversion

Rollback of the New Deal was the specific aim of the ultraconservatives, but they pursued a broader agenda as they fanned fears of a domestic threat of communism to justify "entirely smashing the labor movement and the New Deal," and "rooting out the subversives who supposedly infested Hollywood, the Ivy League, the State Department, and Wall Street" (Berlet and Lyons 2000, 165).

Why do so many ultraconservatives imply, or state outright, that Roosevelt was a tool of a vast subversive communist conspiracy? This tendency, called "countersubversion," dates back to the late 1700s when an early reactionary movement pushed through the Alien and Sedition Acts. Later, in the mid to late 1800s, some xenophobic activists launched "nativist" anti-Catholic and anti-immigrant movements, using fears of subversion to mobilize a mass reaction (Davis 1971, Bennett 1988[1995]). Government surveillance and repression of "radicals" on the political Left was a common feature in modern America from the 1870s to the present day (Goldstein 1978; Donner 1980; Gary T. Marx 1988, 1997;Greenberg 2014).

Widespread public fear of communist subversion "was being developed as a weapon to isolate labor organizations and control the untamed urban masses," writes Heale. This worked in a way that "legitimated the use of strong-arm tactics and the expansion of police powers" (Heale 1990, 27).

In the 1900s the most prevalent form of countersubversion was "Red Scares" such as those that promoted the Palmer Raids of 1919–1920 and the trial of Sacco and Vanzetti in 1921. In the 1930s, according to Leo P. Ribuffo it was no surprise to find conservatives adapting these "venerable countersubversive themes" and deeming "Roosevelt's program un-American as well as unwise." and by 1934, "critics routinely compared the whole New Deal to 'Russianized' government" (Ribuffo 1983, 15).

Some ultraconservative business and industrial leaders "saw the New Deal as proof of a sinister alliance between international finance capital and communist–controlled working–class organizations to destroy free enterprise" (Berlet and Lyons 2000, 163; see also Schrecker 1994). This sector of the U.S. political Right became known as "Business Nationalists," (Lyons 1998, 80–102), and today their views are represented by ultraconservative political figures such as Pat Buchanan (Berlet and Lyons 2000, 279–281).

Back in the mid-1930s, it was firebrand orator Gerald L. K. Smith who carried the banner for the business nationalists, many of whom were isolationist and would later oppose the entry of the United States into World War II (Ribuffo 1983, 128–177; Jeansonne 1988, 64–79). Smith received public and financial support from wealthy businessmen who were "concentrated in nationalist–oriented industries." These included "the heads of national oil companies Quaker State, Pennzoil, and Kendall Refining; and automakers Henry Ford and John and Horace Dodge." Two business nationalists who networked other ultraconservatives were J. Howard Pew, president of Sun Oil, and William B. Bell, president of the American Cyanamid, a chemical company (Berlet and Lyons 2000, 163; see also Jeansonne 1988, 65; Ribuffo 1983, 147).

Pew and Bell were on the executive committee of the National Association of Manufacturers (Berlet and Lyons 2000, 163; see also Seldes 1947, 38–56). Pew also funded the American Liberty League, Sentinels of the Republic, and other groups that flirted with fascism prior to World War II (Seldes 1947, 297). After World War II, Pew funded conservative Christian evangelicals such as the Rev. Billy Graham (Scranton and Fridenson 2013, 90; see also Hart 2011).

The Old Christian Right of the 1930s and 1940s

Leaders of what Ribuffo (1983) calls the "Old Christian Right" mobilized large groups of people in the United States into searching for subversives during the 1930s and 1940s. The fear of the Red Menace in some ultraconservative Protestant circles was fueled by apocalyptic Biblical prophecy. The term "apocalypse" simply means the idea that there is an approaching confrontation of epic proportions after which the world will be changed forever, and hidden truths will be revealed (see Topics Resource: Apocalypse and Millennialism).

For many Christian evangelicals and fundamentalists, communism and anarchism were literally tools of the devil. According to Frank Donner, "Bolshevism came to be identified over wide areas of the country by God–fearing Americans as the Antichrist come to do eschatological battle with the children of light," as prophesied in Revelation. Although based in Christianity, this apocalyptic anti–communist worldview developed a "slightly secularized version," explains Donner, and it was "widely shared in rural and small-town America," where leaders of evangelical and fundamentalist groups regularly "postulated a doomsday conflict between decent upright folk and radicalism—alien, satanic, immorality incarnate" (Donner 1980, 47–48).

Many Protestant evangelicals and fundamentalists have historically connected apocalyptic prophecies in the Bible's book of Revelation to contemporary political and social events (Boyer 1992; Fuller 1995). Robert C. Fuller (1995) notes that trying to match real life political figures with the evil Antichrist (prophesied as the sidekick of Satan in Revelation) became something of an "American obsession" in certain circles. During the Presidential administration of Barack Obama, 15 percent of Republican voters in New Jersey told pollsters in 2009 that they thought it was possible President Obama might be the Antichrist. Another 14 percent were sure of it (Public Policy Polling 2009).

Red scares and revelations

Apocalyptic Biblical prophecy warning of conspiracies in high places during the "End Times" played a major role in Right-wing Protestant movements between World War I and World War II and helped frame the rhetoric used by the leading spokesmen for what Ribuffo calls the "Protestant Far Right:" William Dudley Pelley, Gerald B. Winrod, and Gerald L. K. Smith (Ribuffo 1983, 2–24, 58–72, 83–116, 175–177).

President Roosevelt was seen as not only as promoting "modernist" ideas such as collectivism, but also sliding down "a slippery slope from liberalism to atheism, nudism, and Communism," quips Ribuffo (1983, 110). This form of conspiracist thinking easily fits into past and contemporary narratives of Christian struggles against evil in the millennial End Times (Berlet 1999, 2008, 2011).

Claims about a vast conspiracy to subvert America could remain focused on Communism, or involve suggestions that Jews were responsible for the New Deal. Some authors such as Elizabeth Dilling even claimed, "to have uncovered Roosevelt's Jewish ancestry" (Ribuffo 1983, 113; see also 59–60, 72–74). Dilling's most famous works include *the Red Network: A "Who's Who" and Handbook of Radicalism for Patriots* (1934); and *the Roosevelt Red Record and its Background* (1936).

Dilling is but one example of this antisemitic characterization of Roosevelt and other progressive Democrats (Ribuffo 1983, 16–17, 167, 196–197, 211; Bennett 1995, 269). These bigoted antisemitic characterizations continue today with claims by some participants in the Alt-Right network that Jews are behind the attacks on President Donald Trump and his agenda. Trump as President has himself made antisemitic statements (Kestenbaum 2017).

Most conservative Protestants, however, avoided obvious antisemitism, and were more in tune with the National Association of Evangelicals, founded in 1942, which "assailed the 'revolutionary' activities of the New Deal and the infiltration of government, the unions, and churches by 'reds'" (Heale, 1990, 139). Catholic church leaders, including Francis Cardinal Spellman and Bishop Fulton J. Sheen, were also outspoken anti-communists (Bennett 1995, 287–288; Heale 1990, 139).

After the end of World War II, the 1946 "general elections were greatly influenced by the onset of the Cold War" against communism and the Soviet Union (Oshinsky 1976, 52). In 1947 the passage of the Taft–Hartley Act was facilitated by what would become a new "Red Scare" that eventually morphed into the McCarthy Period. Among the supporters of Joseph McCarthy's 1946 Senate campaign were those who framed the issue as anticommunism, but as one admitted, the real reason for their support of McCarthy was "to force Congress to crack down on militant industrial unionism" (Oshinsky 1976, 54). The Taft–Hartley Act facilitated the linkage of anti–union Right–to–Work organizing by explicitly allowing employers to target their employees with anti–union materials (Diamond 1998, 52; citing Westin 1963). Booklets, reports, and flyers linked labor unions with subversion by communists, and the Chamber of Commerce developed a huge "propaganda campaign … alleging extensive Communist penetration of government and of the labor unions" (Heale 1990, 136; see also Bennett 1995, 287).

Congressional committees, the FBI, and private watchdog groups cooperated both publicly and privately to monitor and "expose" communist influences in film, radio, television, and the theater (Navasky 1980, Schrecker 1998). Fraternal and veteran's organizations published warnings about subversion (Heale 1990, 138–140). The Minute Women organized ultra-conservative women to combat subversion (Scher 1995). The American Security Council began tracking names of alleged communist sympathizers for use by employers screening job seekers (Donner 1980,

422–424). The Right-wing Church League of America also kept a huge collection of files on suspected subversives. For a fee, employers could have the files searched to see if a prospective employee was a troublemaker or radical or union member (Donner 1980).

The Church League of America attacked mainline Protestant denominations for their doctrinal and political liberalism and issued reports claiming the National Council of Churches was infested with subversives and communists. The "internal subversion thesis and the view of liberalism as merely a soft form of communism provided the logic for Christian Rightists' attacks on reputable Church bodies," explains Sara Diamond (1995, 102).

The messages of militant anticommunism continued to be circulated well into the 1950s by NAM, the Chamber of Commerce, and USBIC, as well as early think tanks such as the Hoover Institution at Stanford University and the Foreign Policy Research Institute founded with assistance from the University of Pennsylvania. Conservative media led by the ubiquitous *Reader's Digest*, with its huge reader base, spread similar messages through the 1960s.

Postwar fusionism

After World War II and the Truman Administration, a moderate Republican, Dwight D. Eisenhower, was elected President in 1952. The political Right in the Republican Party, (called the "Taft Wing" after the former President, Robert Taft), had been eclipsed. Three strategists, Frank Meyer, M. Stanton Evans, and William F. Buckley, Jr. decided this required carving a conservative movement out of the fractured remains of the political Right, in part by specifically rejecting the legacy of overt White supremacy and antisemitism. Buckley had gained attention writing for the libertarian journal *Freeman*, but secured his niche in history when in 1955 he founded the influential *National Review* magazine (Himmelstein 1990, 43–44).

Buckley, Evans, and Meyer sought a working coalition—a fusion—bridging three tendencies: economic libertarianism, social traditionalism, and militant anticommunism (Himmelstein 1990, 14). According to Jerome L. Himmelstein, "the core assumption that binds these three elements is the belief that American society on all levels has an organic order—harmonious, beneficent, and self–regulating— disturbed only by misguided ideas and policies, especially those propagated by a liberal elite in the government, the media, and the universities" (Himmelstein 1990, 14). Himmelstein's discussion of how the three strands of "fusionist" conservatism were woven into a movement alliance is illuminating (Himmelstein 1990, 43–60). This coalition plan became known as "Fusionism."

Among the libertarian ideologues were old-timers including former presidents Herbert Hoover and Robert Taft, classical liberal (*laissez–faire*) economists including Ludwig von Mises, Friedrich von Hayek, and Milton Friedman; "and a variety of iconoclastic individualists and objectivists like Albert Jay Nock and Ayn Rand (Himmelstein 1990, 46). Social traditionalist ideologues included Leo Strauss, Eric Vogelin, Robert Nisbet, Russell Kirk, and Richard Weaver (Himmelstein 1990, fn. 26 on 220) They contributed ideas with "arguments rooted in natural law, Christian theology, and nineteenth–century European conservatism and its notions of tradition," reports Himmelstein (1990, 49).

During this same period, a number of industrial interests revisited their long-standing opposition to labor unions. In 1955 they joined to form the National Right-to-Work Committee. Fred A. Hartley—the same Hartley who co-sponsored the anti–union Taft-Hartley Act in 1947—became the first president of the NRTWC. According to Gilbert J. Gall at least one labor leader feared there would be an "organized assault by a coalition of the National Association of Manufacturers, the U.S. Chamber of Commerce," and the new national group (Gall 1988, 72). The NRTWC still opposed labor unions, but reframed the issue, shifting away from anticommunism and claims of subversion used during the New Deal and early Cold War period. The new theme was that greedy and thuggish union bosses were denying the rights of workers their freedom to choose their employer and terms of employment (Dixon 2003).

For some conservatives, however, the hunt for the red menace continued (Berlet 1994). In 1958 the John Birch Society was founded to continue to combat the communist conspiracy. The JBS launched a campaign to get the US out of the UN, and this project peaked in the early 1960s. For Birch members, the main threat was always communist subversion aided by liberal internationalists, collectivists, modernist theologies, and unions (Berlet and Lyons 2000, 175–198). A similar analysis laced with coded (and sometimes obvious) antisemitism was pursued by the now–defunct Liberty Lobby, brainchild of Willis Carto (Berlet and Lyons 2000; Mintz 1985).

A variety of chapter-based, grassroots, fraternal and religious groups continued to carry the anti–communist alerts into the hands of members across the land (Heale 1990, 1998; Kovel 1994). Christian Right icon David A. Noeble wrote books in the 1960s and 1970s with titles including *Communism, Hypnotism and the Beatles* (1965), *Rhythm, Riots and Revolution* (1966), and *Marxist Minstrels: A Handbook on Communist Subversion of Music* (1974). The legacy of anticommunism in shaping political life in the United States sank deep roots, especially among Christian evangelicals and fundamentalists (Berlet and Lyons 2000, 174–227, esp. 201–202; Berlet and Quigley 1992; Scher 1995, 300–301).

The 1964 Goldwater campaign

When John F. Kennedy was elected President in 1960, ultraconservatives sought to build a broad coalition to retake the presidency from the Democrats, and install a *real* Republican, unlike President Dwight D. Eisenhower, the moderate whose Republican administration from 1952 to 1960 was seen as an unmitigated disaster by ultraconservatives.

In 1963 William A. Rusher, publisher of the ultraconservative magazine *National Review,* "urged fellow conservatives to take a risk" in order to "break the New Deal Coalition's lock on the presidency" Schoenwald reports (2001, 258). Rusher predicted: "It will take courage; it will take imagination; it will compel the GOP to break the familiar mould [sic] that has furnished it with every presidential nominee for a quarter of a century—but it can be done" (Schoenwald 2001, 258; citing Rusher 1963, 110).

It was done when "the right wing of the party ... seized control of the G.O.P. In the early 1960s" wrote Ferguson and Rogers (1979); and this was "supported strongly by such protectionist and nationalistically inclined figures as National Steel's George Humphrey, textile magnate Roger Milliken, and independent oil men John Pew and Henry Salvatori." As the Republican Party was tugged to the Right, there was a flotilla of multinational businesses (including a portion of the high technology sector) that sailed from the Republican Party to the Democratic Party (Ferguson and Rogers 1979, 1, 17–20, quote from 18). This would push the Democratic Party away from labor unions and toward Wall Street.

The Republican Party also did a course-correction. In 1964 they turned to Barry Goldwater, a Senator from the state of Arizona who was smart as a tack, photogenic, and very, very conservative.

Some conservative Christian campaigners for candidate Goldwater, such as Phyllis Schlafly and John Stormer, were still worried about subversive conspiracies and communist infiltration. They were skeptical of international treaties and US participation in the United Nations. Nevertheless, with allies in the ultra-conservative John Birch Society, these activists helped secure the 1964 Republican Party nomination for Goldwater. The 1964 Goldwater campaign is best known for the candidate's spectacular failure in the general election. Yet far more important political realignments were in play, as extensively chronicled by Rick Perlstein (2001). Most notably, the Goldwater supporters went on to help build the New Right in the 1970s and 1980s (Hardisty 1999; Berlet and Lyons 2000; Goldberg 2006).

The Goldwater campaign elevated Phyllis Schlafly to a high-profile role in ultraconservative organizing that lasted more than 40 years, as she built the Eagle Forum and led anti-feminist conservative women in organizing the successful blocking of the Equal Rights Amendment (Sims 1973, Hardisty 1999, 74–79; Critchlow 2005).

Lucy Williams (1997) observes that the Old Right rhetoric behind the Goldwater campaign focused on messages stressing the "confluence of poverty, race, labor unions, violence and communism. In this way, the Old Right was able to promote its agenda of lower taxes and reduced government."

Williams notes that during the Goldwater campaign, "rightist publications attacked the welfare state for undermining rugged individualism and private property, fostering immorality and non-productive activity ... contributing to crime (particularly associated with urban riots and the Civil Rights Movement), and ultimately leading to Communism" (Williams 1997). This frame did not propel Goldwater to victory in the general election, but it did begin a process that eventually altered the way ultraconservatism presented itself to appeal to a wider audience.

When Goldwater's presidential campaign wiped out on Election Day, 1964, political conservatism was dismissed as a quaint relic of earlier political turmoil. Robert Mason explains that, "Despite the birth of a modern movement of conservative thought in the 1950s and its growth in the 1960s, conservative ideas remained relatively marginal to intellectual and wider public debate" throughout most of the 1960s (R. Mason 2004, 115–116; see also Rusher 2005).

Defending "free enterprise"

In 1971 corporate attorney, Lewis F. Powell, Jr. wrote a memo claiming that there was an organized "Attack [on the] American Free Enterprise System." to counter this Powell suggested a coordinated campaign to defend "Free Market" capitalism and reshape the ideological debate in the media, on the college campuses, and in the political and legal arenas. The memo was widely circulated among business and political leaders and reached the White House. Within a few months, Powell was named by President Nixon to a seat on the US Supreme Court (see Topics Resource: Powell Memo).

The Powell memo picked up on longstanding complaints about statist collectivism, and big government; as well as a defense of a hands-off *laissez-faire* model of political economy. All of this had previously been aired in the conservative publications *Freeman* and *National Review*. This time, however, a number of wealthy ultraconservatives including Richard Mellon Scaife and Joseph Coors (and soon many others including the Koch Brothers) began funding Right-wing organizations and institutions in a strategic manner to help build a national and state network of think tanks, training centers, watchdog groups, opposition research groups, magazines, and endowed chairs for professors at universities (Diamond 1995;Soley 1995; People for the American Way 1996; Covington 1997; Hardisty 1999; Berlet and Lyons 2000; Berlet and Lyons 2008; Berlet and Lyons 2013; Berlet and Lyons 2016; Berlet and Lyons 2017).

College campuses were seen as a particular target for rectification (Messer–Davidow 1993, 1994). As part of their backlash endeavor, the political Right redefined the term "political correctness" to mock issues involving "leftist" support for diversity (especially involving race); and regulations and language designed to respect and mainstream people with disabilities (Schultz 1993, Scatamburlo 1998).

To implement the Powell Memo plan, conservatives began constructing a network of social movement organizations and institutions that would feed people into their political operation. As Doug McAdam and David A. Snow explain, social movements consist of groups of people who act with "some degree of organization and continuity outside of institutional channels for the purpose of promoting or resisting change in the group, society, or world order of which it is a part" (1997). Just as the Civil Rights Movement pulled the Democratic Party to the political Left, the New Right movement leaders—energized and trained in the Goldwater campaign—were pulling the Republican Party to the Right.

William Simon, an ultraconservative ideologue, chose election year 1978 to renew the call to bolster public support to defend the Free Enterprise system. Simon urged that money "generated by business (by which I mean profits, funds in business foundations and contributions from individual businessmen) must rush by multimillions to the aid of liberty ... to funnel desperately needed funds to scholars, social scientists, writers, and journalists who understand the relationship between political and economic liberty (Alliance for Justice 1986).

Christian conservative nationalism

Christian conservative nationalism was also re–invigorated in the 1970s, and a key organization was the now-defunct Christian Freedom Foundation (CFF), which was for "twenty years the most influential of the 'old' Christian right organizations" (Hadden and Swann 1981).

In 1974, the Pew Freedom Trust contributed $300,000 to the group, and the president of Amway Corporation, Richard M. DeVos, gave $25,000 (Saloma 1984, 53–54). The next year, according to Saloma, a group of wealthy ultraconservative businessman began to change the work of CFF toward more aggressive political activism. They included DeVos, "John Talcott of Ocean Spray Cranberries and Art De Moss, board chairman of the National Liberty Insurance Corporation" (Saloma 1984)

The "New Conservative Labyrinth" is what Saloma called the growth of the interlocking network of Right-wing Republicans that reached out to journalists, academics, students, and grassroots activists. Saloma, a moderate Republican, warned about the "ominous politics" being promoted by the growing New Right infrastructure (Saloma 1984).

The purpose of taking over CFF, reports Saloma, was "to use the foundation's tax-exempt status to further religious right organizing efforts and to channel funds" into a publishing project, including *One Nation Under God*, a text which provided "a political rationale for the religious right" (Saloma 1984, 53–54). Saloma writes that "Art De Moss admitted publicly that the purpose of CFF was to elect Christian conservatives to Congress in 1976" and that DeMoss explained his "vision is to rebuild the foundations of the Republic as it was when first founded—a 'Christian Republic.' We must return to the faith of our fathers" (Saloma 1984, 53–54, quoting DeMoss).

In the mid-1970s, CFF sponsored seminars "on government and politics in Washington," where Christian Right activists were trained. Among those attending was Robert Billings, who later set up shop in the nation's capital "monitoring legislation that had implications for Christian schools." Billings soon changed the name to the National Christian Action Coalition, "and its mission broadened to include lobbying," according to Jeffrey K. Hadden and Charles E. Swann, in *Prime Time Preachers*. Billings reached out to ultraconservative televangelists such as Jerry Falwell (Hadden and Swann 1981, 135).

The resulting political mobilization of millions of conservative Christian evangelicals became known as the "New Christian Right." the core public organizational issues of the New Christian Right were moral, with a focus on stopping abortions and blocking gay rights. But there is more to this story.

Building the New Right

The coalition that emerged in the 1970s to back conservative Republicans became known as the "New Right." It included Christian conservatives in the "New Christian Right," militarists, economic libertarians, and White nationalists, among other tendencies. The "New Right" replicated the strategy of conservative icon William F. Buckley, Jr. in the 1950s by uniting a functional conservative coalition.

Many of the organizers of the New Right had been involved in the failed Presidential bid of Senator Barry Goldwater in 1964. Richard Viguerie, a conservative movement activist, originally built his conservative direct mail empire by collecting names from the 1964 Goldwater campaign, and from the 1972 Presidential campaign of George Wallace, and entering them into a computer database (Viguerie 1980, 26–27; Lesher 1994, 463–464). The blizzard of direct mail from Viguerie and others caused an avalanche of feedback landing on elected representatives in Washington, DC.

By 1973 President Nixon was under pressure from grassroots conservatives to stop funding government programs where they claimed liberals and progressives were on the federal gravy train pursuing collectivist social engineering. In response, in 1973 Nixon appointed conservative activist Howard Phillips to dismantle the Office of Economic Opportunity, the main target of conservative angst. Phillips had been active with the conservative youth group Young Americans for Freedom, and other YAF activists and allies from the American Conservative Union joined in the effort (Diamond 1995, 116). Phillips lasted only a few months before resigning, but for decades remained a key player in the growth of Right-wing Republican organizing.

That rapid growth of the New Right was spectacular. Here are some key early activities:

- Karl Rove (later a key strategy adviser to President George W. Bush), became the executive director of the national College Republicans, which began a transition into more aggressive political activism, especially on college campuses.
- The creation of the Heritage Foundation to represent ultraconservative interests in Washington, DC. Paul Weyrich was the first president of Heritage, and initial funding came from beer baron Joseph Coors (Bellant 1991).
- Paul Weyrich sets up the Committee for the Survival of a Free Congress, "to select, train and fund rightist candidates for Senate and Congressional races" and "target vulnerable incumbents" by smearing them "in direct mail and media campaigns with charges of immorality and/or softness on communism" (Diamond 1989, 54–55).
- Robert Grant founds American Christian Cause.

- The establishment of the Conservative Caucus (TCC); run by Howard Phillips with fundraising support from Viguerie, and ideological support from Jesse Helms, an ultraconservative Senator from North Carolina with whom Phillips briefly worked. For a time, Ed McAteer also worked as the field director at the Conservative Caucus (Crawford 1980, 39–40; Hadden and Swann 1981, 138; Conway and Siegelman 1984, 88, 286; Saloma 1984, 54–56).
- The aggressive and vitriolic National Conservative Political Action Committee (NCPAC) is formed by L. Brent Bozell, III; Terry Dolan, Robert H. Krieble; Leif Noren, Craig Shirley, and Roger Stone. NCPAC successfully spearheaded the defeat of "liberal Senators Frank Church, George McGovern, Birch Bayh, and John Culver" in the 1980 election (Hardisty 1999, 45; Biersack, Herrnson, and Wilcox 1994, 182; Mayer 2016, 89; Oyez 2018).
- Richard Viguerie, William Rusher of *National Review,* Howard Phillips of the Conservative Caucus, and Paul Weyrich at the Heritage Foundation tried to establish a third party by seizing control over Wallace's American Independent Party. When this failed they turned their attention to gaining control over the Republican Party (Viguerie 1980; Himmelstein 1990, 80–94; Bellant 1991, 16, 44; Lesher 1994, 463–464; Diamond 1995, 127–138; Kazin 1995, 255–260; Martin 1996, 88).
- The economic libertarian "Free Market" think tank, the Cato Institute, is founded by Charles G. Koch, Edward H. Crane, and Murray Rothbard (Schulman 2014, Cato 2017).
- Paul Weyrich takes his experience with the Committee for the Survival of a Free Congress and the Heritage Foundation and establishes and runs the Free Congress Research and Education Foundation (usually just called the Free Congress Foundation) (Weber 2008), which is now closed.
- Concerned Women for America is formed by Beverly LaHaye.
- The Religious Roundtable is founded by Christian Right activist, Ed McAteer.

For several decades the Free Congress Foundation (FCF) was the flagship think tank in Washington, DC representing the interests of conservative Protestant evangelicals and fundamentalists as well as conservative Catholics. FCF spearheaded the idea of "cultural conservatism" as the bulwark for defending family values, and helped launch what became known as the Culture Wars (Bellant 1991, 15–35; Schapiro 1994; Berlet and Lyons 2000, 228–242; Krehely 2005). (After Weyrich's death in 2008, the FCF was renamed the American Opportunity Foundation and its core mission was redirected.)

At a meeting in 1979 Christian and conservative activists Billings, Falwell, McAteer, Phillips, Viguerie, and Weyrich discussed a way to more directly link political activism with the growing evangelical subculture being networked through televangelism. What emerged was the idea of a "Moral Majority," which became the name of an organization under the leadership of Falwell. Billings became executive director of the Moral Majority. Another activist who had been thinking along the same lines, Tim LaHaye, became a board member of the Moral Majority, along with D. James Kennedy of Coral Ridge Presbyterian Church in Florida.

While abortion was singled out as a public wedge issue to mobilize a voter base and split the Democratic Party, it was later revealed that White fear fueled the growth of the Christian Right Moral Majority movement. Randall Balmer documented this when he struck up a conversation with Christian Right strategist Paul Weyrich at a meeting in Washington, DC. Balmer reports that Paul Weyrich admitted that maintaining the tax status of segregated all–White Christian academies was the primary issue that provided the glue to bind together the troops in the Religious Right. Balmer adds that other leaders of the Christian Right have verified this (Balmer 2006, 13–17; 2008, 99–101).

Some of the New Right organizers saw America as being established as a White Christian nation run by godly men. That was a legacy of the earliest European setters, the Puritans, which included the Pilgrims who settled around now what is Boston in the state of Massachusetts. These early Christian settlers brought with them the concept of an approaching battle between good and evil—an apocalyptic battle as part of a momentous millennial confrontation between good and evil during which hidden truths would be revealed and society dramatically altered.

Racist populist framing: Producers v. parasites

While the interlocking network of conservative and libertarian national and state policy organizations and think tanks was being built, the rhetorical frame of the Republican Party was also being revamped.

In 1965, M. Stanton Evans had written a book titled: The *Liberal Establishment Who Runs America…and How*. Conservatives, therefore, needed to set up a "Counter-Establishment," to give America back to the people. In 1969 a political strategist close to the Republican Party, Kevin Phillips, outlined a plan for building an "Emerging Republican Majority."

President Nixon, elected in 1968, began to implement Phillips' plan, which became known as the "Southern Strategy." After meeting with Phillips, Nixon's aide H. R. Haldeman wrote a note to use "Phillips as an analyst—study his strategy—don't think in terms of old-time ethnics, go for Poles, Italians, Irish, must learn to understand Silent Majority … don't go for Jews and Blacks."

Instead of bemoaning the failure of Goldwater to attract voters, ultraconservative strategists and organizers repackaged themselves as populists and reframed their messages.

- To the middle class, they offered tax reductions, which also served their goal of reducing the size of federal and state budgets and meddling government programs.
- To the emerging Christian Right, they promised to restore America to its proper status as a Christian nation built on "family values" and to defend the

idealized Christian family against the sinful feminist, homosexual, secular humanist, and socialist subversives (Diamond 1995, 161–197, 228–256; Martin 1996[2005]; Hardisty 1999; Berlet and Lyons 2000, 199–264).

An important factor for the successful growth of the US Christian Right was the effective coordinated campaign to defund the more progressive National Council of Churches of Christ in the USA (Gill 2011). (see Topics Resource: Christian Right Movements).

A major subtext in the campaign of reframing political struggles was exploiting racial anxiety among many White people (Kazin 1995, 246; Carter 1995, 379; 1996; Lowndes 2008). Ultraconservative strategists began to "use welfare and the War on Poverty … to capture the increasing racial fears of much of white America at a time when African Americans were asserting their rights in new ways," explains Williams (1997).

Back in 1975 William Rusher set the tone of the new frame pitting populist producers against parasitic liberal elites and their lazy, sinful, or subversive allies at the bottom of the political system:

> a new economic division pits the producers—businessmen, manufacturers, hard-hats, blue–collar workers, and farmers—against the new and powerful class of nonproducers comprised of a liberal verbalist elite (the dominant media, the major Foundations And research institutions, the educational establishment, the federal and state bureaucracies) and a semipermanent welfare constituency, all coexisting happily in a state of mutually sustaining symbiosis.
>
> *(Rusher 1975, 4; see also Berlet and Lyons 2000, especially 6–13)*

These new Republican frames targeted anxiety caused by changing racial, gender, and class power relationships. They were designed to build a mass base and increase voter turnout for Republicans. Some analysts claim it involved an intentional plan to "mobilize resentment" (Hardisty 1999) through populist and producerist rhetoric (Berlet and Lyons 2000). In this way portions of the electorate were persuaded to vote against their apparent economic self–interest in favor of hot button social issues involving White nationalism, abortion, and heteropatriarchy (Crawford 1980; Hardisty 1999; Berlet and Lyons 2000, Frank 2004). In addition to rhetorical populism and producerism, different sectors of the political Right (and different players in other specific sectors) also use dualism and the demonization of opponents, conspiracist narratives, and an apocalyptic frame that raises the stakes of political struggle to a cosmological level (see Topics Resource: Apocalypse and Millennialism).

In 1978 Howard Jarvis led a "taxpayer revolt" in California, Proposition 13, that garnered national headlines and was replicated in many other states (Lo 1995; Jarvis with Pack 1979).Grover Norquist, who later served as the executive director of the National Taxpayers Union, worked on "Proposition 13 in California and similar tax cutting initiatives in other states that year" (Chapin 2003). An 1978 activist guide on how to run a state initiative targeting the progressive income tax by Engelmayer and Wagman, *the Taxpayer's Guide to Effective Tax Revolt* (1978) was picked up by the ultraconservative Arlington House, publishers of the first edition of the Kevin Phillips book, in the 1980s. Alan Brinkley quipped the new tax policies were "Reagan's Revenge: As Invented by Howard Jarvis," (1994, 36–37).

The New Right was now gaining institutional power and reshaping party politics in the United States. It was the 1978 national election that gave the "first indication that the new conservative movement was nationally viable," states John B. Judis. Among Republican candidates elected were half a dozen governors, a dozen members of the House of Representatives, three Senators, and over 300 representatives on the state level. According to Judis, Republican conservatives made the "most impressive gains" (Judis 2000, 149). The role of racist White nationalism in this transformation has often been neglected, but is well-documented (Carter 1996; Lowndes 2008; Haney-Lopez 2014). This shift to Right-wing populist rhetoric targeting liberals but with a subtext of anti–Black racism presaged the campaign for the Presidency in 2016 with the election of Donald Trump using rhetoric drawn from Rusher's model.

The "New Right" and Reagan

The election of Ronald Reagan as President of the United States in 1980 was in part due to his popularity as a straight–shooting actor; but also, due to a network of conservative and Right-wing ideologues who valued Reagan's anti-communist views as being useful to "rollback" the "collectivist" social policies of the Roosevelt administration seen as favoring "Big Government" and "Big Labor." Reagan was an actor, but also active in trying to squash labor unions in Hollywood and their alleged Red Menace communist subversion of the movie industry. This movement compiled lists of suspected communist infiltrators in America. In a 2012 article in the *Hollywood Reporter,* Gary Baum and Daniel Miller noted that:

> If not for the first and subsequent blacklists, Wisconsin Sen. Joseph McCarthy might have never had the ability to begin his four-year reign of often baseless accusation, which began in earnest in 1950. The so–called Hollywood Ten had been brought before the House Committee on Un-American Activities (HUAC) in November 1947 as part of an investigation into whether communists and communist sympathizers had been sneaking their propaganda into films. People like Walt Disney and Ronald Reagan, then the head of the Screen Actors Guild, testified before the committee about the communist menace; others, like Humphrey Bogart and Lauren Bacall, who were members of the Left-leaning Committee for the First Amendment, flew to Washington to stand up for their colleagues, though ultimately to no avail.

Over the next two decades in rural California powerful agricultural interests were battling attempts by farmworkers to organize (Olmsted 2015), while in the suburbs a conservative rebellion was planting the seeds for what became the "New Right" (McGirr 2002), a movement which was soon "ready to lead" (Gingrich 2011, 2015).

Reagan as president

The election of Ronald Reagan as president in 1980 was significantly shaped by shifts to voting Republican by many previously Democratic-voting White Christians (Diamond 1995; 173, 208–209, 233). Christian conservative organizers played a major role in the Reagan White House. For example, Robert Billings, who had joined the 1980 Reagan presidential campaign as the liaison to the religious community, then assumed the same post in the Reagan White House (Hadden and Swann 1981, 130, 135).

When Ronald Reagan took office as president in 1981, his administration was immediately presented with over one thousand pages of detailed policy recommendations assembled into a book by the Heritage Foundation. Titled *Mandate for Leadership: Policy Management in a Conservative Administration*, the text was written by conservative activists with input from dozens of Right-wing think tanks, political advocacy groups, and social movement organizations that lined the streets around the White House, Congressional office buildings, and the Capitol Building in Washington, DC (Heatherly 1981).

Alan Brinkley quipped the Republican's new tax policies were "Reagan's Revenge: As Invented by Howard Jarvis" (1994, 36–37).

Reagan and the Christian apocalypse

During the US Civil War, the "Battle Hymn of the Republic" included the phrase "Mine eyes have seen the glory of the coming of the Lord." For many it is not a metaphor.

That was a legacy of the earliest European setters, the Puritans, which included the Pilgrims who settled around now what is Boston in the state of Massachusetts. These early Christian settlers brought with them the concept of an approaching battle between good and evil—an apocalyptic battle as part of a momentous millennial confrontation between good and evil during which hidden truths would be revealed and society dramatically altered. Some apocalyptic Christians today even believe they must wage "spiritual warfare" against the agents of Satan (Diamond 1989; 1997). This messianic vision of purification in an apocalyptic battle against evil periodically turns the American Dream into a nightmare for people scapegoated as not worthy of being citizens (O'Leary1994; Quinby 1994, 1999; Fuller 1995; Lamy 1996).

> In 1983 President Reagan told reporters for *People* magazine:theologians have been studying the ancient prophecies [about] what would portend the coming of Armageddon [and] have said that never in the time between the prophecies

up until now has there ever been a time in which so many of the prophecies are coming together. There have been times in the past when people thought the end of the world was coming and so forth, but never anything like this...

(Reagan, Public Papers, 1983; 1714–1715; Sklar 1986)

For Reagan watchers this was no surprise. Back in 1971, then the Governor of California, Reagan remarked to a friend that he noted that:

...in the 38th chapter of Ezekiel it says that the land of Israel will come under attack by the armies of the ungodly nations and it says that Libya will be among them. Do you understand the significance of that? Libya has now gone communist, and that's a sign that the day of Armageddon isn't that far off ... Everything is falling into place ... Ezekiel tells us that Gog, the nation that will lead all of the other powers of darkness against Israel, will come out of the north ... now that Russia has become communist and atheistic, now that Russia has set itself against God. Now it fits the description of Gog perfectly.

(Cited in Sklar 1986)

Reagan also adopted and echoed the framework of apocalyptic millennialism common among evangelicals and fundamentalists active in the Christian Right (FitzGerald 1985, 105–196).

President Reagan spoke of the early Puritan settler legacy when he described America as representing the "shining city on the hill." the original quote is by Puritan minister John Winthrop, who helped found the Massachusetts Bay Colony. Winthrop said of his flock "We shall be as a city upon a hill, the eyes of all people are upon us." These colonists were part of a religious theocracy that executed alleged witches and political dissidents. Punishing the wicked through purifying apocalyptic violence was part of preparing the way for the millennial return of Jesus Christ to the "New Jerusalem" being built by the Puritans. Winthrop was paraphrasing Matthew 5:14, the parable of "Salt and Light," taken from the Sermon on the Mount by Jesus of Nazareth.

President Donald Trump routinely uses apocalyptic warnings about immoral and evil people threatening the existence of the United States. When Trump announced in 2017 the United States would recognize Jerusalem as the capital of Israel (and promised to eventually move the US embassy to Jerusalem) it was credited as a reward for his evangelical Christian constituency, most of which believes Jewish control of all of Jerusalem and the Temple Mount is required for the return of Jesus in the millennial "End Times" (Gorenberg 2000; Schallhorn, Fox News 2017).

Militarism

Nikhil Aziz observes that Ronald Reagan, at his second inaugural in 1984, claimed that as a nation "[p]eace is our highest aspiration and our record is clear. Americans resort to force only when they must. We have never been aggressors."

Aziz charged that this claim was an insult to the suffering of people the world over; and noted the historic record documented the "the imperialist, interventionist, and racist history of the United States from its very origins." Aziz noted that during Reagan's eight years in office there were hundreds of thousands of people "killed in El Salvador, Nicaragua, Grenada, Guatemala, Angola, Mozambique, Afghanistan, and around the world as a direct result of his and his Administration's policies and agendas."

According to Aziz (and many other progressive scholars) Reagan's lasting foreign policy legacy was the "Reagan Doctrine," which, according to Aziz, was for "the vast majority of the world's citizens" resulted in, "war, hunger, poverty, sickness, and human rights violations, of arms races, and the slashing of social spending and increasing inequalities." As of the end of 2017, Trump's blustery rhetoric embraces militarism, but as yet there is not enough of a track record to plot the course of his policies.

Reaganomics

For some of the Right-wing ideologues in the 1950s, the collectivism of labor unions and "big government" inevitably led to totalitarian tyranny like that under Hitler's Nazi genocidal form of fascism and Stalin's brutalist repressive communism. This was outlined in the book *the Road to Serfdom* by the conservative libertarian economist Fredrich von Hayek, who based his work in part on the theories of his ally, economist Ludwig von Mises.

Neither von Mises (1881–1973) nor von Hayek (1899–1992) had any control over the Right-wing conspiracy theories about the Democrats and increased government spending. Nor could they envision this conspiracism overlapping with Christian apocalypticism in the United States (Berlet 2017,131–173). Yet "Reaganomics" was ostensibly based on their theories; and:

> President Ronald Reagan honored the work of both men, as did President George H. W. Bush. Moreover, everyone familiar with American politics of the last few years knows that the Tea Party and Fox News idolized Friedrich von Hayek and that Glenn Beck, a renowned (not to say notorious) Fox–News pundit, caused Hayek's sharpest book, *the Road to Serfdom* [1944] to become a national best seller in 2010.
>
> *(Lindley and Farmelant 2012)*

Reagan's adaptation of the economic theories of von Mises and von Hayek was called "trickle-down theory," which produced tax cuts for the very wealthy but accelerated the economic woes for most wage-earning Americans while increasing the anxiety of most salaried Middle-Class voters. In 2017 the Trump Republicans passed a regressive and brutalist federal budget continuing Reagan's philosophical path.

Legacies: The Council for National Policy

One ongoing New Right elite networking group that at first received little public attention was the Council for National Policy, founded in 1981, they ear President Reagan took office. The CNP brings together "a broad array of Republican elected officials and strategists, top Right–wing evangelicals, secular activists, government officials, retired military and intelligence officers, journalists, academicians, and business leaders," writes Matthew N. Lyons (1998, 91).CNP membership is by invitation only, and pricey since "several thousand dollars a year" are expected as dues (Kirkpatrick 2004, 10). Membership is supposed to be secret, but lists have leaked to progressive watchdog groups and the press over the years. The 2014 CNP "Membership Directory" was published online by the Southern Poverty Law Center (2014). It carried the slogans: "Economic Freedom" "Judeo-Christian Values" "Strong National Defense"

An example of the long-term networking role played by CNP is member Richard M. DeVos, who had funded the Christian Freedom Foundation in its move into political activism in the 1970s. He continued to network religious and fiscal conservatives as finance chairman of the Republican National Committee (Diamond 1989, 60).

Tim LaHaye, a well–known conservative Christian family counselor and author, became the first president of the CNP (Bellant 1991, 26–27, 36–46; 1994). According to Russ Bellant, LaHaye was working with the Moral Majority when he contacted T. Cullen Davis and Nelson Bunker Hunt for assistance in setting up the CNP. During the same period, LaHaye, Paul Weyrich, and Richard Viguerie had been discussing the idea of such a group. (Bellant 1991, 36–37). As a result, there are conflicting stories about the origins of the CNP, although it was clearly a group effort.

The Council for National Policy claims it is just a retreat for like–minded individuals. The Southern Poverty Law Center, however, suggests that the CNP includes as members "individuals whose goals are less benevolent." As an example, they point out that one of the CNP five founders, Tim LaHaye, is:

> …the co-author of the *Left Behind* series of apocalyptic Christian novels and a man who has described gay people as "vile," said the Illuminati are conspiring to establish a "new world order," attacked Catholicism, and once worked for the wildly conspiracist John Birch Society. An important member whose name was revealed early on was John Rousas Rushdoony, who … advocated for a society ruled by Old Testament law requiring, among other things, the stoning of adulteresses, idolaters and "incorrigible" children.
>
> *(Beirich and Potok 2016)*

The CNP, tactical projects, and strategic planning

Scholar Sara Diamond observed that the Christian Right popularized the organizing concept of tactical cultural "projects" which are part of the ongoing CNP game plan (Diamond 1989, 106–107, 174; 1998, 41–55).

Project-oriented tactical campaigns create the space for leaders on the Right to come to the national CNP meetings, listen to presentations, take part in discussions, and then break out into smaller groups where they agree on a specific short-term project. Even if other attendees at a CNP do not want to engage in the project (or even oppose it) these leaders come back to the next CNP meeting and start the tactical project process over again. The tactical project process uses cooperative "principles of unity" to maintain ethical coalitions (Berlet 2017).

The long–term strategic goal of the CNP is moving the nation to the political and cultural Right and gradually taking power to crush Big Government, "tax and spend liberals," and the political and cultural Left (as the members of the CNP define it). It is this combination of strategic vision and tactical cooperation that helps social movements succeed and pull political and electoral agendas in their direction.

Conclusions

Starting in the late 1970s, through the 1980s (and down to today) corporate and alternative journalists have repeatedly exposed the authoritarian, reactionary, and exclusivist agenda of the Right–wing juggernaut in the United States that seeks to roll back the progressive policies of the Roosevelt administration (Berlet 2018a). During the presidential administration of William "Bill" Clinton (1993–2001), the Democratic Party began sliding toward more aggressive militarism and support for "Free Market" economic policies that benefited the wealthiest 1 percent and began pushing the rest of the population down the economic ladder.

At the same time progressive activists and scholars began warning Democratic Party strategists of the need to cooperate with social movements on the Left. We called for the rebuilding of cooperative projects between the Democratic Party and progressive labor and social movement groups that were terminated unilaterally by the Democratic National Committee after the failed Presidential campaign of George McGovern in 1972.

We called for the creation of long-term *strategic* education and training projects to challenge the Right-wing backlash. Tens of millions of dollars were raised for this effort. Much of the funding, however, were diverted away from *strategic* progressive grassroots movement projects to Inside-the-Beltway *tactical* short-term *opposition* political research by groups allied with DNC centrists. The same cohort of DNC centrists supported the candidacy of Hillary R. Clinton for President in 2016—thus facilitating the election of Donald Trump as President of the United States. Some of this funding has now reached some strategic progressive movement organizations—mostly too little and too late.

The rest of this book tracks the details of this story of how we got from Reagan to Alt-Right with its public support for the policies of Republican President Donald Trump in the White House—support that ranges from angry White Democrats to neofascists.

1

THEOCRACY AND WHITE SUPREMACY[1]

Behind the Culture War to restore traditional values

Chip Berlet and Margaret Quigley[2]

As the United States slid toward the twenty-first century, the major mass movements challenging the bipartisan status quo were not found on the Left of the political spectrum, but on the Right.

The resurgent Right contains several strands woven together around common themes and goals. There is the electoral activism of the religious fundamentalist movements; the militant anti-government populism of the armed militia movement; and the murderous terrorism of the neonazi underground–from which those suspected of bombing the Alfred P. Murrah Federal Building in Oklahoma City appear to have crept.

It is easy to see the dangers to democracy posed by far-Right forces such as armed militias, neonazis, and racist skinheads. However, hard Right forces such as dogmatic religious movements, regressive populism, and White racial nationalism

1   This chapter was first published in 1992 in the *Public Eye* magazine. In its early years this publication did not include references. The underlying reference materials were photocopied and placed in a file in the Political Research Associate library and file room and then years later were archived at Tufts University. There is ongoing project to locate fugitive quotations that now can be found online due to efforts to digitalize print materials and make them searchable for specific phrases. See https://tinyurl.com/trump ing-democracy-book-cites. Copyright 1992, 2019 by Political Research Associates. Used by permission of the publisher, all rights reserved. Also collected in Chip Berlet, ed. 1995. *Eye's Right! Challenging the Right: Wing Backlash*. Boston, South End Press.

2   This chapter sketches the alliance of White Nationalists and Christian Right theocrats that decades later helped elect Donald Trump President of the United States. It was Margaret Quigley, then on the staff of Political Research Associates, who first suggested she and I look at the rising wave of reactionary populist movements in Europe to understand the politics of the "New Christian Right" in the United States. Sadly, Margaret Quigley and her partner Susie Chancey O'Quinn were killed by a drunk driver in 1993.

also are attacking democratic values in our country. Consider the following quote uttered at the Republican National Convention in 1992:

> "We are America, they are not America."
>
> *(GOP Party Chief Richard Bond)*

The best-known sector of the hard Right is often called the "Religious Right." It substantially dominates the Republican Party in at least ten (and perhaps as many as 30) of the 50 states. As part of an aggressive grassroots campaign, these groups have targeted electoral races from school boards to state legislatures to campaigns for the US Senate and House of Representatives. They helped elect dozens of hardline ultraconservatives to the House of Representatives in 1994. This successful social movement politically mobilizes a traditionalist mass base from a growing pious constituency of evangelical, fundamentalist, charismatic, Pentecostal, and orthodox churchgoers.

The goal of many leaders of this ultraconservative religious movement is imposing a narrow theological agenda on secular society. The predominantly Christian leadership envisions a religiously-based authoritarian society; therefore, we prefer to describe this movement as the "theocratic Right." A theocrat is someone who supports a form of government where the actions of leaders are seen as sanctioned by God—where the leaders claim they are carrying out God's will. The central threat to democracy posed by the theocratic Right is not that its leaders are religious, or fundamentalist, or Right-wing—but that they justify their political, legislative, and regulatory agenda as fulfilling God's plan.

Along with the theocratic Right, two other hard Right political movements pose a grave threat to democracy: regressive populism, typified by diverse groups ranging from members of the John Birch Society out to members of the patriot and armed militia movements; and White racial nationalism, promoted by Pat Buchanan and his shadow, David Duke of Louisiana.

The theocratic Right, regressive populism, and White racial nationalism make up a hard-Right political sector that is distinct from and sometimes in opposition to mainstream Republicanism and the internationalist wing of corporate conservatism.

Finally, there is the militant, overtly racist far Right that includes the open White supremacists, Ku Klux Klan members, Christian Patriots, racist skinheads, neonazis, and Right-wing revolutionaries. Although numerically smaller, the far Right is a serious political factor in some rural areas, and its propaganda promoting violence reaches into major metropolitan centers where it encourages alienated young people to commit hate crimes against people of color, Jews, and gays and lesbians, among other targets. The electoral efforts of Buchanan and Duke serve as a bridge between the ultraconservative hard Right and these far-Right movements. The armed militia movement is a confluence of regressive populism, White racial nationalism, and the racist and antisemitic far Right.

All four of these hard-Right activist movements are antidemocratic in nature, promoting in various combinations and to varying degrees authoritarianism, xenophobia, conspiracy theories, nativism, racism, sexism, homophobia, antisemitism, demagoguery, and scapegoating. Each wing of the antidemocratic Right has a slightly different vision of the ideal nation.

The theocratic Right's ideal is an authoritarian society where Christian men interpret God's will as law. Women are helpmates, and children are the property of their parents. Earth must submit to the dominion of those to whom God has granted power. People are basically sinful and must be restrained by harsh punitive laws. Social problems are caused by satanic conspiracies aided and abetted by liberals, homosexuals, feminists, and secular humanists. These forces must be exposed and neutralized.

Newspaper columnist Cal Thomas, a long-standing activist in the theocratic Right, recently suggested that churches and synagogues take over the welfare system "because these institutions would also deal with the hearts and souls of men and women." the churches "could reach root causes of poverty"—a lack of personal responsibility, Thomas wrote, expressing a hardline Calvinist theology. "If government is always there to bail out people who have children out of wedlock, if there is no disincentive (like hunger) for doing for one's self, then large numbers of people will feel no need to get themselves together and behave responsibly" Thomas, wrote in 1994.

For regressive populism, the ideal is America First ultra-patriotism and xenophobia wedded to economic Darwinism, with no regulations restraining entrepreneurial capitalism. The collapsing society calls for a strong man in leadership, perhaps even a benevolent despot who rules by organically expressing the will of the people to stop lawlessness and immorality. Social problems are caused by corrupt and lazy government officials who are bleeding the common people dry in a conspiracy fostered by secret elites, which must be exposed and neutralized.

Linda Thompson, a latter-day Joan of Arc for the patriot movement, represents the most militant wing of regressive populism. She appointed herself "Acting Adjutant General" of the armed militias that have formed cells across the United States. Operating out of the American Justice Federation of Indianapolis, Thompson's group warns of secret plots by "corrupt leaders" involving "Concentration Camps, Implantable Bio Chips, Mind Control, Laser Weapons," and "neuro-linguistic programming" on behalf of bankers who "control the economy" and created the illegal income tax.

The racial nationalists' ideal oscillates between brutish authoritarianism and vulgar fascism in service of White male supremacy. Unilateral militarism abroad and repression at home are utilized to force compliance. Social problems are caused by uncivilized people of color, lower-class foreigners, and dual-loyalist Jews, who must all be exposed and neutralized.

Samuel Francis, the prototypical racial nationalist, writes columns warning against attempts to "wipe out traditional White, American, Christian, and Western Culture," which he blames on multiculturalism. Francis's solutions:

> Americans who want to conserve their civilization need to get rid of elites who want to wreck it, but they also need to kick out the vagrant savages who

have wandered across the border, now claim our country as their own, and impose their cultures upon us. If there are any Americans left in San Jose, they might start taking back their country by taking back their own city. ... You don't find statues to Quetzalcoatl in Vermont.

For the far Right, the ideal is White revolution to overthrow the corrupt regime and restore an idealized natural biological order. Social problems are caused by crafty Jews manipulating inferior people of color. They must be exposed and neutralized.

The Truth at Last is a racist far Right tabloid that features such headlines as "Jews Demand Black Leaders Ostracize Farrakhan," "Clinton Continues Massive Appointments of Minorities," and "Adopting Blacks into White Families Does Not Raise Their IQ," which concluded that "only the preservation of the White race can save civilization ... Racial intermarriage produces a breed of lower-IQ mongrel people."

There are constant differences and debates within the Right, as well as considerable overlap along the edges. The relationships are complex: in the 1990s the members of the John Birch Society feuded with supporters of conservative Reform Party billionaire politician Ross Perot on trade issues in the 1990s, even though their other basic themes were similar. The theocratic Right has much in common with regressive populism, though the demographics of their respective voting blocs appear to be remarkably distinct.

These antidemocratic sectors of the hard Right are also distinct from traditional conservatism and political libertarianism, although they share some common roots and branches.

All of these antidemocratic tendencies are trying to build grassroots mass movements to support their agendas which vary in degrees of militancy and zealousness of ideology, yet all of which (consciously or unconsciously) promote varieties of White privilege and Christian dominion. These are activist movements that seek a mass base. Across the full spectrum of the Right one hears calls for a new populist revolt.

Many people presume that all populist movements are naturally progressive and want to move society to the Left, but history teaches us otherwise. In his book the Populist Persuasion, Michael Kazin explains how populism is a style of organizing. Populism can move to the Left or Right. It can be tolerant or intolerant. In her 1981 book *Populism*, Margaret Canovan defined two main branches of Populism: agrarian and political Agrarian populism worldwide has three categories: movements of commodity farmers, movements of subsistence peasants, and movements of intellectuals who wistfully romanticize the hard-working farmers and peasants. Political populism includes not only populist democracy, championed by progressives from the LaFollettes of Wisconsin to Jesse Jackson, but also politicians' populism, reactionary populism, and populist dictatorship. The latter three antidemocratic forms of populism characterize the movements of Ross Perot, Pat Robertson, and Pat Buchanan, three straight White Christian men trying to ride the same horse.

Of the hundreds of hard Right groups, the most influential is the Christian Coalition led by televangelist and corporate mogul Pat Robertson. Because of Robertson's smooth style and easy access to power, most mainstream journalists routinely ignore his authoritarianism, bigotry, and paranoid dabbling in conspiracy theories.

Robertson's gallery of conspirators parallels the roster of the John Birch Society, including the Freemasons, the Bavarian Illuminati, the Council on Foreign Relations, and the Trilateral Commission. In Robertson's book the New World Order, he trumps the Birchers (their founder called Dwight Eisenhower a communist agent) by alluding to an anti-Christian conspiracy that supposedly began in ancient Babylon—a theory that evokes historic anti-Jewish bigotry and resembles the notions of the late fascist demagogue Lyndon LaRouche, who is routinely dismissed by the corporate media as a crackpot. Robertson's homophobia is profound. He is also a religious bigot who has repeatedly said that Hindus and Muslims are not morally qualified to hold government posts. "If anybody understood what Hindus really believe," says Robertson, "there would be no doubt that they have no business administering government policies in a country that favors freedom and equality."

Robertson's embrace of authoritarian theocracy is equally robust:

> There will never be world peace until God's house and God's people are given their rightful place of leadership at the top of the world. How can there be peace when drunkards, drug dealers, communists, atheists, New Age worshipers of Satan, secular humanists, oppressive dictators, greedy money changers, revolutionary assassins, adulterers, and homosexuals are on top?

Mainstream pundits are uncertain about the magnitude of the threat posed by the theocratic Right and the other hard Right sectors. Sidney Blumenthal warned recently in the New Yorker that "Republican politics nationally, and particularly in Virginia, have advanced so swiftly toward the Right in the past two years that [Oliver] North's nomination [for the US Senate] was almost inevitable." But just a few years ago, after George Bush was elected President, Blumenthal dismissed the idea that the theocratic Right was a continuing factor in national politics. "Journalists like Blumenthal are Centrists who believe that America always fixes itself by returning to the center. They have the hardest time appreciating the danger the Right represents because they see it as just another swing of the political pendulum," says Jean Hardisty, a political scientist who has monitored the Right for more than 20 years:

> As the McCarthy period showed, however, if you let a right-wing movement go long enough without serious challenge, it can become a real threat and cause real damage. Centrists missed the significance of the right-wing drive of the past fourteen years as it headed for success.

The defeat of George Bush in 1992 did not deter the hard Rightists as they increasingly turned toward state and local forums, where small numbers can transform communities. They learned from the humiliating defeat of Barry Goldwater in 1964 that to construct a conservative America would take strategic planning that spanned decades.

Now, after decades of organizing, the Right has managed to shift the spectrum of political debate, making conservative politics look mainstream when compared with overt bigotry, and numbing the public to the racism and injustice in mainstream politics. When, for example, Vice President Dan Quayle was asked by ABC what he thought of David Duke, Quayle sanitized Duke's thorough racism and said: "the message of David Duke is … anti-big-government, get out of my pocketbook, cut taxes, put welfare people back to work. That's a very popular message. The problem is the messenger. David Duke, neonazi, ex-Klansman, basically a bad person."

The pull of the antidemocratic hard Right and its reliance on scapegoating, especially of people of color, is a major factor in the increased support among Centrist politicians for draconian crime bills, restrictive immigration laws, and punitive welfare regulations. The Republican Party's use of the race card, from Richard Nixon's southern strategy to the Willie Horton ads of George Bush's 1988 campaign, is made more acceptable by the overt racism of the far Right. Racist stereotypes are used opportunistically to reach an angry White constituency of middle- and working-class people who have legitimate grievances caused by the failure of the bipartisan status quo to resolve issues of economic and social justice.

Scapegoating evokes a misdirected response to genuine unresolved grievances. The Right has mobilized a mass base by focusing the legitimate anger of parents over inadequate resources for the public schools on the scapegoat of gay and lesbian curriculum, sex education, and AIDS-awareness programs; by focusing confusion over changing sex roles and the unfinished equalization of power between men and women on the scapegoats of the feminist movement and abortion rights; by focusing the desperation of unemployment and underemployment on the scapegoat of affirmative-action programs and other attempts to rectify racial injustice; by focusing resentment about taxes and the economy on the scapegoat of dark-skinned immigrants; by focusing anger over thoughtless and intrusive government policies on environmental activists; and by focusing anxiety about a failing criminal justice system on the scapegoat of early release, probation, and parole programs for prisoners who are disproportionately people of color.

Such scapegoating has been applied intensively in rural areas which see emerging social movements of "new patriots" and "armed militias" who are grafting together the conspiracy theories of the hard-Right John Birch Society with the ardor and armor of the paramilitary far Right.

These hard Right and far Right forces are beginning to influence state and local politics, especially in the Pacific Northwest and Rocky Mountain states, through amorphous patriot and armed militia groups, sovereignty campaigns, and county autonomy movements as well as some portions of the anti-environmentalist "Wise Use" movement. The same regions have seen contests within the Republican Party on the state level between mainstream Republicans and the theocratic Right. Some Republican candidates pander to the patriot and militia movements as a source of constituent votes. The political spectrum in some states now ranges from repressive corporate liberalism in the "center" through authoritarian theocracy to nascent fascism.

The road to backlash politics

How did we get here? Despite the many differences, one goal has united the various sectors of the antidemocratic Right in a series of amorphous coalitions since the 1960s: to roll back the limited gains achieved in the United States by a variety of social justice movements, including the civil rights, student rights, antiwar, feminist, ecology, gay and lesbian rights, disability rights, and antimilitarist movements.

Hard Right nativists formed the core of Joseph McCarthy's constituency after World War II. After McCarthy's fall, they retreated until the late 1950s and early 1960s, when a network of anti-communists spread the gospel of the communist and secularist threats through such books as Dr Fred Schwartz's 1960 You Can Trust the Communists (to be Communists). At the 1964 Republican convention, the growth of hard Right forces became apparent. Goldwater's candidacy represented a reaction to the values of modernity. Unlike traditional conservative politics, which sought to preserve the status quo from the encroachments of the modern world, Goldwater's politics sought to turn back the political clock. This reactionary stance remains a key component of the US hard Right today. In 1961, Goldwater said, "My aim is not to pass laws but to repeal them." Twenty years later, Paul Weyrich, chief architect of the New Right, said, "I believe in rollback."

Hard Right activists such as Phyllis Schlafly and John Stormer had helped engineer Goldwater's nomination. Schlafly was a convention delegate in 1964, and went on to found the Eagle Forum, which fought the Equal Rights Amendment. Stormer wrote a book called *None Dare Call It Treason*. Their aggressive anti-communist militarism worried many conventional voters, and their conspiracy theories of secret collusion between corporate Republican leaders and the communists—Schlafly called them the "secret kingmakers" in her pro-Goldwater book *A Choice Not an Echo*—brought the hard Right and far Right out of the woodwork as Goldwater supporters, which cost votes when they began expounding on their byzantine conspiracy theories to the national news media.

Most influential Goldwater supporters were not marginal far Right activists, as many liberal academics postulated at the time, but had been Republican Party regulars for years, representing a vocal reactionary wing far to the Right of many persons who usually voted Republican. This hard Right reactionary wing of the Republican Party had an image problem, which was amply demonstrated by the devastating defeat of Goldwater in the general election. The Right-wing avalanche began when a group of conservative strategists decided to brush off the flakes who had burdened the unsuccessful 1964 Goldwater presidential campaign. They decided it was time to build a "New Right" coalition that differentiated itself from the old, nativist Right in two key ways: it embraced the idea of an expansionist government to enforce the hard Right's social policy goals, and it eschewed the old Right's explicitly racist rhetoric.

Overt White supremacists and segregationists had to go, as did obvious anti-Jewish bigots. The wild-eyed conspiratorial rhetoric of the John Birch Society was unacceptable, even to William F. Buckley, Jr., whose National Review was the authoritative journal of the Right.

While the old Right's image was being modernized, emerging technologies and techniques using computers, direct mail, and television were brought into play to build the New Right. After Goldwater's defeat, Richard Viguerie painstakingly hand-copied information on Goldwater donors at the Library of Congress and used the results to launch his direct-mail fundraising empire, which led to the formation of the New Right coalition. and to reach the grassroots activists and voters, Right-wing strategists openly adopted the successful organizing, research, and training methods that had been pioneered by the labor and civil rights movements.

When Richard Nixon was elected president in 1968, his campaign payoff to the emerging New Right included appointing such Right-wing activists as Howard Phillips to government posts. Phillips was sent to the Office of Economic Opportunity with a mandate to dismantle social programs allegedly dominated by liberals and radicals. Conservatives and reactionaries joined in a "Defund the Left" campaign. As conservatives in Congress sought to gut social-welfare programs, corporate funders were urged to switch their charitable donations to build a network of conservative think tanks and other institutions to challenge what was seen as the intellectual dominance of Congress and society held by such liberal think tanks as the Brookings Institution.

Since the 1960s, the secular, corporate, and religious branches of the Right have spent hundreds of millions of dollars to build a solid national Right-wing infrastructure that provides training, conducts research, publishes studies, produces educational resources, engages in networking and coalition building, promotes a sense of solidarity and possible victory, shapes issues, provides legal advice, suggests tactics, and tests and defines specific rhetoric and slogans. Today, the vast majority of "experts" featured on television and radio talk shows, and many syndicated print columnists, have been groomed by the Right-wing infrastructure, and some of these figures were first recruited and trained while they were still in college.

Refining rhetoric is key for the Right because many of its ideas are based on narrow and nasty Biblical interpretations or are of benefit to only the wealthiest sector of society. The theocratic Right seeks to breach the wall of separation between church and state by constructing persuasive secular arguments for enacting legislation and enforcing policies that take rights away from individuals perceived as sinful. Matters of money are interpreted to persuade the sinking middle class to cheer when the rich get richer and the poor get poorer. Toward these ends, questionable statistics, pseudo-scientific studies, and biased reports flood the national debate through the sluice gates of the Right-wing think tanks.

Thus, the Right has persuaded many voters that condoms don't work but trickle-down theories do. The success of the Right in capturing the national debate over such issues as taxes, government spending, abortion, sexuality, childrearing, welfare, immigration, and crime is due, in part, to its national infrastructure, which refines and tests rhetoric by conducting marketing studies, including those based on financial response to direct-mail letters and televangelist pitches.

Corporate millionaires and zealous Right-wing activists, however, can't deliver votes without a grassroots constituency that responds to the rhetoric. Conveniently, the New Right's need for foot soldiers arrived just as one branch of Christianity, Protestant evangelicalism, marched onward toward a renewed interest in the political process. Earlier in the century, Protestant evangelicals fought the teaching of evolution and launched a temperance campaign that led to Prohibition. But in the decades preceding the 1950s, most Protestant evangelicals avoided the secular arena. Their return was facilitated by the Reverend Billy Graham, perhaps the best known proponent of the idea that all Protestants should participate in the secular sphere to fight the influence of Godless communism at home and abroad, and others ranging from the international Moral ReArmament movement to local pastors who helped craft theological arguments urging all Christians to become active in politics in the 1950s and 1960s.

A more aggressive form of Protestant evangelicalism emerged in the 1970s, when such Right-wing activists as Francis A. Schaeffer, founder of the L'Abri Fellowship in Switzerland and author of *How Should We Then Live?*, challenged Christians to take control of a sinful secular society. Schaeffer (and his son Franky) influenced many of today's theocratic Right activists, including Jerry Falwell, Tim LaHaye, and John W. Whitehead, who have gone off in several theological and political directions, but all adhere to the notion that the Scriptures have given dominion over the Earth to Christians, who thus owe it to God to seize the reins of secular society.

The most extreme interpretation of this "dominionism" is a movement called Reconstructionism, led by Right-wing Presbyterians who argue that secular law is always secondary to Biblical law. While the Reconstructionists represent only a small minority within Protestant theological circles, they have had tremendous influence on the theocratic Right (a situation not unlike the influence of Students for a Democratic Society or the Black Panthers on the New Left in the 1960s). Reconstructionism is a factor behind the increased violence in the anti-abortion movement, the nastiest of attacks on gays and lesbians, and the new wave of battles over alleged secular humanist influence in the public schools. Some militant Reconstructionists even support the death penalty for adulterers, homosexuals, and recalcitrant children.

One key theocratic group, the Coalition on Revival, has helped bring dominionism into the hard-Right political movement. Militant antiabortion activist Randall Terry writes for their magazine, Crosswinds, and has signed their Manifesto for the Christian Church, which proclaims that America should "function as a Christian nation" and that the "world will not know how to live or which direction to go without the Church's Biblical influence on its theories, laws, actions, and institutions," including opposition to such "social moral evils" as "abortion on demand, fornication, homosexuality, sexual entertainment, state usurpation of parental rights and God-given liberties, statist-collectivist theft from citizens through devaluation of their money and redistribution of their wealth, and evolutionism taught as a monopoly viewpoint in the public schools." Taken as a whole, the manifesto is a call for clerical fascism in defense of wealth and patriarchy.

While dominionism spread, the number of persons identifying themselves as born-again Christians was growing, and by the mid-1970s, Rightists were making a concerted effort to link Christian evangelicals to conservative ideology. Sara Diamond, author of *Spiritual Warfare*, assigns a seminal role to Bill Bright of the Campus Crusade for Christ, but traces the paternity of the New Right to 1979, when Robert Billings of the National Christian Action Council invited rising tel-evangelist Jerry Falwell to a meeting with Right-wing strategists Paul Weyrich, Howard Phillips, Richard Viguerie, and Ed McAteer. According to Diamond, "Weyrich proposed that if the Republican Party could be persuaded to take a firm stance against abortion, that would split the strong Catholic voting bloc within the Democratic Party." Weyrich suggested building an organization with a name involving the idea of a "moral majority."

While Falwell's Moral Majority began hammering on the issue of abortion, the core founding partners of the New Right were joined in a broad coalition by the growing neoconservative movement of former liberals concerned over what they perceived as a growing communist threat and shrinking moral leadership. Reluc-tantly, the remnants of the old Right hitched a ride on the only electoral wagon moving to the Right. The New Right coalition was built around shared support for anti-communist militarism, moral orthodoxy, and economic conservatism, the themes adopted by 1980 presidential candidate Ronald Reagan.

The ardor and activism of the paranoid nativist and Americanist wing of the New Right made many mainstream Republicans nervous. Even Goldwater divorced himself from the more extreme New Right partisans, saying, "These people are not conservatives. They are revolutionaries."

The Reagan Administration was masterful at buying the loyalty of the paranoid nativist wing of the New Right. While Reagan gave mainstream Republicans a green light for the lucrative trade with such communist countries as the Soviet Union and the People's Republic of China, he gave the meager markets in Central America, Africa, and Afghanistan to the hard Right as a testing ground for their plans to fight communism and terrorism through covert action. While he nego-tiated with the Soviet Union, he continued to celebrate Captive Nations Day.

Under Reagan, the nativist-Americanist Rightists received appointments to executive agencies, where they served as watchdogs against secular humanism and subversion. For example, a Phyllis Schlafly protege in the Department of Education succeeded in blocking for several years all federal funds for the Boston-area Facing History and Ourselves project, which produces a curriculum on the Holocaust, genocide, and racism; the staffer denounced the program as secular humanist psy-chological manipulation.

The first attempt to build a broad theocratic Right movement failed in part because Jerry Falwell's Moral Majority, with its Baptist roots and pragmatic fun-damentalist Protestant aura, had only a limited constituency; it failed to mobilize either the more ethereal charismatic and Pentecostal wings of Christianity or the more moderate branches of denominational Protestantism. Apart from the abortion issue, its appeal to conservative Catholics was microscopic.

But as early as 1981, Falwell, Weyrich, and Robertson were working together to build a broader and more durable alliance of the theocratic Right through such vehicles as the annual Family Forum national conferences, where members of the Reagan Administration could rub shoulders with leaders of dozens of Christian Right groups and share ideas with rank-and-file activists. This coalition-building continued through the Reagan years.

Most Christian evangelical voters who had previously voted Democratic did not actually switch to Reagan in 1980, although other sectors of the New Right were certainly influential in mobilizing support for Reagan the candidate, and new Christian evangelical voters supported Republicans in significant numbers. But by 1984, the theocratic Right had persuaded many traditionally Democratic but socially conservative Christians that support for prayer in the schools and opposition to abortion, sex education, and pornography could be delivered by the Republicans through the smiling visage of the Great Communicator. Reagan did try to push these issues in Congress, but many mainstream Republicans refused to go along.

Despite its successes, the hard Right felt that Reagan lacked a true commitment to their ideology. In 1988, during Reagan's second term, some key New Right leaders, including Weyrich, Viguerie, and Phillips, began denouncing Reagan as a "useful idiot" and dupe of the KGB, and even a traitor over his arms control negotiations with the Soviet Union.

Under the Bush Administration, this branch of the Right had less influence. It was this perceived loss of influence within the Republican Party, among other factors, that led to the highly publicized schism in the late 1980s between the two factions of the New Right that came to be called the paleoconservatives and the neoconservatives.

Patrick Buchanan, who says proudly, "We are Old Right and Old Church," emerged from this fracas as the leader of the paleoconservatives. (The term neoconservatives, once restricted to a small group of intellectuals centered around Commentary magazine, came within this context to refer to all conservatives to the left of the paleoconservatives, despite substantial differences among them. For example, traditional neoconservatives like Midge Decter were concerned with a perceived deterioration of US culture, while the conventional conservatives at the Heritage Foundation were concerned almost exclusively with the economy.)

The paleoconservatives' America First policy supports isolationism or unilateralism in foreign affairs, coupled with a less reverent attitude toward an unregulated free market and support for an aggressive domestic policy to implement New Right social policies, such as the criminalization of sodomy and abortion.

The paleoconservatives are also more explicitly racialist and anti-democratic than the neoconservatives, who continue to support immigration, civil rights, and limited government.

The strongest glue that bound together the various sectors of the New Right's pro-Reagan coalition was anti-communist militarism. Jewish neoconservatives were even willing to overlook the long-standing tolerance of racist and antisemitic sentiments among some paleoconservatives. This led to some strange silences, such as the failure to protest the well-documented presence of a network of émigré reactionaries and anti-Jewish bigots in the 1988 Bush campaign. The neocons could not be budged to action even when investigative writer Russ Bellant revealed that one aging Republican organizer proudly displayed photos of himself in his original Waffen SS uniform, and that Laszlo Pasztor, who had built the Republican emigre network, was a Nazi collaborator who had belonged to the Hungarian Arrow Cross, which aided in the liquidation of Hungary's Jews. (Pasztor was still a key adviser to Paul Weyrich when this was written.)

The hard-Right saw Bush as an Eastern elite intellectual, and even his selection of Dan Quayle as his running mate to pacify the theocratic Right was not enough to offset what they perceived as Bush's betrayal over social issues.

When the scandals of Jimmy Swaggart and Jim Bakker rocked televangelism and Pat Robertson failed in his 1988 presidential bid, some predicted the demise of the theocratic Right. But they overlooked the huge grassroots constituency that remained connected through a Christian Right infrastructure of conferences, publications, radio and television programs, and audiotapes. Robertson lost no time in taking the key contacts from his 1988 presidential campaign and training them as the core of the Christian Coalition, now the most influential grassroots movement controlled by the theocratic Right.

Still, the theocratic Right kept its ties to the Bush White House through chief of staff John H. Sununu, who worked closely with the Free Congress Foundation and even sent a letter on White House stationery in July 1989 thanking Weyrich for his help and adding, "If you have any observations regarding the priorities and initiatives of the first six months or for the Fall, I would like to hear them." The Bush White House also staffed an outreach office to maintain liaison with evangelicals.

After the election of Clinton, the New Right alliance eventually collapsed. That became clear during the Gulf War, when Buchanan's bigotry was suddenly discovered by his former allies in the neoconservative movement. Neoconservatives who championed the anti-Sandinista Nicaraguan contras were offered posts in the Clinton Administration. And Barry Goldwater, toast of the reactionaries in 1964, lambasted the narrow-minded bigotry of the theocratic Right, which owes its birth to his failed presidential bid.

The 1992 Republican Party convention represented the ascendancy of hard Right forces, primarily the theocratic Right. The platform was the most conservative ever, and speakers called repeatedly for a cultural war against secular humanism.

The similarities between Goldwater's 1964 campaign and the 1992 Republican convention were marked. Phyllis Schlafly was present at both, arguing that liberals were trying to destroy the American way of life. In 1964, Goldwater had targeted the deterioration of the family and moral values; in 1992, the Republicans targeted traditional values.

The genius of the long-term strategy implemented by Weyrich and Robertson was their method of expanding the base. First, they created a broader Protestant Christian Right that cut across all evangelical and fundamentalist boundaries and issued a challenge to more moderate Protestants. Second, they created a true Christian Right by reaching out to conservative and reactionary Catholics. Third, they created a theocratic Right by recruiting and promoting their few reactionary allies in the Jewish and Muslim communities.

This base-broadening effort continued through the mid1990s, with Ralph Reed of the Christian Coalition writing in the Heritage Foundation's Policy Review about the need for the Right to move from such controversial topics as abortion and homosexuality toward bread-and-butter issues-a tactical move that did not reflect any change in the basic belief structure. Sex education, abortion, objections to lesbian and gay rights, resistance to pluralism and diversity, demonization of feminism and working mothers continued to be core values of the coalition being built by the theocratic Right.

John C. Green is a political scientist and director of the Ray C. Bliss Institute at the University of Akron in Ohio. With a small group of colleagues, Green has studied the influence of Christian evangelicals on recent elections, and has found that, contrary to popular opinion, the nasty and divisive rhetoric of Pat Buchanan, Pat Robertson, and Marilyn Quayle at the 1992 Republican Convention was not as significant a factor in the defeat of Bush as were unemployment and the general state of the economy. On balance, he believes, the Republicans gained more votes than they lost in 1992 by embracing the theocratic Right. "Christian evangelicals played a significant role in mobilizing voters and casting votes for the Bush-Quayle ticket," says Green.

Green and his colleagues, James L. Guth and Kevin Hill, wrote a study entitled Faith and Election: The Christian Right in Congressional Campaigns 1978–1988. They found that the theocratic Right was most active–and apparently successful– when three factors converged:

- the demand for Christian Right activism by discontented constituencies;
- religious organizations that supplied resources for such activism; and
- appropriate choices in the deployment of such resources by movement leaders.

The authors see the Christian Right's recent emphasis on grassroots organizing as a strategic choice, and conclude that "the conjunction of motivations, resources, and opportunities reveals the political character of the Christian Right: much of its activity was a calculated response to real grievances by increasingly self-conscious and empowered traditionalists."

The roots of the Culture War

Spanning the breadth of the antidemocratic hard Right is the banner of the Culture War. The idea of the Culture War was promoted by strategist Paul Weyrich of the Free Congress Foundation. In 1987, Weyrich commissioned a study, Cultural Conservatism: Toward a New National Agenda, which argued that cultural issues provided antiliberalism with a more unifying concept than economic conservatism. Cultural Conservatism: Theory and Practice followed in 1991.

Earlier, Weyrich had sponsored the 1982 book *the Homosexual Agenda* and the 1987 *Gays, AIDS, and You*, which helped spawn successive and successful waves of homophobia. The Free Congress Foundation, founded and funded with money from the Coors Beer family fortune, is the key strategic think tank backing Robertson's Christian Coalition, which has built an effective grassroots movement to wage the Culture War. For Robertson, the Culture War opposes sinister forces wittingly or unwittingly doing the bidding of Satan. This struggle for the soul of America takes on metaphysical dimensions combining historic elements of the Crusades and the Inquisition. The Christian Coalition could conceivably evolve into a more mainstream conservative political movement, or—especially if the economy deteriorates—it could build a mass base for fascism similar to the clerical fascist movements of mid-century Europe.

For decades anti-communism was the glue that bound together the various tendencies on the Right. Ironically, the collapse of communism in Europe allowed the US political Right to shift its primary focus from an extreme and hyperbolic anti-communism, militarism, and aggressive foreign policy to domestic issues of culture and national identity. Multiculturalism, political correctness, and traditional values became the focus of this new struggle over culture. An early and influential jeremiad in the Culture War was Allan Bloom's 1987 book *the Closing of the American Mind*. But neither the collapse of communism in the former Soviet Union, nor the publication of Bloom's book accounts for the success of this Culture War in capturing the high ground in popular discourse. Instead, it resulted from the victory of hard-Right forces within the New Right (which helped lead to its demise as a coalition), and the concomitant embrace by hard Right activists of a nativist, theocratic ideology that challenged the very notion of a secular, pluralistic democracy.

At the heart of this Culture War, or *kulturkampf*, as Patrick Buchanan calls it, is a paranoid conspiratorial view of Leftist secular humanism, dating to the turn of the century and dependent upon powerful but rarely stated presumptions of racial nationalism based on Eurocentric White supremacy, Christian theocracy, and subversive liberal treachery.

The nativist Right at the turn of the century first popularized the idea that there was a secular humanist conspiracy trying to steer the US from a God-centered society to a socialist, atheistic society. The idea was linked from its beginnings to an extreme fear of communism, conceptualized as a "red menace." the conspiracy became institutionalized in the American political scene and took on a metaphysical nature, according to analyst Frank Donner:

> the root anti-subversive impulse was fed by the [Communist] Menace. Its power strengthened with the passage of time, by the late twenties its influence

had become more pervasive and folkish ... A slightly secularized version, widely shared in rural and small-town America, postulated a doomsday conflict between decent upright folk and radicalism—alien, satanic, immorality incarnate.

This conspiratorial world-view continued to animate the hard Right. According to contemporary conspiratorial myth, liberal treachery in service of Godless secular humanism has been "dumbing down" schoolchildren with the help of the National Education Association to prepare the country for totalitarian rule under a "One World Government" and "New World Order." This became the source of an underlying theme of the armed militia movement.

This nativist-Americanist branch of the hard Right (or the pseudo-conservative, paranoid Right, as Richard Hofstadter termed it in his classic essay, "the Paranoid Style in American Politics") came to dominate the Right wing of the Republican Party, and included Patrick Buchanan, Phyllis Schlafly's Eagle Forum, Pat Robertson's Christian Coalition, the Rockford Institute, David Noebel's Summit Ministries, and Paul Weyrich's Free Congress Foundation and Institute for Cultural Conservatism. of more historical importance are the John Birch Society, the Christian Anti-Communism Crusade, and Billy James Hargis' Christian Crusade, although the John Birch Society's membership doubled or tripled since the Gulf War in 1991 to over 40,000 members. Despite some overlap at the edges, reactionary hard Right electoral activists should be distinguished from the extra-electoral Right-wing survivalists, militia members, and armed White racists on their right, and from the Eastern establishment conservative branch of the Right wing represented by George Bush on their left.

Secular humanism has been called the bogey-man of Right-wing fundamentalism; it is a term of art, shorthand for all that is evil and opposed to God. While historically there has been an organized humanist movement in the United States since the mid-1800s, secular humanism as a large religious movement exists more in the Right's conspiracy theories than in actual fact. Secular humanism is a non-theistic philosophy with roots in the rationalist philosophies of the Enlightenment that bases its commitment to ethical behavior on the innate goodness of human beings, rather than on the commands of a deity.

The conspiracy that the Right wing believes has resulted in secular humanism's hegemony is both sweeping and specific. It is said to have begun in 1805, when the liberal Unitarians, who believed that evil was largely the result of such environmental factors as poverty and lack of education, wrested control of Harvard University from the conservative Calvinists, who knew that men were evil by nature. The Unitarian drive for free public schools was part of a conscious plan to convert the United States from capitalism to the newly postulated socialism of Robert Owen.

Later, according to the conspiracy theorists, John Dewey, a professor at Columbia University and head of the progressive education movement (seen as "the Lenin of the American socialist revolution"), helped to establish a secular, state run (and thus socialized) educational system in Massachusetts. To facilitate the communist takeover, Dewey promoted the look-say reading method, knowing it would lead to widespread illiteracy. As Samuel Blumenfeld argued in 1984, "[T]he goal was to produce inferior readers with inferior intelligence dependent on a socialist education elite for guidance, wisdom and control. Dewey knew it..."

For the hard Right, it is entirely reasonable to claim both that John Dewey conspired to destroy the minds of American schoolchildren and that contemporary liberals carry on the conspiracy. As Rosemary Thompson, a respected pro-family activist, wrote in her 1981 book, *Withstanding Humanism's Challenge to Families* (with a foreword by Phyllis Schlafly), "[H]umanism leads to feminism. Perhaps John Dewey will someday be recognized in the annals of history as the 'father of women's lib.'"

To these Rightists, all of the evils of modern society can be traced to John Dewey and the secular humanists. A typical author argued:

> Most US citizens are not aware that hard-core pornography, humanistic sex education, the "gay" rights movement, feminism, the Equal Rights Amendment, sensitivity training in schools and in industry, the promotion of drug abuse, the God-Is Dead movement, free abortion on demand, euthanasia as a national promotion ... to mention a few, highly publicized movements ... have been sparked by humanism.

According to the Right, by rejecting all notions of absolute authority and values, secular humanists deliberately attack traditional values in religion, the state, and the home.

The link between liberalism and treachery is key to the secular humanist conspiracy. In 1968, a typical book, endorsed by Billy James Hargis of the Christian Crusade, claimed, "the liberal, for reasons of his own, would dissolve the American Republic and crush the American dream so that our nation and our people might become another faceless number in an internationalist state." Twenty-five years later, Allan Bloom, generally put forth as a moderate conservative, argued that all schoolteachers who inculcated moral relativism in school children "had either no interest in or were actively hostile to the Declaration of Independence and the Constitution."

The Culture War and theocracy

Most analysts have looked at the Culture War and its foot soldiers in the traditional family values movement as displaying a constellation of discrete and topical beliefs. These include support for traditional, hierarchical sex roles and opposition to feminism, employed mothers, contraception, abortion, divorce, sex education, school-based health clinics, extramarital sex, and gay and lesbian sex, among other issues.

Traditional values also include an antipathy toward secular humanism, communism, liberalism, utopianism, modernism, globalism, multiculturalism, and other systems believed to undermine US nationalism. Beliefs in individualism, hard work, self-sufficiency, thrift, and social mobility form a uniquely American component of the movement. Some traditional values seem derived more immediately from Christianity: opposition to Satanism, witchcraft, the New Age, and the occult (including meditation and Halloween depictions of witches). Less often discussed but no less integral to the movement are a disdain for the values of egalitarianism and democracy (derived from the movement's anti–modernist orientation), and support for Western European culture, private property, and laissez-faire capitalism.

This orthodox view of the traditional values movement as an aggregate of many discrete values, however, is misleading, for it makes it appear that Judeo-Christian theism is simply one value among many. Rather, Judeo Christian theism, and in particular Christianity, is the core value of the traditional values movement and the basis for the Crusades-like tone of those in the hard Right calling for the Culture War.

Traditional values start from a recognition of the absolute, unchanging, hierarchical authority of God (as one commentator noted, "the Ten Commandments are not the Ten Suggestions") and move from there to a belief in hierarchical arrangements in the home and state.

As Pat Robertson said at the Republican convention, "Since I have come to Houston, I have been asked repeatedly to define traditional values. I say very simply, to me and to most Republicans, traditional values start with faith in Almighty God." Robertson has also said, "When President Jimmy Carter called for a 'Conference on Families,' many of us raised strenuous objections. To us, there was only one family, that ordained by the Bible, with husband, wife, and children."

In part, the moral absolutism implicit in the Culture War derives from the heavy proportion of fundamentalist Christians in the traditional family values movement. Their belief in the literal existence of Satan leads to an apocalyptic tone: "the bottom line is that if you are not working for Jesus Christ, then you are working for someone else whose name is Satan. It is one or the other. There is no middle of the road."

The hard-Right activist, as Richard Hofstadter noted, believes that all battles take place between forces of absolute good and absolute evil, and looks not to compromise but to crush the opposition.

A comment by Pat Robertson was typical:

> What is happening in America is not a debate, it is not a friendly disagreement between enlightened people. It is a vicious one-sided attack on our most cherished institutions. ... Suddenly the confrontation is growing hotter and it just may become all out civil war. It is a war against the family and against conservative and Christian values.

Paul Weyrich saw the struggle today between those "who worship in churches and those who desecrate them."

The root desire behind the Culture War is the imposition of a Christian theocracy in the United States. Some theocratic Right activists have been quite open about this goal. Tim LaHaye, for example, argued in his book *the Battle for the Mind* that "we must remove all humanists from public office and replace them with pro-moral political leaders."

Similarly, in Pat Robertson's *the New World Order: It Will Change the Way You Live* (which argues that the conspiracy against Christians, dating back to Babylon, has included such traditional conspirators as John Dewey, the Illuminati, the Free Masons, the Council on Foreign Relations, and the Trilateral Commission), the question of who is fit to govern is discussed at length:

> When I said during my presidential bid that I would only bring Christians and Jews into the government … the media challenged me, "How dare you maintain that those who believe the Judeo Christian values are better qualified to govern America than Hindus and Muslims?"
>
> My simple answer is, "Yes, they are." If anybody understood what Hindus really believe, there would be no doubt that they have no business administering government policies in a country that favors freedom and equality … There will never be world peace until God's house and God's people are given their rightful place of leadership at the top of the world.
>
> How can there be peace when drunkards, drug dealers, communists, atheists, New Age worshipers of Satan, secular humanists, oppressive dictators, greedy moneychangers, revolutionary assassins, adulterers, and homosexuals are on top?

The most extreme position in the Culture War is held by Christian Reconstructionists who seek the imposition of Biblical law throughout the United States. Other hard Right activists, while less open or draconian, share an implicitly theocratic goal. While it denies any desire to impose a theocracy, the Center for Cultural Conservatism, which defines cultural conservatism as the "necessary, unbreakable, and causal relationship between traditional Western, Judeo-Christian values … and the secular success of Western societies," breaks with conservative tradition to call upon government to play an active role in upholding the traditional culture which they see as rooted in specific theological values.

The Culture War and White supremacy

The theory of widespread secular subversion spread by proponents of the Culture War was from the beginning a deeply racialized issue that supported the supremacy of White Anglo-Saxon Protestants. To the nativist Right, in the 1920s as well as now, the synthesis of traditional values constituted "Americanism," and opponents of this particular constellation of views represented dangerous, un-American forces.

As John Higham argued in *Strangers in the Land: Patterns of American Nativism 1860–1925*, subversion has always been identified with foreigners and anti-Americanism in the United States, and particularly with Jews and people of color. In the 1920s, subversion was linked to Jews, and the immigration of people of color was opposed in part because they were seen as easy targets for manipulation by Jews.

While antisemitism was never the primary ingredient in anti-radical nativism, the radical Jew was nevertheless a powerful stereotype in the "communist menace" movement. For example, some members of the coercive immigrant "Americanization" movement adopted the startling slogan, "Christianization and Americanization are one and the same thing."

Virtually any movement to advance racial justice in the US was branded by the reactionary Right as a manifestation of the secular humanist conspiracy. The National Education Association's bibliography of "Negro authors," foundation support for "Black revolutionaries," and the enlistment of Gunnar Myrdal as an expert on the "American Negro" were all framed in this way. Similarly, the African American civil rights movement was from its beginning identified by the Right wing as part of the secular humanist plot to impose communism on the United States.

In 1966, David Noebel (then of Billy James Hargis' Christian Crusade, and later head of the influential Summit Ministries) argued, "Anyone who will dig into the facts of the Communist involvement in the 'civil rights' strife will come to the conclusion that these forces have no stopping point short of complete destruction of the American way of life." (In the preface, Noebel thanks Dr R. P. Oliver, who is now perhaps best known as a director of the Institute for Historical Review, which denies that the Holocaust took place.) (See bibliography for references to Noebel's books 1965, 1966, 1974.)

In 1992, the civil rights movement is still seen in this light, as the Rightist Catholic magazine *Fidelity* makes clear:

> It is no coincidence that the civil rights movement in the United States preceded the largest push for sexual liberation this country had seen since its inception … the Negro was the catalyst for the overturning of European values, which is to say, the most effective enculturation of Christianity.
>
> The civil rights movement was nothing more than the culmination of an attempt to transform the Negro into a paradigm of sexual liberation that had been the pet project of the cultural revolutionaries since the 1920s.

The identification of sexual licentiousness and "primitive" music with subversion and people of color is an essential part of the secular humanist conspiracy theory, and one that has been remarkably consistent over time. The current attacks on rap music take place within this context.

In 1966, David Noebel argued that the communist conspiracy ("the most cunning, diabolical conspiracy in the annals of human history") was using rock music, with its savage, tribal, orgiastic beat, to destroy "our youths' ability to relax, reflect, study and meditate" and to prepare them "for riot, civil disobedience and revolution."

Twenty years later, these views were repeated practically verbatim by Allan Bloom, who wrote that rock music, with its "barbaric appeal to sexual desire," "ruins the imagination of young people and makes it very difficult for them to have a passionate relationship to the arts and thought that are the substance of liberal education."

The hard Right's attack on multiculturalism derives its strength from the Right's absolutism, as well as from its White racial nationalism. Samuel Blumenfeld was among the first to attack multiculturalism as a new form of secular humanism's values relativism, writing in 1986 that multiculturalism legitimized different lifestyles and values systems, thereby legitimizing a moral diversity that "directly contradicts the Biblical concept of moral absolutes on which this nation was founded."

Patrick Buchanan bases his opposition to multiculturalism on White racial nationalism. In one article, "Immigration Reform or Racial Purity?" Buchanan himself was quite clear:

> the burning issue here has almost nothing to do with economics, almost everything to do with race and ethnicity. If British subjects, fleeing a depression, were pouring into this country through Canada, there would be few alarms.
>
> The central objection to the present flood of illegals is they are not English-speaking white people from Western Europe; they are Spanish speaking brown and black people from Mexico, Latin America and the Caribbean.

Buchanan explicitly links the issue of non-White immigration with multiculturalism, quoting with approval the xenophobic and racist American Immigration Control Foundation, which said:

> the combined forces of open immigration and multi-culturalism constitute a mortal threat to American civilization. The US is receiving a never-ending mass immigration of non-Western peoples, leading inexorably to white-minority status in the coming decades [while] a race-based cultural-diversity is attacking, with almost effortless success, the legitimacy of our Western culture.

The Free Congress Foundation's Center for Cultural Conservatism disavows any racial nationalist intent while bluntly arguing that all non-White cultures are inferior to traditional Western cultures.

Race and culture

The major split inside the Right-wing crusaders for the Culture War is based on whether or not race and culture are inextricably linked. Buchanan and the authors of the Bell Curve argue for biological determinism and White supremacy, while Weyrich and Robertson argue that people of all races can embrace Americanism by adopting northern European, Christian, patriarchal, values—or, in their shorthand: traditional family values.

It's important to state clearly that neoconservatives, for the most part, share Buchanan's distaste for multiculturalism. The *American Spectator*, for example, has argued:

> the preservation of the existing ethnocultural character of the United States is not in itself an illegitimate goal. Shorn of Buchanan's more unhygienic rhetoric, and with the emphasis on culture rather than ethnicity, it's a goal many conservatives share. If anything, a concern that the ethnocultural character of the United States is being changed in unwholesome ways is the quality that distinguishes the conservatism of Commentary and the Public Interest from the more economically minded conservatism that pervades the Washington think tanks.

In part, it is legitimate to argue that the distinction between the old and new conservatives on the issue of race is slim. At the same time, however, the distinction between the approaches the old and new conservatives take on race is the distinction between White racism and White racial nationalism. While systemic racism enforced by a hostile, repressive state is dangerous, the massed power of racial nationalism, as expressed in the activities of the racial nationalist, clerical fascist regimes in Eastern Europe during World War II, is vastly more dangerous.

The embrace of White racial nationalism by the paleo conservatives has been extensive. *Chronicles* magazine wrote in July 1990:

> What will it be like in the next century when, as Time magazine so cheerfully predicts, white people will be in the minority. Our survival depends on our willingness to look reality in the face. There are limits to elasticity, and these limits are defined in part by our historical connections with the rest of Europe and in part by the rate of immigrations. High rates of non-European immigration, even if the immigrants come with the best of intentions in the world, will swamp us. Not all, I hasten to add, do come with the best intentions.

In his distaste for democracy, Buchanan has explicitly embraced racial nationalism. In one column, titled "Worship Democracy? A Dissent," Buchanan argued, "the world hails democracy in principle; in practice, most men believe there are things higher in the order of value-among them, tribe and nation, family and faith." in April 1990, he made a similar statement: "It is not economics that sends men to the barricades; tribe and race, language and faith, history and culture, are more important than a nation's GNP."

Buchanan has also stated:

> the question we Americans need to address, before it is answered for us, is: Does this First World nation wish to become a Third World country? Because that is our destiny if we do not build a sea wall against the waves of

immigration rolling over our shores … Who speaks for the Euro-Americans, who founded the USA? … Is it not time to take America back?

The basic thesis of White racial nationalism is expressed by David Duke, who won 55 percent of the White vote in Louisiana while arguing:

I think the basic culture of this country is European and Christian and I think that if we lose that, we lose America … I don't think we should suppress other races, but I think if we lose that White—what's the word for it—that White dominance in America, with it we lose America.

It is difficult not to see the fascist undercurrents in these ideas.

The hard Right's disdain for democracy and modernity

In the 1920s, at a time, not unlike today, of isolationism, anti-immigrant activism, and White racial nationalism, democracy was seriously challenged. With its anti-elitist, egalitarian assumptions, democracy did not appeal to the reactionary Rightists of the 1920s, who insisted that the US was not a democracy but a representative republic. Today, Patrick Buchanan, Paul Weyrich, and the John Birch Society also insist on this distinction, which can more easily accommodate the anti-egalitarian notion of governmental leadership by an elite aristocracy. As Hofstadter pointed out, the pseudo conservatives' conspiratorial view of liberals leads them to impugn the patriotism of their opponents in the two-party system, a position that undermines the political system itself.

While hard Rightists claim to defend traditional US values, they exhibit a deep disdain for democracy. Dismissive references to "participatory democracy, a humanist goal," are common; Patrick Buchanan titled one article, "Worship Democracy? A Dissent." Like many hard Rightists, Allan Bloom mixes distaste for humanism and democratic values with elitism when he argues:

Humanism and cultural relativism are a means to avoid testing our own prejudices and asking, for example, whether men are really equal or whether that opinion is merely a democratic prejudice.

More specific rejections of democracy are common currency on the hard Right these days. Paul Weyrich, for example, called for the abolition of constitutional safeguards for people arrested in the drug war. Murray Rothbard called for more vigilante beatings by police of those in their custody. Patrick Buchanan has supported the use of death squads, writing, for example:

Faced with rising urban terror in 1976, the Argentine military seized power and waged a war of counter-terror. With military and police and freelance operators, between 6,000 and 150,000 leftists disappeared. Brutal, yes; also successful. Today, peace reigns in Argentina; security has been restored.

Perhaps the most disturbing manifestation of antidemocratic sentiment among the reactionary Rightists has been their apparently deliberate embrace of a theory of racial nationalism that imbues much of the protofascist posturings of the European New Right's Third Position politics. Third Position politics rejects both communism and democratic capitalism in favor of a third position that seems to be rooted historically in a Strasserite interpretation of National Socialism, although it claims to have also gone beyond Nazism.

Third Position politics blends a virulent racial nationalism (manifested in an isolationist, anti immigrant stance) with a purported support for environmentalism, trade unionism, and the dignity of labor. Buchanan has endorsed the idea of antidemocratic racial nationalism in a number of very specific ways, arguing for instance, "Multi-ethnic states, of which we are one, are an endangered species" because "most men believe there are things higher in the order of value [than democracy]-among them, tribe and nation." In support of this view, Buchanan even cites Tomislav Sunic, an academic who has allied himself with European Third Position politics.

Over the past several years, Third Position views have gained currency on the hard Right. The Rockford Institute's magazine *Chronicles* recently praised Jorg Haider's racial nationalist Austrian Freedom Party, as well as the fascist Italian Lombardy League. In a sympathetic commentator's description, the Third Position politics of *Chronicles* emerge with a distinctly volkish air:

> Chronicles is somewhat critical of free markets and spreading democracy. It looks back to agrarian society, small towns, religious values. It sees modern times as too secular, too democratic. There's a distrust of cities and of cultural pluralism, which they find partly responsible for social decay in American life.

Similarly, Paul Weyrich's Center for Cultural Conservatism praised corporatism as a social model and voiced a new concern for environmentalism and the dignity of labor.

In the wake of the schism within the Right wing, the formation of coalitions is just beginning. Whether the US is indeed endangered because it is multicultural may depend on whether mainstream conservatives embrace a paranoid, conspiratorial world view that wants a White supremacist theocracy modeled on the volatile mix of racial nationalism and corporatism that escorted fascism to Europe in the mid-century.

Defending democracy and diversity

If the Left of the current political spectrum is liberal corporatism and the Right is neofascism, then the political Center is likely to be conservative authoritarianism. The value of the Culture War as the new principle of unity on the Right is that, like anti-communism, it actively involves a grassroots constituency that perceives itself as fighting to defend home and family against a sinister threatening force.

Most Democratic Party strategists misunderstand the political power of the various antidemocratic Right-wing social movements, and some go so far as to cheer the theocratic Right's disruptive assault on the Republican Party. Democrats and their liberal allies rely on short-sighted campaign rhetoric that promotes a Centrist analysis demonizing the "Radical Right" as "extremists" without addressing the legitimate anger, fear, and alienation of people who have been mobilized by the Right because they see no other options for change.

That there is no organized Left to offer an alternative vision to regimented soulless liberal corporatism is one of the tragic ironies of our time. The largest social movements with at least some core allegiance to a progressive agenda remain the environmental and feminist movements, with other pockets of resistance among persons uniting to fight racism, homophobia, and other social ills.

Organized labor, once the mass base for many progressive movements, continues to dwindle in significance as a national force. It was unable to block the North American Free Trade Agreement, and it has been unwilling to muster a respectable campaign to support nationalized health care. None of these progressive forces, even when combined, amount to a fraction of the size of the forces being mobilized on the Right.

"It's a struggle between virtual democracy and virulent demagoguery," says author Holly Sklar, whose books on Trilateralism document the triumphant elitist corporate ideology implemented in the United States, Europe, and Japan. Trilateralist belt-tightening policies have caused material hardships and created angry backlash constituencies.

The Right has directed these constituencies at convenient scapegoats rather than fostering a progressive systemic or economic analysis. Ironically, among the Right-wing's scapegoats is a conspiratorial caricature of the Trilateralists as a secret elite rather than the dominant wing of corporate capitalism that currently occupies the center and defends the status quo.

Suzanne Pharr, an organizer from Arkansas who moved to Oregon to help fight the homophobic initiative Measure Nine, is especially concerned that even in states where the theocratic Right has lost battles over school curricula or homophobic initiatives, it leaves behind durable Right-wing coalitions poised to launch another round of attacks. Pharr says:

> Progressives need to develop long-term strategies that move beyond short-term electoral victories. We have to develop an analysis that builds bridges to diverse communities and unites us all when the antidemocratic right attacks one of us.

Obviously, individuals involved with the antidemocratic Right have absolute constitutional rights to seek redress of their grievances through the political process and to speak their minds without government interference, so long as no laws are violated. At the same time, progressives must oppose attempts by any group to pass laws that take rights away from individuals on the basis of prejudice, myth, irrational belief, inaccurate information, and outright falsehood.

Unless progressives unite to fight the rightward drift, we will be stuck with a choice between the non-participatory system crafted by the corporate elites who dominate the Republican and Democratic parties and the stampeding social movements of the Right, motivated by cynical leaders willing to blame the real problems in our society on such scapegoats as welfare mothers, immigrants, gays and lesbians, and people of color.

The only way to stop the antidemocratic Right is to contest every inch of terrain. Politics is not a pendulum that automatically swings back and forth, Left and Right. The "Center" is determined by various vectors of forces in an endless multidimensional tug of war involving ropes leading out in many directions. Whether or not our country moves toward democracy, equality, social justice, and freedom depends on how many hands grab those ropes and pull together.

2

SWASTIKAS IN CYBERSPACE[1]

Ultra-Right White supremacy and antisemitism online

Chip Berlet and Carol Mason

A variety of scholars have documented the rise of the US Right in terms of media and technological innovation. The Ku Klux Klan in the 1920s was organized in part through a network of newspapers (McVeigh, 2009); while Catholic antisemite Father Coughlin took to the airwaves when radio was in its infancy (until his religious superiors pulled his plug) (Warren, 1996). Stories of evangelical Christian and anti-communist broadcasting have brought to light just how important harnessing new technologies was for the ascendency of conservatism and the Christian Right in America starting in the 1970s (Diamond 1995; Hendershot, 2011; Kintz and Lesage 1998; Snyder-Hall and Burack 2014).

The story of how ultra-Right-wing agitators adopted new online technologies in the US, however, is less well known, and it begins with a man named George P. Dietz (1928–2007) who arrived in the US from Germany at the age of 29 in 1957. Dietz became an American citizen in 1962 while living in New Jersey; he then relocated in 1971 to Roane County, West Virginia, where he worked as a real estate broker and set up a print shop (*Hur Herald* 2007). Eventually Dietz ran an international operation of neonazi publications, set up the first online communication among White supremacists in the US, and influenced other ultra-Right organizers who went digital.

---

1   This chapter first appeared as "Swastikas in Cyberspace: How Hate Went Online" by Chip Berlet and Carol Mason. It appeared in *Digital Media Strategies of the Far-Right in Europe and the United States*, edited by Patricia Anne Simpson and Helga Druxes. It was published in 2015 by Lexington Books, Rowman & Littlefield. All rights reserved.

    The neofascist Alt-Right phenomenon that bolstered the Trump campaign in 2016 was preceded by the early adoption of online media technology by various hard Right and neonazi sectors in the United States.

From *American Opinion* to White power

In May 1974, George Dietz joined the John Birch Society and opened an American Opinion Bookstore, which featured John Birch Society material, in Reedy, West Virginia (Mason 2009, 69–78). *American Opinion* was the name of the flagship periodical publication of the JBS. At the time, about an hour away in the state capital of Charleston, an important conflict over school curriculum was brewing in Kanawha County. Several historians have identified the Kanawha County textbook controversy of 1974–75 as a significant part of the shift to conservatism in US politics and as an early indicator of the rise of the Christian Right in the late 1970s or the more recent Tea Party movements (Moffett 1989; McGirr 2002, 331–339; Martin 2005[1996]; Mason 2009; Perlstein 2014).

Dietz's role in this controversy highlights how ultra-Right forces were affected by the conflict, in which protesters opposed the implementation of a multiracial and multi-language arts curriculum in public schools. Protesters objected to the selected textbooks for a variety of reasons, some of which were overtly racist. Dietz's print shop produced a steady stream of advertisements and flyers (more than 200,000 by one estimate) that textbook protesters used early in the controversy to garner mass opposition to the school board (*World Magazine*, 22 February 1975; National Education Association 1975, 48).

Dietz also published a magazine, *the Liberty Bell*, which fanned the flames of the curriculum dispute and became a precursor of White supremacist online activity. The Liberty Bell at first was in accordance with John Birch Society rhetoric, but became more blatantly attuned to Dietz's neonazi outlook, which was promoted internationally in print and online (Hearst, Ernest, Berlet, and Porter 2007, 74–82).

During the textbook controversy, Dietz's *Liberty Bell* showcased stock arguments from the John Birch Society regarding the general failure of American education, attributing it to a communist conspiracy to turn children against parents and society by indoctrinating them with militant multiracial literature, situational ethics, and psychological conditioning. The motivation behind the "tyranny" was "to convert the great American republic into a helpless branch of their One World-Socialist society" (Sheppe 1974, 5).

The pages of the Liberty Bell indicated an interesting tension between at least two kinds of Right-wing visions of the textbook controversy: one in which racial politics—be they school integration by bussing or multiracial textbooks—were a matter of competing cultures; and one in which they were a matter of biological difference. It would not be long after the publication of "A Message to All True Sons" that Dietz would reveal the kind of Right-wing politics to which he and the Liberty Bell were more devoted.

Dietz's politics were to the Right of the JBS. Born in Kassel, Germany, in 1928, Dietz was a member of the Hitler Youth during the Third Reich (White Power Report 1976, 34). A review of archival materials offers little to suggest he ever wavered from his upbringing. The aftermath of the textbook controversy saw George Dietz resigned from the John Birch Society and launch bolder neonazi programs locally, nationally, and internationally. "I met you at the Charleston Textbook Rally in November 1974," a correspondent wrote to Dietz, who published the letter in his overtly neonazi journal, *White Power Report*. "I have received your publications since then," the fan noted, signing off with a "Heil Hitler!" (White Power Report 1977, 36). By 1977, Dietz was showing Triumph of the Will, Leni Riefenstahl's unforgettable and visually stunning, though morally repulsive, Nazi propaganda film to select audiences in Reedy (White Power Report 1977, 51). At this point, the Anti-Defamation League of B'nai B'rith considered Dietz the world's leading producer of antisemitic materials.

Ten years after the Liberty Bell was first published, George Dietz reported to its subscribers that he had been "working, for the past two weeks, until 4–5 o'clock in the morning, trying to learn 'computerese' so that so that Yours Truly may talk to that monster in ITS language and on ITS terms" (Dietz letter to Joseph Dilys, August 10, 1983). One advantage to learning computer skills was security: "from now on, there will be in our offices no more written records, or any of the bulky address plates we have been using in the past, which are prone to 'inspection' by 'undesirables,' and everything will be safely stored on 'disposable' disks" (Dietz letter to Dilys, August 10, 1983).

Another advantage was expanding communication among White supremacists, an upgrading perhaps of "the Liberty Net," a ham radio network that "as far back as the early '70s, before [personal] computer technology was developed," brought Right-wing thinkers into conversation with one another three nights a week (McCune 1986, 10). With computer skills mastered, Dietz initiated the first White supremacist electronic bulletin board system (or BBS). A BBS is run on a single personal computer connected to a phone line through a modem-connecting device, allowing one visitor at a time to access a selection of text material being made available for online reading.

Calling his first BBS the Liberty Bell Network, Dietz in 1983 launched a new era of White supremacist organizing in cyberspace. Dietz saw the new bulletin board system as a way to thwart the Jews. Reportedly, Dietz exclaimed with delight to his colleague, "Boy, are the Yids going to scream when they learn about this!" (National Socialist Vanguard Report 1992, 3). A selling point for the early network was its being the "only computer bulletin board system and uncontrolled information medium in the United States of America dedicated to the dissemination of historical facts—not fiction!" Not surprisingly, some of the first postings on the BBS were electronic versions of *Liberty Bell* articles (Berlet and Mason 2015).

Aryan cyberspace after Dietz

Shortly after the launching of his BBS, Dietz "helped Louis Beam to establish the Aryan Liberty Network with computers in Texas, North Carolina, Illinois, Michigan and Idaho." Beam is often wrongly credited with developing the concept of "Leaderless Resistance." Beam, however, in his newsletter properly credited another newsletter editor, former U.S. Intelligence operative, Col. Ulius Louis Amoss, who first wrote of the idea in the mid-1950s as part of an anticommunist

Cold War strategy in Eastern Europe. Beam confirmed this in an interview with author Berlet (2008).

Known for his influential discussions of independent paramilitary cells and their capacity for "leaderless resistance," Beam no doubt saw computer communication networks as instrumental for the type of decentralized action he was promoting in response to government crackdowns on Right-wing organizing (Burlein 2002, 91; National Socialist Vanguard Report 1992, 3).

Beam's "Aryan Liberty Net" went online sometime in the spring of 1984 and quickly surpassed Dietz's Liberty Bell as the preferred online communication for White supremacists (It appears that notices for Dietz's online system were sometimes referred to as the Liberty Bell network and sometimes the Info International network.) As the leader of various Texas Ku Klux Klan (KKK) factions that worked closely with Richard Butler, who presided over an Aryan Nations Christian Identity compound in Idaho. Beam may have discussed the idea of a computer network as early as July 1983 at a meeting at Aryan Nations (Stern 2000, 139–157).

Next to come online (in late 1984 or early 1985) was the White Aryan Resistance BBS in Fallbrook, California, under the auspices of Tom Metzger. Metzger announced the "W.A.R. Computer Terminal" in *War '85*, the newspaper of his White Aryan Resistance (Metzger, n.d.). This system originally ran on a Commodore 64 computer with a 300 bits per second (bps) modem (Sills 1989, 144–149). At the time, this speed was cutting-edge technology. Today pocket-sized smart phones can deliver content at over 9,600,000 bps. Back then you could read articles as the computer screen as it displayed sentences at about one word a second. One of the first messages sent out by Metzger was directed at "any Aryan patriot in America who so desires" willing to arrange for local cable access channel broadcast of Metzger's new cable TV program "the World as We See It," later renamed "Race and Reason."

During this same period, there were over one dozen call-in telephone hot lines with recorded messages containing racist and antisemitic material (Berlet and Mason 2015). Thus, White supremacists were using all available technology to proliferate their hateful ideas, which continued to spread online, hence across national borders. Around August 1984, a one-page flyer circulated in Canada, announcing remote access (through the Aryan Liberty Net) to racist material otherwise banned under Canadian laws against hate speech (King 1985; Bohy 1985).

The White supremacist US-based BBSs allowed people in Canada and in European countries, where distribution of bigoted literature is often restricted by law, to gain access to these race-hate texts through their computer. This was a major goal of the early racist BBS operators Metzger bragged that his system had "ended Canadian Censorship" (Lowe 1985) "Already White Aryan comrades of the North have destroyed the free speech blackout to our Canadian comrades," wrote Metzger (1985).

In early 1985, Aryan Nations Liberty Net consisted of the Aryan Nations BBS near Hayden Lake, Idaho, a KKK BBS's with two additional phone lines near Dallas, Texas, and a KKK BBS in the Raleigh/Durham area of North Carolina. In June of 1985 a message announced the new network:

Finally, we are all going to be linked together at one point in time. Imagine if you will, all of the great minds of the patriotic Christian movement linked together and joined into one computer. All the years of combined experience available to the movement. Now imagine any patriot in the country being able to call up and access those minds, to deal with the problems and issues that affect him. You are on line with the Aryan Nations brain trust. It is here to serve the folk.

Clearly excited by the possibilities of unprecedented electronic outreach, these wired White supremacists signed off with the tagline, "Aryan Nation liberty net (an Aryan communications system). Please call again! One Nation—One race —One God."

The early 1990s online systems operated with text-only communications; this was before a graphic interface produced the World Wide Web. During this transitional period online bigotry was often posted to early Internet USENET news groups, a system of message-based topical conferences. There was vigorous debate over policy within the USENET community, often by critics of hate, but also among far-Right activists. neonazi skinheads dominated one online skin conference, but their views were attacked by anti-racist "skins," as they called themselves. In the US many skinheads are culturally identified youth rebels who are not explicitly racist, and in some cases, are actively anti-racist (Hamm 1994).

As the graphic interface for the early Internet evolved into the World Wide Web, a few sporadic web pages carrying racist, antisemitic, or other bigoted material began to appear. In May 1995, for example, Don Black set up the neonazi Stormfront site, the first major website by a national race hate organization. Stormfront remains online as of 2014, and a handful of its participants have gone on to carry out acts of terrorism and murder (Beirich 2014). White supremacists like Don Black and his Internet associates carried forward George Dietz's introduction of swastikas in cyberspace.

"Those who shrink from the Swastika today," wrote Dietz in *White Power Report*, "will next shrink from wearing their White skins" (Mason 2009, 193). Perhaps it is ironic that someone so emphatic about "White skins" was a pioneer in White supremacist organizing online where, at that early phase of internet development, no one could see skin color. For this reason, cyberspace was first theorized as a free arena in which one could escape the social confines of race or gender, and the physical constraints of corporeal being. Cultural historians of the Internet know that William Gibson's novel, *Neuromancer,* introduced "cyberspace" in 1984 in terms of a "consensual hallucination." While 1980s authors and artists like Gibson offered a radical vision of a new online world in which identity was mutable and inessential, George Dietz and other White supremacists at the same time were using computers to promote their own consensual hallucination of fascism in which identity was paramount and essentialist. The efforts to translate print media into digital documents, to circumvent national prohibitions on antisemitic materials, and to inspire Right-wing revolutionaries made the Internet—and beyond—an unsafe, unfree place to be without "White skins."

3

THE EUROPEAN NEW RIGHT AND US POLITICS[1]

Margaret Quigley

The European New Right (ENR) arrives at its call for a new form of Gramscism from the Right in part because it rejects traditional economic analyses.

What is important to the ENR is not economic, but cultural power. The European New Right bears no organizational or thematic similarity to the US "New Right," centered around the Reagan Revolution and such organizations as the Heritage Foundation, Free Congress Foundation, and the (now defunct) Moral Majority. The ENR can be linked ideologically to what has come to be called the US paleoconservative Right, the result of a schism within the US New Right at the time of the Gulf War over issues such as Israel, antisemitism, and the relative importance of racial/cultural and economic issues. Neoconservatives continued to assert conservatism's roots in a form of classical liberalism.

Differences between the European New Right and the traditional US Right include the latter's generally unquestioning acceptance of constitutionalism, rule of law, and democracy, coupled with its distrust of untrammeled state authority. Sunic (1988) also notes that there is a deep strain of pessimism, even nihilism, on the European New Right that contrasts with the Judeo–Christian values in the US context.

One ENR trait that appeals to progressives is its critique of capitalism, which is more than a shallow rejection of capitalism. The ENR condemns the cultural

---

1   Written in 1991 by Ms. Quigley as an internal memo for the staff of Political Research Associates. Ms. Quigley was fluent in reading and speaking French, and translated many of the quotes used in this text. We now know that the ideas of the European New Right in the 1990s inspired many of the theorists such as Steve Bannon who helped create the Alt-Right networks that bolstered Donald Trump's Presidential campaign in 2016. Sadly, Ms. Quigley and her partner Susie Chancey O'Quinn were killed by a drunk driver in 1993. A set of updated resource materials is online here at https://www.researchforprogress.us/top ic/41173/ and https://www.researchforprogress.us/topic/47284/.

imperialism of the US, which is the milieu in which they call for a "Gramscism of the Right." the European New Right rejects what it calls the "economism" of both capitalistic democracy and socialism, under which all transactions are reduced to their economic meaning and value (Benoist speaks of "this world of calculated thought which weighs all values to the right price". See similar themes in Benoist and Champetier 2000.)

The ENR critique of the Neoconservatives in the United States is based in part on the contention that the Neoconservatives reject the economic system of Marxism, without recognizing the deeper problem is that it is egalitarianism itself that led to the Soviet Gulag prison. This connects to the ENR theme from Hobbes that the human condition is a "war of everyone against everyone" (2017 [1651]). European New Rightists argue that in a world which aspires to egalitarianism, those who reject its precepts will always be treated with utter brutality because they have placed themselves outside the principle on which the society is organized.

This theory derives in part from Carl Schmitt, a German jurist and Nazi supporter, who the European New Rightist claims as an intellectual forerunner. Schmitt identifies politics as the distinction between friend and foe, claims it is the basis of man's humanity, and argues that liberal and socialist societies wrongly seek to de-politicize societies. The perpetual peace they seek to impose is not just unlikely but dangerous: in the depoliticized sphere, violence is unrestrained and universal; in the political world, its imposition is limited to the enemy. For a nation to choose a politics of peace is to commit suicide (1922, 1923).

Another favored ENR theorist is Vilfredo Pareto, who argued that force was the only language people understand. Pareto once said, "Whoever becomes a lamb will find a wolf to eat him" (1906).

From Schmitt as well, the European New Rightists take the idea that democracies are false and shallow because they claim to believe in universal egalitarianism while they in fact make distinctions between citizens and others, and exclude foreigners from positions of power and affluence.

The ENR is, in general, very critical of the role of intellectuals, although it is itself a quintessentially intellectual movement. According to the ENR intellectuals are not rooted in an ethnic historical context … are not committed to a mission, and thus are vulnerable to adoption of any dominant ideology. De Benoist notes that intellectuals provided the backbone of French collaborationism in the 1940s, and that intellectuals today prop up the discredited liberal and communist systems. The ENR adopts Gramsci's notion of "organic intellectuals," who are both popular leaders and scholars. Thus, intellectuals of the European New Right are expected to be engaged in building and organizing the movement, not merely in sterile academic discussions.

The ENR argues that its embrace and use of fascist ideology does not make the movement itself fascist. It claims that the intellectual terrorists of the post-war era consigned many scholars and ideas to oblivion because they were branded fascist. Such ideas grew out of a larger milieu and it is the ENR's goal to rehabilitate much of that thought. Another connection can be found in the context of the US debate on multiculturalism. The ENR introduced the term "cultural terrorists" to refer to its critics, in a usage that presaged the obsession of Right-wing ideologues in the United States with the term "political correctness."

The ENR "has also become parasitic on other movements, mostly on the far left, that preach anti-Americanism, environmentalist controls, and the demilitarization of Western Europe. The French European New Right now seems to be divided between support for the Right-wing National Front [Le Pen's group] and for the leftist Greens. Its members move back and forth, without apparent embarrassment, between extolling Catholic counter- revolutionaries and calling for tighter enforcement in French Public schools of the Laic Laws of 1905 (Sunic and De Benoist 2011).

It has become almost obligatory to refer to the insufficiency of "right" and "left" as organizing categories in political analysis. De Benoist has claimed, "Personally, I am totally indifferent to the issues of being or not being on the right. At the moment being, the ideas which it espouses are on the right, but they are not necessarily "of the right," I can easily imagine situations where these ideas could be on the left" (Sunic 1988, 13).

The ENR dates back to 1979 (it held its first press conference on September 18th of that year), although it claims intellectual roots in the French national socialist movements of 1890–1920, and the German conservative revolution of the teens, as well as other thinkers such as Nietzsche, Spengler, and Hegel. There are ENR movements across Europe:

- in Germany, the principal organs and individuals of the ENR are "Elemente", "Thule Seminar", *Neue Kultur*, Pierre Krebs, and Wigbert Grabert, Sigrid Hunke;
- in England, it is Michael Walker and his publication *Scorpion*, although it is possible to trace other influences with the British National Front;
- in France, it is Alain De Benoist, Guillaume Faye, Jean Haudry, Julien Freund GRECE, and the journals *Nouvelle Ecole, Krisis*, and *Elements*;
- in Belgium, Robert Steuckers and his journal *Orientation*; and
- in Italy, *La Destra* and *Elementi*.

Among other scholars who are identified with the European New Right are Jurgen Eysenck, Julien Freund, Armin Mohler, Thomas Molnar, Tomislav Sunic, Paul Gottfried, Gorgio Locchi, and Robert Steuckers.

One group of thinkers is centered around the organization calling itself GRECE which is used to identity the (Groupement de Recherche et d'Etudes de la Civilisation Europeenne [Group for the Research and Study of European Civilization]). The name used as an acronym is G.R.E.C.E. When spelled GRECE, however, it is a homonym for the French word for Greece and indicates the European New Right's desire to reject Europe's Judeo-Christian roots for the polytheism of classical antiquity.

The ENR 's embrace of polytheistic paganism at the expense of monotheistic Judeo-Christianity (which came to be known in Parisian circles as the European New Right's game of mono-poly) is layered. The ENR argues that Christianity presupposed a universalistic world view (the one truth) and fostered a dualistic way of looking at the world (right vs. wrong). To the European New Right, Christianity itself represents a prototype of totalitarianism, because of its beliefs in egalitarianism and universalism. The European New Right also counters the Christian values of humility and fear, to paganism's support for courage, strength, and personal honor.

It is within the ENR 's criticism that its anti-Jewish sentiment can be seen perhaps most clearly. ENR theorists make it quite clear that Judaism is the basis of such pernicious ideas as egalitarianism and human rights. Tomislav Sonic, in a revealing turn of phrase, commented that the ENR's "believes that the ideal of equality, human rights, constitutionalism, and universalism represent the secular transposition of non-European, Oriental and Judeo-Christian eschatology" (Sunic 1988, 94).

The ENR's critique of socialism and liberalism (both of which it sees as the secular descendants of the "alien" philosophy of Judeo-Christianity) starts from a belief that both movements advocate similar ideals of egalitarianism, globalism and economism, and both want to impose on all nations concepts about equality, human rights, democracy, and economic policy. As between, socialism and liberalism, the ENR's European New Right has rather more respect for the former. According to de Benoist (1986, 219) the US is itself a totalitarian system, as is the USSR, and that of the two, the US version, which "air-conditions hell and kills the soul" is the more dangerous. The ENR's belief in democratic totalitarianism is facilitated by its belief that totalitarianism cannot be defined by its methods, such as gas chambers or police terror.

Michael Walker, editor of the English European New Rightist magazine, *Scorpion*, argues:

> There exists a totalitarian liberalism. If this expression appears to be an oxymoron, it goes to show how far we have been trained to disassociate liberalism from any whiff of totalitarianism. Our criteria for judging what is totalitarian (extreme ideas, concentration camps, secret police, the cult of masculinity, the veneration of the state) are, as though by chance, the criteria which nicely exclude all possible liberal methods of exercising power.
>
> *(Walker cited in Sunic 1988, 133)*

While other thinkers, including a number of progressives, have pointed out that the exercise of power in the liberal state may also be (repressive), the assumption of the moral equivalency of the concentration camp and the ad campaign is unique to the ENR's European New Right. That this train of thought results is apologia for fascism is obvious, as this comment from de Benoist indicates, "For the European New Right, the secular results of Judeo-Christianity were egalitarianism, economism, and individualism, which in turn merged into 'soft' liberal totalitarianism, "continued" into communist totalitarianism, and triggered a 'defense' against them by the rise of Nazi totalitarianism (de Benoist quoted in Sunic 1988, 136).

Democracy, by professing an ideology of equality, and then limiting its enforcement to the sphere of political rights, is felt to contain the seeds of its own destruction. Socialism may enforce an equality of poverty, but at least it is consistent with its ideals by insisting on both factual and political equality. The ENR is also opposed to US dominance in the world.

The ENR's recapitulation of anti-Jewish themes should be clear: appeals to anti-Jewish bigotry have a long history in French progressive circles: significant numbers of leftists were pro-fascist and pro-Nazi during the Occupation, while French leftists during the 1920s argued that heroic antisemitism was quintessentially French. In lieu of the liberal belief in egalitarianism, individualism, and human rights, the ENR puts forward its belief in the importance of the ethnic, national and historical identities of people. The European New Right believes that people are born with different degrees of ability that correspond in large measure to racial and ethnic differences.

The European New Right's turn away from concern with economistic factors for cultural factors was as much ideological as practical: in addition to believing that people will support issues of culture and race, the European New Right itself believes that such issues are more important than the nature of a nation's government. The European New Right is a firm supporter of the eugenics movement, which explores purported racial differences in ability and genetic heritage. (See for example the writings of Hans Eyesenk and Roger Pearson.)

The ENR believes that multi-ethnic societies are untenable because some ethnic groups will not be able to adapt to the larger group's identity, or will not wish to. This failure to join together in an organic national mission will lead the majority to feel uprooted, and will result in turn in racism and violent nationalism. The ENR critique of human rights grows out of its nationalism, both in its specific arguments for national rights in the place of human rights, and in its support of organicism.

The ENR wants national rights in lieu of human rights, and it fears that the individualism presupposed by a notion of human rights will contradict the idea of an organic society, led by a powerful organic leader toward its own destiny. The ENR does not just argue that human rights provisions or advocates may be mistaken in specific cases, it argues that human rights are bad in themselves: human rights ideology "arose as a protest against love of fatherland," it generally emerges when a nation is "plagued by hyper individualism" and undergoing "rapid disintegration."

The language of the European New Right resounds with a demagogic appeal to mythic, heroic values that are curiously empty of content other than opposition. Alain de Benoist, for instance, says:

> That which we feel ourselves strangers from, it is not a particular political formation, it is to the world in which these political formations are discussed. To participate in our enterprise, it is not to choose one group against another. It is to change the universe. It is to give the world again its colors: To the

memory, its dimensions; to the people, a historical possibility. It is to be at the listening post of history and to feel there again the call of the gods gone by and the gods to come.

(de Benoist 1982, 9–21)

The claim of the ENR is that Christianity is a slave religion that insists people are spiritually equal because they are equal before God. The French Revolutionaries (and democracy in general) further argues that people should be politically equal as well as equal before the law. Bolshevism goes beyond both to put forth the specious argument that people are equal in fact, equal in the eyes of science.

The main thing that makes Patrick Buchanan's views fundamentally different from the ENR is his fervent Catholicism. (In the United States one of the first major political figures to adopt many of the themes of the ENR was Right-wing Republican firebrand Patrick Buchanan.) But this is not without precedent among the pagans of the European New Right. In France, the ENR often praises Catholic theorists, such as the distributionism of G. K. Chesterton and the anti-egalitarian philosophy of Joseph de Maistre.

The ENR argues that its philosophy is something more than a recycled fascism. De Benoist, for example, "insists on the sui generis character of 'his' right." Without such a caveat, it might be difficult to see how the positions of the European New Right differ from classical fascism: both despise democracy. The ENR, like fascism, rejects reason as a guide for human behavior, embracing the mystical and irrational. The *Neue Kultur* manifesto, published in Germany by Thule Seminar, states: "Our school stresses the primacy of life over all transmitted world views, the primacy of soul over spirit, the primacy of feelings over intellect, and finally of character over reason," (Thule Seminar cited in Sunic 1988, 160).

The ENR says that its anti-egalitarianism is its starting point. Because it opposes egalitarianism in any form, it opposes Marxism and liberalism, both universalist and egalitarian systems. Any political system the ENR institutes must start from an understanding that people are not equal–not spiritually, politically or factually equal. One commentator sympathetic to the European New Right has claimed that the essence of the German conservative revolution movement was "the absolute subordination of individuals to the collectivity and the negation of individual autonomy" (Sunic 1988, 41). This subordination is the basis on any concept of an organic society and is closely related to the ENR's critique of egalitarianism, a political doctrine based on the primacy of the individual.

It is difficult to summarize the European New Right's political positions. It is opposed to egalitarianism, democracy, capitalism, US multi-nationals and US cultural, diplomatic and military presence in Europe and the third World, and the modern mass society, economism, liberalism, communism, socialism, modernism, universalism, individualism, Christianity, monotheism, belief in the inevitability of human progress, parliamentary procedures and the rule of law, excessive technology and the loosening of social ties brought about by the Industrial Revolution. The ENR urges a repudiation of any sense of responsibility or guilt for the racist and imperialistic actions of the countries of Europe in the Third World. Such concerns, they argue, paralyze Europeans, and leave them defenseless against the new conquerors.

The ENR favors organicism, paganism, pantheism, strong government, strong leaders, and the fostering of a sense of a community's spirit and sense of its historical destiny. That sense of historical destiny is derived from Hegel's concept of community world spirit, Nietzsche's will to power, and Spengler, who argued that each person was born into a specific time, people, religion, culture, etc., and that all attempts at changing one's destiny were helpless.

4

MILITIA NATION[1]

Chip Berlet and Matthew N. Lyons

Many of us thought that April 19 would bring a physical confrontation of some sort, given that Waco is the central icon of this movement. No one imagined a horror of the magnitude of what happened in Oklahoma City. The bombing of the Alfred P. Murrah federal building on April 19 and the reported involvement of perpetrators linked to armed Right-wing militias finally made the danger of these groups evident to all. But the warning signs were there all along.

The growth of armed militias has been rapid, with new units appearing on a weekly basis. An educated guess about the number of militia members ranges from 10,000 to 40,000. There is at least one militia unit up and running in 40 states, with militia organizing most likely happening in all 50 states.

Anyone with an ear to the ground could have heard the rumblings. The Oklahoma bombing was not by any means the first act of public violence with connections to the armed militias and the Patriot movement they grow out of. John Salvi, who is accused of shooting reproductive-rights workers in Brookline, Massachusetts, last year, told his former employer that he was interested in the armed militias. And Francisco Duran, who was convicted of spraying the White House with bullets, was linked to the Patriot movement and armed militias.

Two years ago, even before the militias had settled on a name, alternative journalists began writing about them. Small research groups issued report after report, but no one seemed to be listening. The best early research came from such groups as the Coalition for Human Dignity, People Against Racist Terror, Western States Center, Institute for First Amendment Studies, Alternet, the Montana Human

---

1   Written for the *Progressive Magazine* after the April 19, 1995 bombing of the Oklahoma City Federal Building by Timothy McVeigh (a neonazi) and Terry Nichols (a patriot/ militia activist). Copyright 2010, The *Progressive Magazine*, all rights reserved.

Rights Network, Political Research Associates, the Center for Democratic Renewal, and many others.

The first national groups that tried to get reporters to pay attention to the threat included Planned Parenthood, Greenpeace, the Sierra Club, and the Environmental Working Group. The first national conference on the threat posed by the militias was held near Seattle in January 1995 and was organized by the Northwest Coalition Against Malicious Harassment. The Southern Poverty Law Center wrote to Janet Reno on October 25, 1994, alerting her to the danger of the militias. The Anti-Defamation League of B'Nai B'rith and the American Jewish Committee published reports on the militias.

So how were the warnings of scores of groups and hundreds of people so systematically ignored by government officials? Activists and researchers had been pleading with Congress to hold hearings on the ongoing Right-wing violence for years. It took a stack of bodies to force the hearing onto the calendar, and now we see that Congressional attention is focused on terrorism rather than the underlying causes that fuel the Right-wing militia movement.

If there had been a movement set on violent confrontation with the US government and consisting of 10,000 to 40,000 armed militia members who were African-American, you can bet they would have been investigated months ago, with many members arrested. And you can bet that Congress and the media would have played up the danger.

The armed militias are the militant wing of the Patriot movement, which has perhaps 5 million followers in this country. This diverse Right-wing populist movement is composed of independent groups in many states, unified around the idea that the government is increasingly tyrannical. This anti-government ideology focuses on federal gun control, taxes, regulations, and perceived federal attacks on constitutional liberties.

Many militia members also believe in a variety of conspiracy theories that identify a secret elite that controls the government, the economy, and the culture. Variations on these themes include theories of a secular-humanist conspiracy of liberals to take God out of society, to impose a "One World Global Government" or a "New World Order" under the auspices of the United Nations. Though many militia members appear unaware of this, these theories conform to longstanding antisemitic ideologies dating to the Nineteenth Century. White-supremacist states' rights arguments and other theories rooted in racial bigotry also pervade the militia movement.

The Patriot movement is bracketed on the "moderate" side by the John Birch Society and some of Pat Robertson's followers, and on the more militant side by Liberty Lobby and avowedly white supremacist and antisemitic groups, such as neo-Nazi groups. The leadership of pre-existing far-Right groups, such as the Posse Comitatus, the Aryan Nations, and the Christian Patriots are attempting to steer the armed militia movement toward these white supremacist and racist ideologies.

Attending a Patriot meeting is like having your cable-access channel video of a PTA meeting crossed with audio from an old Twilight Zone rerun.

In November 1994, there was a Patriot meeting at a high school in Burlington, Massachusetts, a short distance from Boston and Brookline. Speakers included John Birch Society stalwart Samuel L. Blumenfeld, Sandra Martinez of Concerned Women for America, and leading antiabortion organizer Dr Mildred Jefferson. Both the John Birch Society and the Concerned Women for America are also active in the anti-abortion movement. Jefferson began to speak, tying groups such as NOW and Planned Parenthood to a conspiracy of secular humanists tracing back to the 1800s. Jefferson is a founder and former officer of the National Right to Life committee and a board member of Massachusetts Citizens for Life.

During the meeting, attendees browsed three tables of literature brought by Den's Gun Shop in Lakeville, Massachusetts. One book offered instruction in the use of the Ruger .22 rifle, the weapon used by Salvi. Other books contained diagrams on how to build bombs and incendiary devices. One title was *Improvised Weapons of the American Underground*. You could even purchase the book *Hunter* by neo-Nazi William Pierce of the National Alliance. Hunter is a book about parasitic Jews destroying America, and the need for armed civilians to carry out political assassinations to preserve the white race. Pierce's previous book, *The Turner Diaries*, was the primary sourcebook of racist terror underground organizations, such as The Order, in the 1980s, and still is favored by the neo-Nazi wing of the militias. The Turner Diaries includes a section on the bombing of a federal building by the armed underground.

One speaker, Ed Brown, runs the Constitutional Defense Militia of New Hampshire. Brown passed out brochures offering "Firearms Training, Combat Leadership, Close Combat, and Intelligence Measures." The featured afternoon speaker was Robert K. Spear, a key figure in training armed civilian militias. Spear is the author of *Surviving Global Slavery: Living Under the New World Order* (1992). According to Spear, we are living in the "End Times" predicted in the book of Revelations. Spear cited the Bible's Book of Revelation, in Chapter 13, warning that Christians will be asked to accept the Satanic "Mark of the Beast" and reject Christ. True Christians, Spear said, must defend their faith and prepare the way for the return of Christ. Spear believes the formation of armed Christian communities is necessary to prepare for the End Times. Spear's idea that we are in the End Times is growing in Right-wing Christian evangelical circles. While predominantly a Protestant phenomenon, there are small groups of orthodox and charismatic Catholics that also are embracing End Times theology.

These views are hardly marginal within the Christian Right. Pat Robertson has been emphasizing this theme on his 700 Club television programs. Just after Christmas last year, the 700 Club carried a feature on new dollar-bill designs being discussed to combat counterfeiting. The newscaster then cited Revelations and suggested that if the Treasury Department put new codes on paper money, it might be the Mark of the Beast. Other End Timers believe the Mark of the Beast is hidden in supermarket bar codes or computer microchips.

It is the convergence of various streams of fanatical Right-wing beliefs that seems to be sweeping the militia movement along. Overlapping Right-wing social movements with militant factions appear to be coalescing within the militias. These include:

- militant Right-wing gun-rights advocates, anti-tax protesters, survivalists, far-Right libertarians;
- pre-existing elements of racist, antisemitic, or neo-Nazi movements, such as the Posse Comitatus, Christian Identity, or Christian Patriots;
- advocates of "sovereign" citizenship, "freeman" status, and other arguments rooted in a distorted analysis of the Fourteenth and Fifteenth Amendments. Among this group are those who argue that African Americans are second-class citizens;
- the confrontational wing of the anti-abortion movement;
- apocalyptic millennialists, including some Christians who believe we are in the period of the End Times;
- the dominion theology sector of the Christian evangelical Right, especially its most zealous and doctrinaire branch, Christian Reconstructionists;
- the most militant wing of the anti-environmentalist Wise Use movement; and
- the most militant wing of the county movement, the Tenth Amendment movement, the states'-rights and the state-sovereignty movements.

This coalescence created a potential for violent assaults against certain targeted scapegoats: federal officials and law-enforcement officers, abortion providers and their pro-choice supporters, environmentalists, people of color, immigrants, welfare recipients, gays and lesbians, and Jews.

Militia-like organizations have existed within the right for many years in the form of Ku Klux Klan klaverns, the Order cell (out of Aryan Nations), and the Posse Comitatus. But today's citizens' militias, which have sprung up across the country over the last three years, represent a new and ominous development within the US Right-wing.

But we need to be very careful that we describe the militia phenomenon accurately. Otherwise, we will not blunt the threat, and we may only aid those in this country who are all too eager to curtail our civil liberties. The first point to underscore about the militias is that not all militia members are racists and anti-semites. While some militias clearly have emerged, especially in the Pacific Northwest, from old race-hate groups such as the Ku Klux Klan or Aryan Nations, and while the grievances of the militia movement as a whole are rooted in white supremacist and antisemitic conspiracy theories, many militia members do not appear to be consciously drawn to the militia movement on the strength of these issues. Instead, at least consciously, they focus on blaming a caricature of the government for all the specific topical issues that stick in their craw.

To stereotype every armed militia member as a Nazi terrorist not only increases polarization in an already divided nation; it also lumps together persons with unconscious garden-variety prejudice and the demagogues and professional race-hate organizers.

Similarly, it would be wrong to assume, as some in the media have, that all members of the armed militias are marginal individuals on the fringes of society who have no connection to mainstream politics. In this view, there are always a number of fragile people who are subject to political histrionics. When they snap, they adopt an increasingly paranoid style and make militant and unreasonable demands. But this "crackpot" theory is not an accurate picture of everyone in the militia movement; it dismisses out of hand every political grievance they have, and it denies the social roots of the militia movement.

Nor would it be wise to accept the view of the law-enforcement and intelligence agencies, which see the militia movements as the creation of outside agitators who comprise a crafty core of criminal cadre at the epicenter of the movement. These leaders, the theory goes, use the movement as a front to hide their plans for violent armed revolution. Advocates of this view conclude that widespread bugging and infiltration are needed to penetrate to the core of the movement, expose the criminal cadre, and restore order. The larger movement, they claim, will then collapse without the manipulators to urge them to press their grievances, which were never real to begin with.

The problem with these interpretations is that some of the grievances are real. We need to remember that the growth of the militias is a social by-product, coming on the heels both of economic hardship and the partial erosion of traditional structures of white male heterosexual privilege. It is at times of economic dislocation and social upheaval that the Right has grown dramatically throughout our history. Indeed, the most famous militia movement in the United States, the Ku Klux Klan, arose as a citizens' militia during the turmoil of Reconstruction.

The armed militias are riding the crest of a historically significant Right-wing populist revolt in America. This revolt has arisen from two major stresses:

- actual economic hardship, caused by global restructuring; and
- anger over gains by oppressed groups within US society.

Among militia members, there is a great sense of anger over unresolved grievances, over the sense that no one is listening, and this anger has shifted to bitter frustration. The government is perceived to be the enemy because it is the agency by which the economy is governed, and by which equal rights for previously disenfranchised groups are being protected.

But militia members have a point about economic deterioration, and about the systematic expansion of the state's repressive apparatus. These are tenets of populism, which can be participatory and progressive, or scapegoating and regressive.

The last 20 years have seen a decline in real wages for millions of Americans. The farm belt has been particularly hard-hit, and the government shares part of this responsibility, since it urged farmers to borrow heavily and plant fence-to-fence for the Soviet grain deal, then collapsed the farm economy by canceling the deal, which nearly destroyed the family farm.

And the government has abused its power in pursuing and killing Right-wing militants without benefit of due process in a series of incidents since 1983 of which

Waco was merely the most murderous example. (For details see Wilson (2017) and https://figshare.com/articles/US_Government_Abuse_of_Power/8985707.)

These wrongs reflect real structures of political and economic inequality central to US policy. Anti-elitism, properly directed, would be a healthy response. But the Patriot movement diverts attention away from actual systems of power by the use of scapegoating and by reducing complex reasons for social and economic conditions to simple formulaic conspiracies.

There is an undercurrent of resentment within the Patriot movement against what are seen as the unfair advantages the government gives to people of color and women through such programs as affirmative action. Thus, the militias are now only the most violent reflection of the backlash against the social-liberation movements of the 1960s and 1970s. The Patriot movement represents an expression of profound anger, virtually a temper tantrum, by a subculture made up primarily, but not exclusively, of white, Christian males.

This temper tantrum is fueled by an old tenet of conspiracy theories: that the country is composed of two types of persons–parasites and producers. The parasites are at the top and the bottom; the producers are the hard-working average citizens in the middle. This analysis lies at the ideological heart of Right-wing populism. The parasites at the top are seen as lazy and corrupt government officials in league with wealthy elites who control the currency and the banking sector. The parasites at the bottom are the lazy and shiftless who do not deserve the assistance they receive from society. In the current political scene, this dichotomy between parasites and producers takes on elements of racism because the people at the bottom who are seen as parasites are usually viewed as people of color, primarily black and Hispanic, even though most persons who receive government assistance are white.

Yet it is not only the angry defense of white male heterosexual privilege that fuels Right-wing populism, but also the real economic grievances of working-class and middle-class people. Unless society adapts to address these legitimate grievances, the scapegoating will spread, and Right-wing populism can turn to violent authoritarian revolt or move towards fascism.

But even if the society never becomes fascist, the period of turmoil can be dangerous, since it is almost inevitable that someone will conclude that the most efficient solution is to kill the scapegoats.

INTERLUDE B

Defending the four freedoms[1]

My dad, Memorial Day, and democracy

Chip Berlet

We all need to spend some time considering how best to defend liberty and free-dom, and what unites us as a nation concerned with democratic values. In doing so, we need to commit to a process that respects civil liberties, and civil rights, and civil discourse.

My dad wouldn't talk with me about World War II except to say it was brutal and bloody and that he lost many friends. So, when he swapped war stories in the basement with his drinking buddies, I would sit in the dark at the top of the stairs and listen.

I learned how his hands and feet had been frostbitten during the Battle of the Bulge, and that one of his Bronze Star citations was for taking out a Nazi machine gun nest. He thought the Germans were decent people whose big mistake was not standing up to the thugs like the Brownshirts who broke the windows of Jewish-owned stores on *Kristalnacht*. As I remembered this, I watched mountains of broken glass being swept up in Oklahoma City as the death count rose. It was 1995.

---

1 This chapter was first published a few days after the bombing of the Oklahoma City Federal Building on April 19, 1995. A small group of progressive and human rights researchers had been studying the increase in violence of the 1990s Patriot Movement and its armed wing, the Militia Movement. A meeting was convened in the Pacific Northwest and we compared notes. One of us, Ken Stern of the American Jewish Committee, was tasked with writing a report warning the federal government of the potential for imminent violence. The warning was ignored. Stern went on to write a book, *A Force Upon the Plain: the American Militia Movement and The Politics of Hate* (1996).

The original text was written in 1995 and later appeared in *Eye's Right: Challenging the Right-Wing Backlash*, South End Press and Political Research Associates (1995). The edited collection was conceived at the Blue Mountain Working Group mentioned in the appendices. Minor revisions have been made.

News of the domestic terrorist bombing of the federal building in Oklahoma City reached our family on vacation in coastal Georgia. I had been writing about the historic and social roots of the militia movement and, after visiting a museum preserving a former rice plantation, had talked with my son about how the Ku Klux Klan had formed as a militia during the economic and cultural turmoil following the Civil War. I had little doubt that the blast was somehow linked to the armed militia movement.

Reports of the carnage at the Oklahoma City federal building, the selfless efforts of rescue crews, and the horror of even some militia members, mingled eerily with stories commemorating the 50th anniversary of the end of World War II in Europe and the 20th anniversary of the end of the Vietnam War. I found history lessons connecting these events in an old brass-bound wooden chest, inherited after we buried my dad at Arlington National Cemetery years ago. Inside were brittle photos of a young lieutenant, a dried flower sent to my Mom from "somewhere in Belgium," crumbling newspaper clippings on the fighting near Bastogne, and a leather case filled with war medals.

Like many White Christians in the late 1950s, Dad held stereotyped views about Blacks and Jews. His actions spoke differently, though, and were the durable lesson. When neighbors in Hackensack, New Jersey, told him that our town was not ready for the Little League team he coached—with a Black player, a Jewish player, and a Jewish assistant coach—Dad simply said he had picked the best, and shut the door. He told me he had seen Jews and Blacks die along with everyone else fighting the Nazis; then he pointedly invited the entire team and their families to our yard for a very public picnic. Later, the stones crashing through our windows at night merely hardened his resolve.

In the 1960s we moved up the commuter rail line to Hillsdale, New Jersey. My brother went to New York Military Academy and played in the marching band. In college he was sports editor of the campus newspaper and joined ROTC. After graduation he shipped out to fight in Vietnam. I went to church-basement coffee houses and marched with the civil rights movement. In college I edited the campus newspaper at the University of Denver and joined the anti-war movement. After the killings at Kent State and Jackson State in 1970, I editorialized in favor of a student strike.

The next year, after a commemoration of Kent and Jackson, a veteran on the teaching staff sent me his Korean war medals as an act of protest against our government's policies. After hearing an anti-war speech, the veteran felt a need to stand up, and his conscience told him that "it is all of us that are guilty—we who sit there and do nothing." We sent the newspaper with a story about the medals to the printers, then I sat up all night trying to unravel conflicting emotions over family expectations, my hope for my brother's safe return from war, career plans, and what my personal moral obligations demanded of me, given my views about peace and social justice. When morning came, I quietly joined other anti-war protestors and took part in non-violent civil disobedience at a federal building near Denver.

My dad was Grand Marshall of Hillsdale's Memorial Day parade. When a tiny peace group in the early 1970s asked to participate, it created a furor. Dad was a lifelong Republican, pro-war, and anti-communist, and his idea of America came right out of a Norman Rockwell painting. He told the town officials that if the peace marchers followed the rules, they were entitled to march. And they did. Mom told me he came home from the debate shaking his head, asking how people could forget those who gave their lives to defend such rights.

Reunited as a family one Thanksgiving, we all toasted my brother's safe return from Vietnam with the crystal wine glasses my father brought back from Germany. It was a mirrored tableau of Rockwell's "Freedom from Want," a painting of a family sharing abundant food. The "Four Freedoms" series appeared as *Saturday Evening Post* covers during World War II; and as corny and steeped in stereotyping as they were, the theme helped unify and rally our nation at a time of crisis. Sure, politicians had other more cynical and pragmatic justifications for the war, but most Americans were willing to fight because they believed in the four freedoms.

Years later, battling cancer, my dad was determined to don his uniform one last time on Memorial Day. As I helped him dress, I asked him about the war. His only reply was to hand me one of his medals. Inscribed on the back were the words "Freedom from Fear and Want. Freedom of Speech, and Religion." The four freedoms. My dad fought fascism to defend these freedoms, not just for himself, but also for people of different religions and races, people he disagreed with … even people he was prejudiced against.

Today, the four freedoms that millions fought to defend are under attack–in part because we forget why people fought World War II, we deny what led to the Holocaust, we fail to live up to the promise of the civil rights movement, and we refuse to heal the wounds of the Vietnam War era.

Freedom of speech needs to be defended because democracy depends on a public dialogue to build informed consent. This is impossible when the public conversation—from armed militia members to talk-show hosts to mainstream politicians—is typified by shouting, falsehoods, and scapegoating. The Nazi death camps proved that hateful speech linked to conspiracy myths can lead to violence and murder. The solution is not censorship, but citizenship—people need to stand up and speak out in public against the bigots and bullies. Democracy works. The formula for democracy is straightforward: over time, the majority of people, given enough accurate information, and access to a free and open debate, reach the right decisions to preserve liberty. Thus, democracy depends on ensuring freedom of speech.

Freedom from fear is manipulated by those demanding laws that would undermine freedom of speech. The same agencies that spied on the civil rights and anti-war movements are again peddling the false notion that widespread infiltration of social movements is effective in stopping terrorism. Meanwhile, demagogues fan the flames of fear to urge passage of even more authoritarian crime control measures—while doing little to find real societal solutions that would bring freedom from fear to crime-ridden communities.

Freedom of religion is twisted by those seeking to make their private religious views into laws governing the public. But it is also abused by liberal critics who patronize sincere religious belief as ignorance, and litter the landscape with histrionic and divisive direct mail caricaturing all religious conservatives as zealots. Freedom of religion means we must have a serious debate on the issues with our devout neighbors, while condemning the theocrats who claim to speak for God as they pursue secular political goals.

Freedom from want has been shoved aside in a mean-spirited drive to punish the hungry, the poor, the children, the elderly, the disabled, the infirm, the homeless, the disenfranchised.

For many in our country, the four freedoms remain only a dream, but at least in 1945 it was a dream worth fighting for. How many of us today are willing to stop shouting and just talk with each other about how best our nation can defend the four freedoms?

5

WHY NOW?[1]

Jean V. Hardisty

The election results indicate that the American public has repudiated the liberalism that has been the dominant method of social reform since the New Deal. The resurgent right has consolidated its power and is now implementing its agenda. There appears to be a new mood of meanness that expresses itself in spiteful ridicule of liberals, feminists, environmentalists, and those in a weak or dependent position, such as welfare recipients and immigrants. The response from liberals, progressives, and centrists alike has been a mixture of anger, disbelief, denial, and paralysis.

This is not the first time the United States has swung dramatically to the right. Periodically throughout US history, right-wing forces have thrived, promoting such themes as white supremacy, scapegoating of Jews, violent opposition to unions, and rabid anti-communism. During Reconstruction in the South after the Civil War racial hatred was mobilized to destroy gains made by Blacks, and then in the 1920s racial scapegoating created a period of unchecked lynchings of Black men. Immigrants, Catholics, and Jews were scapegoated as "carriers of socialism" and "Papal loyalists" during the first several decades of this century, and union members were violently attacked during the 1930s. The communist witch-hunts of the McCarthy era in the 1950s is a recent example of rightist resurgence.

---

1   This chapter first appeared in the Fall/Winter 1995 issue of *The Public Eye* magazine, copyright 1995 Political Research Associates, used by permission, all rights reserved. A revised version appeared as "The Resurgent Right: Why Now" in Jean's book *Mobilizing Resentment: Conservative Resurgence from The John Birch Society to the Promise Keepers*, 1999, Beacon Press. This version, from Ms Hardisty's website, is copyright 2019 The Estate of Jean V. Hardisty, All Rights Reserved. The original article came with footnotes that are most easily found in the full text version online at the late Dr. Hardisty's personal website at: https://jeanhardisty.com/essay_theresurgentright.html.

The history of US government repression of dissenters, the imperialistic adventures of the 19th and 20th centuries, the grim record of racism directed against people of color that dates to slavery, and the resistance to extending full rights to women are consistent and persistent themes in US history. In truth, a close examination of that history reveals it is more often out of sync with democratic values than aligned with them.

Just 20 years ago it looked as if this dismal historical record might be overcome. Certain commitments to equality and justice had been established in American political culture. These commitments were expressed in policy reforms, such as guaranteed access to the vote, legal services for the poor, or food and shelter for the elderly, the disabled, and those who cannot provide for themselves. These reformist policies tended to cluster under the general heading of liberalism, with those who saw liberalism's reforms as inadequate to bring about real equality and justice—the left and progressives—acting as agents of conscience to expose the failings and shortcomings of liberalism.

Now the political swing to the right is so complete that liberalism has become a political orphan: not because it is a compromised ideology of reform, but because it has been painted as socialism in disguise. Secular humanism—one ideological source of enlightened liberal reformism—is now under attack from religious fundamentalism. The left, defeated and in disarray, is unable to exploit the widespread disillusionment with liberalism to promote its own analysis. Altogether, these political conditions add up to a formidable package of reaction which has an iron grip on the country. It is not surprising that those least able to protect themselves will suffer most from the right's power grab. The growing gap between rich and poor is simply the most obvious indicator of the fate of the poor and dependent.

Mindful that we have been here before, the obvious question is why now? This is not a moment created simply by the hard work of a few right-wing white male leaders; nor is it entirely a product of the potential for repression and inequality inherent in capitalism; nor is it merely a swing of the political pendulum, a backlash against women, a result of the collapse of the family, a spiritual crisis; or any of the other magic bullet explanations that have been popularized since the alarming political debut of the New Right in 1980. Each of these explanations gets at an aspect of the country's rightward swing.

This discussion will address the US right within the electoral sphere, and right-wing movements that operate within the Republican Party. Variously called the New Right, the new Republicans, the Religious Right, or the hard right, this sector does not include the extremist, paramilitary right, such as the Ku Klux Klan, neo-Nazi groups, the Aryan Nations, and other violent white supremacist groups. Violent members of the anti-abortion movement, Christian Reconstructionists, David Duke, Pat Buchanan, and Pat Robertson represent "bridges" that link these two sectors. Though the paramilitary right is not discussed here, much of what is said in this article applies to that sector as well.

The complexity of a full explanation cannot be exaggerated. There are too many factors at play to say with certainty what they all are, or how much each contributes. However, that must not prevent a good-faith effort to lay out ideas and interpretations that hold the potential for insight. In order to chart a course for the next decade, it is important to assess the 1994 election, the mood of the country in general, and especially the apparent sweeping success of the right in hopes that such an understanding will provide some guidance for action.

An explanation that attempts to be comprehensive must take into account the widespread public sentiment that is finding expression in the right, and also the role of the leadership of the right in creating and mobilizing that sentiment. This discussion will draw on both factors in attempting to explain the contemporary rise of the right. To organize the discussion, I suggest that we take one step back in the causal chain and focus on five major economic, social, and political forces that provide the setting for the expression of a rightist agenda, and thereby underlie the success of the resurgent right. These forces are:

- a conservative religious revitalization,
- economic contraction and restructuring,
- race resentment and bigotry,
- backlash and social stress, and
- a well-funded network of right-wing organizations.

Each of these conditions has existed at previous times in US history. While they usually overlap to some extent, they also can be seen as distinct, identifiable phenomenon. The lightning speed of the right's rise can be explained by the simultaneous existence of all five factors. Further, in this period they not only overlap, but also reinforce each other. This mutual reinforcement accounts for the exceptional force of the current rightward swing.

In fact, the right has created a juggernaut—an overwhelming force that has now gained state power. For many progressives and liberals, the specter of fascism is alarming. That alarm is justified. We must remember that fascism begins as a mass movement that combines reactionary political policies and revolutionary fervor. The contemporary right combines a set of reactionary social policies with the fervor provided by fundamentalist religious beliefs and long-standing racism. That is hauntingly similar to the Weimar Republic in Germany, where the fervor was provided by nationalism rather than religious convictions. Further, the alienation created by a restructuring of the economy that is negatively affecting large numbers of workers can be compared with other economic settings in which fascism has attained power. Howard Phillips, an early New Right leader who is a right-wing ideological purist, has said, "the French Revolution was, to some degree, fueled by economic concerns. So I think what will trigger [a right-wing Christian revolution] is the economic problems" (Stan 1995).

One important distinction between the US setting and other settings in which fascism has risen is that the US right's leadership is driven by fairly rigid ideological principles. Fascist leadership is characterized by craven opportunism—an apparent lack of consistent political principles that allows the leadership to change its ideology in order to adapt whatever strategy is necessary to attain and consolidate state power. Another distinction is that in the contemporary right there is not one leader who serves as the strongman. These differences are important, but it is not far-fetched to fear that the appearance of a right-wing charismatic leader with exceptional political skills might create the environment that would transform the current right-wing resurgence into fascism.

Religious revitalization

In the United States, as in many places throughout the world, there is a dramatic growth in the number and influence of people who identify themselves as religious fundamentalists. In fact, it can be argued that the US is in the midst of a religious revitalization. The term "revitalization movement" has been used by anthropologist Anthony F. C. Wallace in a classic 1956 essay to describe a conscious, organized effort by members of a society to construct a more satisfying culture by seeking to bring about change in the whole cultural system, or at least substantial parts of the system (Wallace 1956, 264–281).

People create a revitalization movement because they perceive that a part of the society's cultural system is unsatisfactory. Their discontent leads them to commit themselves to work with urgency for an intended shift in the society's worldview. The catalyst for dissatisfaction can be social stress caused by outside forces (such as war or famine) or social imbalances caused by changes within the society. That is, when people feel ill at ease within their society, or feel that they are losing ground relative to their expectations, they will often turn to religion as a vehicle for the restoration of meaning, purpose, and comfort in their lives. Their explicit goal is to revitalize their society through movement activism.

Wallace identifies a type of revitalization movement that he calls a "revivalistic movement." We are all familiar with the American religious tradition of the "revival meeting"—part entertainment, part inspiration, and often depicted as a traveling "show" that came to small towns. The meetings featured charismatic preachers who won converts to a very conservative version of Christianity. It is associated with an earlier, more innocent and less sophisticated time, when people were less influenced by the media and peer pressure was the major disciplinary force in small-town and rural settings.

Revivalistic movements are an extension of the concept of a revival meeting. They are movements that appeal to large numbers of recruits because they emphasize the customs, values, and even the natural world that were thought to have been characteristic of previous, more satisfactory times. The movement's strength comes from its promise that it will restore these characteristics that have been lost in the corruption of the contemporary world. When revivalistic movements are religious in nature, it is religious values revered in the past, such as the importance of adherence to a literal reading of biblical teaching, that inspire people's interest in religious values as a source of healing and restoration. The movement's message may even create a sense of longing for qualities now lost.

The contemporary movement known as the Religious Right is such a revivalistic movement. Based on evangelical, fundamentalist, Pentecostal, Charismatic, and Reconstructionist religious practices and values, it is made up of a broad array of very conservative Christian sectors, augmented by much smaller conservative religious sectors of Judaism, Catholicism, and Islam.

Distilling the research and writing of George Marsden (1991) and Sara Diamond (1995a, 1995b, 1996, 1998) it becomes clear that the specific "definitions of evangelical and fundamentalist are murky because they describe movements" rather than formal institutions. Especially significant is the rise of the Christian Right within evangelical movements. According to Marsden:

> Christian evangelicalism includes any Christian who is traditional enough to affirm the basic beliefs of:
>
> 1. the final authority of the Bible,
> 2. the reality of scripture,
> 3. redemption through Christ,
> 4. the importance of missionary work, and
> 5. the importance of a spiritually transformed life
>
> A Christian fundamentalist is an evangelical who is militant in opposition to liberal theology or to changes in cultural values or mores.
>
> *(1991)*

Pentecostalism, which dates to the 1920s, is associated with faith healing and speaking in tongues, signifying dramatic intervention of the supernatural. A slightly different and more modern form of supernatural religious practice is practiced by "Charismatics." To be born-again refers to a conversion experience in which one surrenders his or her life to Jesus Christ, thus making Jesus your personal Lord and saviour.

The political power of the Religious Right is nearly unprecedented in US history. With the exception of mobilizations against the teaching of evolution, a prominent role in the promotion of the restrictions of Prohibition, and the supportive efforts of many Black churches in the civil rights struggle, Christian fundamentalists and evangelicals have, in 20th century US history, most often been only marginally involved in politics and political activism. Though Father Charles Coughlin, the reactionary and antisemitic "radio priest" of the 1930s, and a few other charismatic, firebrand preachers rabble-roused for political goals, rank-and-file fundamentalist and evangelical religious sects have, for the most part, stayed out of the power struggles of the political sphere.

There were solid theological reasons for this lack of involvement in politics. For those who read the Bible literally, the focus is on the "end times"—an area of Christian theology formally known as eschatology. There is an important theological debate about the nature of the end times, a debate between those who are pre-millennialists and those who are post-millennialists. The differences between these two positions are so important that it was previously very difficult to bring the two groups together.

As predicted in the Book of Revelations certain events will happen when the world ends. These include the Rapture; a period of chaos known as the Tribulations; the return of Christ; and 1,000 years of peace and harmony under his rule or that of his saints. For those who take the Bible literally, the prescription for a virtuous life is one spent in preparation for this Second Coming of Christ. Thus, involvement in day-to-day political struggles in contemporary secular society held little interest. Focused on the future, the moral health and godliness of this material world was somewhat irrelevant.

When the New Right began its political recruitment of Christian evangelicals and fundamentalists in the 1970s, it faced the question of how to bring them into the political sphere. It was crucial that shrewd organizing skills and convincing theological arguments be developed to inspire and justify their political involvement. A further complication lay in the division between pre-millennialists and post-millennialists about the nature of the Second Coming. For pre-millennialists, great events will precede the return of Christ—perhaps a rapture of Christian believers into heaven, but definitely a period of Tribulation that will culminate in the final battle of Armageddon. Only then will Christ return to rule on earth for 1,000 years; this period's end will mark the end of history. For post-millennialist evangelicals and fundamentalists, the great events of Rapture, Tribulation and Armageddon will follow the millennium. During the millennium, which some post-millennialists believe has begun, God's elect will rule the earth. God's elect are self-evidently Christian, and they bear a heavy burden to rule in a way befitting Christian principles (Diamond 1989).

Each theological position (and I have named only two here) dictates a different order of commitments in the conduct of daily life. In order to capture the large US evangelical and fundamentalist population for a massive political mobilization, the New Right's religious leadership had to develop arguments that harmonized the differences and placed political activism at the top of all those different lists of commitments.

Two such arguments have achieved wide acceptance. First, whether one is a pre-millennialist or a post-millennialist, it can be argued that to do God's work here on earth is to oppose earthly evil at all times. Because moral decay and behavior not consistent with biblical teachings are evil, they should be actively opposed. Second, agreement has emerged that it is Christians who have been given dominion (rule) over the earth by God. Thus, it is wrong and worthy of opposition when secular persons inappropriately take that dominion. These arguments compel the involvement of evangelicals and fundamentalists (and charismatics and Pentecostals) in contemporary politics. Further, they resonate strongly with the "values" questions that are at the center of the agenda of both the religious and secular Right.

Certain individuals, especially Robert Billings, Ed McAteer, Jerry Falwell, Paul Weyrich, and, most recently, Pat Robertson get credit for recruiting Christian fundamentalists and evangelicals into politics. They organized in the 1970s, at a time when the number of citizens identifying themselves as born-again Christians was skyrocketing. By the 1980s, Christian revivalism had become a movement: a locus of righteous fervor, individual meaning, and political organizing. As early as 1981, a Gallup Poll found that 38 percent of the population claimed to have been "born-again" (Gallup Opinion Index, 184: 1–77). While not all those born-again Christians are fundamentalists, nearly all are evangelicals.

As this growth occurred, so too did the political sophistication of the Christian Right leadership. The strategic decision in the 1970s to take the movement into electoral politics, specifically within the Republican Party, was evidence of this growing interest in political power (Diamond 1995). Mainstream Protestant and Catholic churches, meanwhile, were plagued with low growth, dwindling finances, and a decline in those entering the priesthood or ministry.

The foot soldiers of the Religious Right precisely meet Wallace's definition of members of a society who are dissatisfied and driven to introduce a new worldview. In this case, dissatisfaction over "moral decay" which they see as resulting from secular values was augmented by decline in their own status in society. Many evangelicals and fundamentalists felt that their lifestyle and values had become devalued (and in many cases nearly invisible) at least in popular culture. Such feelings of status deprivation and conflict with the dominant values are powerful forces that promote a sense of alienation.

Equally important is the positive pull of the Christian Right. Membership in a movement- in this case one with a spiritual dimension—offers an antidote to a sense of alienation. Further, the theological authoritarianism characteristic of New Right Christian groups provides rules to live by and answers to life's problems with absolute clarity, not fuzzy relativism. Thus, it is no surprise that activists in the Christian Right score exceptionally high on tests of intolerance. In a 1990/91 stratified random sampling of members of Dr James Dobson's Focus on the Family, one of the largest Religious Right organizations, and activists in Beverly LaHaye's Concerned Women for America, researchers associated with the Bliss Institute at the University of Akron found that only 2 percent of Concerned Women for America activists and 6 percent of Focus on the Family members agreed with the statement, "A diversity of moral views is healthy" (Smidt et al 1994). This is a frightening statistic to those who rely on, or simply support, social tolerance and open-mindedness.

What does a growing and politically powerful Christian revivalistic movement mean for Jews in the US? Many conservative Jews may feel a similar sense of alienation from secular society and threat to their traditional religious practices, but it is unlikely that the Christian Right can provide answers that are satisfactory for Jews.

Certainly, there are Jews who align themselves with the Christian Right—an example is the conservative Jewish group Toward Tradition, headed by Rabbi Daniel Lapin. Lapin argues that the proper practice of Jewish faith dictates a belief in moral values that are more closely aligned with those of conservative Christians than with those of liberals whose secular humanism runs against the grain of religious practice.

Another argument for Jewish support for the Christian Right is its consistent support for Israel. Because conservative Christian biblical teachings maintain that the Jews must return to Israel in order for the Second Coming to occur, the Christian Right has firmly supported US aid to Israel. The role of Israel as a buffer against communism in the Middle East was another appealing aspect of this alliance. For Jews who equate support for Israel with support for Jews, the Christian Right is a dependable and valuable ally.

Nevertheless, the relationship between Jews and the Christian Right is a source of considerable debate within the Jewish community. For, in fact, the political platform of the Religious Right promotes the return of America to its Christian roots. The slogan "America is a Christian country" has been the Christian Right's motto. Their advocacy for prayer in schools and the erosion of a separation between church and state inevitably implies discrimination against Jews. Worse yet is the Christian Right's belief that those who are not born-again are not in an appropriate relationship with God.

Even in its support for Israel, the Christian Right has simultaneously pursued a greater Christian presence in Israel and proselytized for Jews to convert to Christianity (Mouly 1985).

Despite the recent Christian Right practice of referring to their religious beliefs as "Judeo-Christian," and the recent statement by Ralph Reed that he had not realized that the slogan "America is a Christian country" might be offensive to Jews, there is a substantial part of the Jewish community that remains suspicious that the Christian Right is antisemitic. A recent, long-overdue publication by the Anti-Defamation League of B'nai B'rith presents a thorough and accurate review of the beliefs and practices of major Religious Right organizations. This book, the Religious Right: The Assault on Tolerance and Pluralism in America, presents clear evidence of the latent and active antisemitism that runs throughout the Christian Right (Cantor 1994).

The writings of Rev Pat Robertson, whose Christian Coalition is now the preeminent organization of the Christian Right, are especially revealing. In his 1994 book, the *New World Order*, Robertson presents his own variation on a longstanding antisemitic conspiracy theory—a sinister plot by secret elites to rule the world, financed by Jewish bankers. Thus, we see the leader of the Christians Right's largest and most powerful organization publishing blatant antisemitic rhetoric as "education" for his members (Lind 1995).

Much like its antisemitism, the misogyny of the Religious Right is not always explicit. Women appear to be accorded very high respect within the tenets of conservative Christianity. In fact, one of the Christian Right's largest and most active organizations is Concerned Women for America, a Christian women's organization headed by Beverly LaHaye. LaHaye teaches that it is in her religion and her family that a woman finds her greatest fulfillment, not in the incorrect and misled principles of feminism. She leads her members to demonize and mobilize against liberal women by portraying them as pleasure-seeking, man-hating, and secular-minded purveyors of sex, abortion, and divorce.

For conservative Christian women, the proper place of the woman in the home is beneath the authority of her husband, who in turn is beneath the authority of God. Far from being a place of subservience, this is a woman's life in its natural form, as intended by God and by a Godly society. Leadership should be in the hands of men; thus, it is entirely appropriate that in the case of the anti–abortion movement– perhaps the first of the New Right's "social issues" to bring together a coalition of secular and religious Rightists– the movement has consistently been led primarily by men.

In addition to its opposition to a range of reproductive rights that give women some control over their own bodies, the Religious Right opposes equal pay, single motherhood, sex education in the schools, lesbianism, feminist curriculum, and even daycare. Logically then, the women's movement's struggle for equality and independence for women is considered to be wrong by conservative Christian women. It is, in fact, seen as threatening to the health of the society as a whole.

The Christian Right's agenda for women is explicitly anti-feminist, but perhaps more dangerous is its implicit attack on poor women. Because women are divided into those who are worthy (living by Godly practices) and unworthy (engaging in an ungodly lifestyle), many poor women who receive AFDC assistance, are single mothers, or are otherwise independent of men but dependent on the state, are also to be condemned. The Christian Right's support for welfare "reform," given that a majority of welfare recipients are women, belies any claim of concern for all women.

In fact, even conservative Christian women can become targets within the Christian Right. The evangelical men's organization known as the Promise Keepers, which draws tens of thousands of men to its rallies in big-city stadiums, encourages men to take back the leadership within the family that they have given over to their wives through their own weakness and sloth. If the wife is not willing to give back the leadership of the family, then the Promise Keepers are urged to *"take it back"* (italics in original) (Evans, 1994).

To the extent that mainstream feminist goals are associated with liberalism, both the secular and religious right can be expected to portray feminists as abnormal, predatory, and dangerous. That is not surprising. It is notable, however, that conservative Christian women collaborate in the demonization of poor women, especially women receiving welfare, and women who are judged to have made mistakes. In their respect for and trust in authority, right-wing women find dignity and a sense of security and order in their proper and natural place under the authority of men. It is far less virtuous to pursue a wrong-headed notion of equality than to behave appropriately and be assured of respect (Dworkin 1983). For those women who do not understand the need for women to remain in their place and make the necessary sacrifices, there is disapproval that often turns to disgust and disdain.

Economic contraction, redistribution, restructuring

The US economy, once based in industrial capital, is being structurally transformed by the declining significance of industrial production and the increasing role played by finance capital and the service and information sectors of the economy. The loss of US blue-collar industrial jobs, as even small corporations now locate production facilities in Third World countries, combined with the downsizing of lower and middle management corporate structures, have left a large part of the US work-force dislocated and disillusioned.

Much of the motivation for this restructuring comes from greater international competition, which has necessitated increasingly speculative business behavior in order to maintain a high level of profits. Profits now are chased with increasingly arcane schemes- including the takeovers, mergers, and buy-outs of the 1980s, which have continued in the 1990s.

How does the contemporary right-wing political movement relate to the changing US economic scene? In order to understand a part of the political motivation of the right, it is important to identify the economic interests it represents. It is clear that the right's economic agenda (corporate tax cuts, changes in tax rates to benefit the wealthy, deregulation, privatization, anti-union legislation, and defunding the left) benefits business interests and high-income individuals. Yet there is conflict within the economic elite- with some corporate interests aligning with the right, while some align with the moderate wing of the Republican Party, and some with the Democrats. It is not until the differing interests of various sectors of business are distinguished that this conflict makes sense.

In the late 1970s, when the New Right became the focus of media attention, its leadership openly declared its allegiance to venture capitalism. Based largely in the West, especially the Southwest and California, and to a lesser extent in the South, venture capitalism represents a sector of corporate business that is young, often small and independent, and characterized by high risk. Oil, electronics, software, and some pharmaceutical companies are examples. In contrast, larger, older, multinational corporate entities, such as the "blue chip" companies often located in the Midwest and North Atlantic regions, represent a sector of capital with a different identity and different needs from the political system. The two sectors are sometimes called the Cowboys and the Yankees.

(The sectors are drawn in an over-simple fashion for the sake of the argument. Many New Right organizations received financial support from sources within the multinational sector, and many aspects of the political agendas of each overlap; most notably in the cultural sphere and the area of the "social issues.")

Liberalism pursued an agenda that, for some years, could be tolerated by the Yankee sector of capital. Large, older corporate structures needed the stability that unionization provided, and could afford to "buy" that stability with benefits and relatively high wages. Thus, during much of the post-World War II period, liberalism and corporate America were able to co-exist in an uneasy alliance. However, with the arrival of national economies that threatened US hegemony (such as Japan, Germany, Western Europe and the emerging Pacific rim countries), the larger, multinational corporate sector could no longer afford liberalism's programs and, in the later 1970s, began its own assault on regulatory laws and labor's pay rates and benefits packages. When the unions objected, they were eliminated.

Simultaneously, the venture capital sector of capital was represented by the New Right. For this sector, stability was less important than an economic environment that was hospitable for fast growth. Therefore, deregulation, de-unionization, and lower corporate taxes were the agenda. As the 1980s progressed, the needs of the two sectors converged, until there was no voice left to defend the economic policies of liberalism- regulation, strong unions, and corporate taxation (Lyons 1994). The attack on these policies was most viciously mounted by the New Right (and continues to be central to the agenda of the "new Republicans"), but it is also supported, though more quietly, by big business.

The result has been the preservation (even inflation) of profits, but at a high social cost. The right's economic agenda has been the equivalent of a "shock" treatment for the US economy. In order to maintain slipping profits, a formula of increased economic speculation, downsizing of the labor force, and concentration of profits in the hands of upper management and stockholders has been followed. The result is a redistribution of wealth, so that profits are maintained but at a punishing cost to the average wage earner. Thus, some are getting richer, many are getting poorer, and the American dream—the belief that hard work will equal success and a better standard of living for the next generation—has been shattered (Sklar 1995).

The discontent that inevitably results from such a blow to the working and middle class has taken the form of a right-wing populist political revolt. We have seen the appeal of rightist rhetoric in the midst of economic decline elsewhere—in Germany during the rise of National Socialism, and more recently in England during the rise of Margaret Thatcher's Tory movement. Some political themes are common to all three cases: nationalism, tax protest, anti-government rhetoric, a nostalgia for a more "moral" time, and scapegoating.

Race resentment and bigotry

White supremacism and racial bigotry pervade the economy and culture of US society, taking different forms at different times. Yet, when discussing the right, many journalists do not refer at all to race and racism. Others see racism as the principal social, psychological and economic motivation for right-wing politics. Certainly, the theme of white resentment of a perceived increase in the power of racial/ethnic minority groups plays heavily in the agenda of the right. That resentment is fanned and augmented by the decreased sense of economic security of many working—and middle-class white people (such as suburban, white, Republican males, white rural males, or women whose status is attached to those men) as a result of economic restructuring. There is no doubt that racial resentment and racial bigotry are major factors in the current resurgence of the right.

(The term "white" is used here to refer to Americans of European descent who are non-Jews. Needless to say, skin color and racial identification are far more complex than allowed by schemes of racial classification. They are, to a large extent, social constructions.)

But how does it work? It is easy to see why so much contemporary analysis of the right does not discuss racism. The New Right in the early 1980s explicitly renounced racism, claiming to turn its back on its past association with the Ku Klux Klan and the George Wallace Presidential campaign. Whenever a racist slur, or an indiscreet racist joke is made public, apologies are made, and the culprit is chastised. It appears that, in public political discourse, only David Duke and his ilk are allowed to "speak race," and even there, the Republican Party national leadership creates a public distance and disavowal.

(The Republican Party refused to back David Duke in his 1991 campaign for Governor of Louisiana, despite the certain victory of the Democratic candidate, Edwin Edmunds.)

Another factor that obscures the right's racism is the intersection of race and class in the US. Because there now exists a substantial Black middle class (and increasingly a Latino and Asian middle class, though as yet only a tiny Native American middle class), there are groups of people of color who are less culturally threatening to the right. In an effort to broaden the tent of Republican voters, these middle-class communities of color have, in some cases, been courted and promoted by the right (Toler 1993).

Most journalists, working within the institutional racism of their own newspapers or television stations, often accept right-wing politicians' self-portrayal as non-racists at face value, and because Americans get most of their information from journalists, the racial motivation of much of the current right's program is not properly understood. What is needed in order to accurately assess the racial politics of the right is an examination of the consequences of the right's political agenda for people of color.

Three public policy initiatives sponsored by the right are examples of the important role of racial bigotry and resentment in the right's political agenda: welfare "reform," the anti-immigrant campaign, and the attack on affirmative action. Here, racist language is barely concealed. Stereotypes such as the "welfare queen," used to attack welfare recipients, "illegal aliens" to attack immigrants, and "reverse discrimination" to misrepresent affirmative action, are promoted for the political punch inherent in the equation of people of color and negative qualities. If people of color are grouped under the umbrella of unseemly characteristics, then to disdain or dismiss them is less easily identified as racism.

In many cases, the racist results of right-wing policies are built on racially encoded concepts. A sampling of some of the most powerful are: individual responsibility, states' rights, and dependency. In both blatant and encoded racial slurs, the central political and psychological ploys used are stereotyping and scapegoating. Scapegoating is fixing blame for social stress, economic loss, or loss of political power on a target group whose constructed guilt provides a simplistic explanation. Scapegoating in turn depends on stereotyping—assigning characteristics (usually negative) not to individuals but to entire groups of people. In a society experiencing painful economic contraction, anger increases, lines harden, and hated stereotypes increasingly become scapegoats. When the dominant political force is actually promoting scapegoating and stereotyping, as the right has done so effectively, the practice is bound to thrive.

In a society founded on the system of enslavement of Blacks, the target of scapegoating is most often the African American population. The dominant culture-white, Protestant, and male- has historically held power in part by oppressing people of color and other hated out-groups, understanding that in order to maintain dominance it cannot tolerate true pluralism.

As always, the effectiveness of the hold of those in power depends in part on the strength of those challenging that control. Currently, the political cohesion of communities of color is diminished. The leadership of the African American community has been in a weakened and fragmented state for some time, and the results of civil rights and anti-poverty legislation, while significant, have not fulfilled their promise of transformation in the fortunes of Black people. Among Latinos, Asian Americans, and African Americans, economic competition and cultural differences create divisions that are easily exploited and make a movement across race and ethnicity difficult to hold together.

For many whites of all classes, however, the advances that have been made by people of color seem to hold particular symbolic significance. In a climate in which many whites feel anxious and vulnerable, there is a simmering racial resentment of those who appear favored by affirmative action, so-called "preferential treatment," and a perception that Blacks have made gains faster than whites. Bilingualism, multiculturalism, and other hard-won gains are now the focus of white backlash. This backlash, often expressed in a form sanitized of racist slurs, attacks African American gains by arguing that Blacks no longer suffer discrimination and therefore do not "deserve" a helping hand. This dismissal of the continuing racism within US society, when combined with the anxiety and anger created in whites by economic contraction, results in whites scapegoating Blacks and other people of color for the slip in status of groups of whites.

In the world of the far right, of course, white supremacism is endemic, and no obligation is felt to obscure it. The far right is more extremist and ideologically alienated than the sector of the right that works within the political power structure. While there is important cross-pollination between the far right and the electoral right, this discussion is not addressing the racism and bigotry of the paramilitary far right.

Would the right have such success with its stereotyping and scapegoating if the economy were expanding? Perhaps not, simply because the economic pain would be less severe, and scapegoating would be less needed as a foil to draw anger away from more accurate targets.

Backlash and social stress

An important factor in explaining the success of the right is a shift in the values held by the majority of the US public. Since the end of the 1970s, a climate of stress and discord has reflected the confusion, resentments, and fears of a society undergoing rapid social change. That climate has been nurtured and exploited by the organized right to promote social conservatism and capture power. One method has been to encourage cynicism about the intentions of government, and especially the evil of liberal reformism. The right's success in transforming public attitudes is a testimony to its own self-conscious organizing, as well as the failure of liberalism to counter with an emotionally compelling vision.

A central goal of the right is to restore the norms of social conservatism that dominated in the 1950s. In the late 1970s, the New Right's leadership skillfully identified deep strains of discontent within the American public: fears, resentments, hatreds, and confusion that bubbled beneath the surface of public life. By organizing this public unhappiness and confusion into anger targeted at the liberation/reform movements of the 1960s and 1970s, they both built on and aggravated social strain. An important vehicle for this organizing was the promotion of a romanticized view of what seems a simpler and more manageable time. The resulting change in public attitudes is a shift in political culture.

This shift is in the core values held by people in both the public sphere and in their private lives. Of course, there is enormous variation in the political culture of any society—by class, race, gender, ethnicity, and by idiosyncratic preferences. But what is identified as a society's political culture is the body of values and attitudes held by the bulk of people as expressed in the voting booth and captured in randomized opinion polls and focus group research. The concept of political culture is too broad a generalization to reflect the vast numbers of subcultures in the US.

Generalization though it is, to talk about a shift in the political culture of the US does capture a real social transformation. It should not be surprising that such a shift is not a matter of smooth transition. The potential winners and the potential losers are locked in struggle, as those who were dominant try to hold on and the challengers try to consolidate power. The power struggle is easiest to track in the political sphere, and in the economic sphere. It is harder to track in the social/cultural sphere- though this is a vital part of the struggle. For this reason, it is a mistake to watch only the right's success in public policy. It is equally important to pay attention to the "values questions." For without capturing the cultural sphere, no economic and political shift will hold.

The struggle is between the liberalism that traces its roots to the New Deal and a right-wing countermovement that opposes the values and policies of that liberalism. The liberal reforms now under attack—or example, legalization of abortion, gains in rights for lesbians and gay men, public support for free expression, and the extension of civil rights protections to people of color—are matters of public policy, but also of values. Those who support these reforms, and the values that underlie them, are prime targets for this countermovement.

Movements and counter-movements do battle at almost any period. In a complex dance that journalists describe as the swinging pendulum, progressive and reactionary forces vie for dominance and influence, and each works to expose the other's agenda. When the Republicans dominate, the pendulum is said to have swung to the right. When Democrats dominate, it has swung to the left.

Occasionally, however, there is a shift in the "center"—the majority of voters who act as the fulcrum or anchor for the swinging pendulum. This is a period of enormous confusion, when scapegoating increases.

Political science literature makes much of the strength of the center in US politics. It is often lionized as the reason for US political stability. The durability and common sense said to characterize the center is also often associated with the large US middle class. Common sense is thought to reside in that stable body of average Americans, whose wisdom keeps a democracy on course.

For nearly 20 years, the US political center has been moving to the right, attracted by the right's platform of family values, nationalism, race resentment, and a rhetoric of the work ethic. The most skillful of the right's strategists, especially Paul Weyrich and Howard Phillips, targeted areas in which liberalism was vulnerable, and with great skill, identified the themes of dependence, crime, taxes, and family values. Crucial to the right's success is the mix of these themes known as the "social issues"- such as sexual promiscuity, the decline of the family, the rights of children, the legitimacy of a gay or lesbian sexual orientation, etc. The right has appealed to age-old American cultural strains: Calvinism, self-reliance, patriarchy, Christian worship, and patriotism, to create a backlash countermovement of enormous effectiveness. The right's organizing has been documented in a number of cases, perhaps most impressively by Ellen Messer-Davidow in her articles on the right's attack on higher education (Messer-Davidow,1993).

A move to the right usually means a shoring up of the "establishment." But the contemporary US right's conservatism is not of the system-supporting type. Classical conservatism favors respect for government, reverence for the church as an institution, support for the nuclear family, and free market economics. It holds the individual as the most important unit in society. In major respects, the shift now occurring does not conform to classical conservatism. The right—both religious and secular—is more extreme in its ideology. It fosters suspicion- if not hatred- of government, dismissal of the mainstream Protestant churches, and a punitive and intrusive role toward individual sexual conduct and sexual orientation.

Rather than a familiar brand of conservative "Father Knows Best" Republicanism, this right-wing social movement organizes the expression of more extreme instincts. It is built on a backlash fueled by anger—in the form of resentment, spite, vengeance, envy, loss, and bitterness over declining status—on the part of those who feel that they have not benefited from the changes of the last 30 years (Gusfield 1963; Crawford 1980). This social anger is also fed by the current religious revitalization, economic contraction and race resentment discussed above. This volatile combination of reactionary instincts is fanned by the right and directed toward the targets of liberals, feminists, people of color (especially through stereotyping of welfare recipients, criminals, immigrants, and drug users), and lesbians and gay men, all perceived to be the beneficiaries of liberal social change.

A number of specific grievances and deprivations underlie the right's successful organizing of a countermovement. First is anxiety on the part of the white, suburban middle-class Protestants who were dominant for generations and in the

1980s began to see themselves as losing status and therefore willing to join backlash movements. The assurance of a secure and predictable place in society, while never guaranteed, was certainly expected as part of the heritage associated with white skin, education, and middle-class family of origin. Policies designed to fortify the liberal ideals of tolerance and pluralism and increased equality seemed to threaten the standing of white heterosexual middle-class Protestants and Catholics, especially males. In the heat of disillusionment and right-wing propaganda, this sector of white voters abandoned the Democratic coalition (Edsall and Edsall 1990).

But the right's resurgence is not based exclusively in the middle class. Working class whites also suffer social stress and perceived loss of status, and especially resent their obvious competitors—African American men, women, gays and lesbians, and immigrants. They also resent the New Class, the small but visible young urban professional nouveau riches of the 1980s. These yuppies, as they are known, are stockbrokers, professional couples with no children, single women corporate executives, MBAs who specialize in mergers and buy-outs, and lawyers who specialize in large real estate transactions. In short, they do not work with their hands, they have excess income that they spend on luxury items, and they are unattached or only loosely attached to church or family.

Across class lines there is a shared anxiety and confusion over the speed of social and cultural change- change that is perceived as making the society more violent, more sexually permissive, less orderly, and less predictable. There is particular anxiety in raising children, because it is in this sphere that so much of the perceived decline in American society becomes concrete.

It is in the raising of children that much of the American dream is most vividly enacted. The United States as the world's dominant economic power, ever growing and bringing increased prosperity to each succeeding generation, is a revered image in our political folklore. Though the American dream is itself a social invention, it is a particularly powerful one. One successful strategy of the contemporary right has been to wrap itself in the American dream, and to portray liberals as killers of that dream (Quigley 1992). The right's caricature of an all-powerful liberalism has proved elastic enough to have caused any grievance.

For middle- and working-class white Protestants anxious about their own status and resentful of the loss of the American dream, the demonization of liberals and progressives deflects anger away from upper-class Republicans—the only group that has remained relatively untouched by the economic contraction, social changes, and shift in political culture of the last three decades. Whether or not a right-wing backlash movement prevails, this group will remain stable. In fact, due to deregulation, and changes in the tax code, it is expanding. While upper-class Republicans may not be culturally comfortable with the "resentment constituency," there is little in this movement that appears to threaten their position in society. Thus, the takeover of the Republican Party by its right wing is unlikely to be opposed by any upper-class elites except the weakened and faltering Republican moderates, who support a more traditional brand of classical conservatism.

Media plays an important role in the current shift and should be mentioned as a factor in the right's resurgence. The right has vilified the mainstream media as liberal and biased against conservative and Christian views. By creating new media outlets, such as Pat Robertson's Christian Broadcast Network, and by pressuring mainstream media through boycotts of advertisers' products and letter-writing campaigns, the right has gained remarkable media access. As documented by the newsletter of Fairness and Accuracy in Reporting, the opinions represented even within the television outlet most attacked by the right, PBS, range from centrist to right wing (Extra! 1993). With the exception of past sporadic appearances by the late Erwin Knoll on the McNeil/Lehrer News Hour or an occasional independent film with a progressive theme, there is no voice of the left on television. Pacifica Radio is one of only a handful of left radio outlets. As the political "center" moves to the right, public debate increasingly takes place between the moderate right and the extreme right.

Before the electronic age—specifically satellite television transmission, cable TV and talk-radio programming—a diversity of values existed in greater distance from each other. Decision-making elites and opinion makers were thought to have more information than the average person, and for that reason were often accorded the role of representing their constituents. Today, people feel that they have enough information to be direct decision-makers (Inglehart 1990). This has encouraged a strong streak of populism that is a crucial ingredient in the right's social movement.

The right has promoted a belief that wisdom resides in the average (white) person and that elites and intellectuals are no longer needed as mediators between government and the people. Thus, an important part of the culture shift is a demand by middle- and working-class white voters for a more direct democracy, in order to express their discontent. This has allowed those who understand and utilize that demand- in this case the right, not the left- to gain political advantage by quickly providing an outlet for it. And it has led to further disenfranchisement of the poor and underserved, who are less well-trained and well-equipped for the challenges of direct democracy.

Social stress and culture shift might equally cause a leftist resurgence—an identification of the source of the problem within capitalism, its power structure and the owning class that controls it. At times this has been the case, but the strength of the right has succeeded in suppressing and deflecting such political impulses, in part through the vehicle of an effective, coordinated, and well-funded movement infrastructure.

Right-wing movement building

Social, political, and economic discontent, no matter how strongly powered by mutually reinforcing causes, does not result in revolutionary change unless there is a political movement to capture the anger and direct it in a certain direction. The right's ability to capitalize on the economic chaos, racial tensions, and social discontent of the current historical moment can be explained, in large part, by its stronger political movement.

(In the case of religious and social movements, often something as specific as a campaign mounted by a group of like-minded citizens is labeled a movement. In this discussion the term movement will be reserved for umbrella movements rather than their sub-movements. Thus, the term social movement will refer to the collectivity of active campaigns mobilized by the right around the social issues. Economic, political, and religious movements will refer to the collectivity of active campaigns mobilized by the right around economic, political, and religious issues. All these movements unite under the rubric of the contemporary US right.)

This (complex and right-wing) movement is well-financed and well-run, combining shrewd strategic planning for political success with a rigid set of ideological principles backed by a certitude based in religious beliefs. The membership organizations, networks, think tanks, media outlets, campus publications, coalitions, interest groups, PACs, and funders that work to advance the right's political movement make up its "movement infrastructure."

While a movement cannot succeed without substantial mass sentiment to support it, its precise level of success is shaped by the strength and effectiveness of its infrastructure (Hixson 273). Public education, which is key to any change in political direction, depends on movement-oriented think tanks, research centers, publishing houses, TV and radio outlets, and schools and universities. Legislative initiatives to press movement goals require legal firms. Mobilization for popular campaigns to pressure legislators requires grassroots membership organizations. Capturing electoral power requires political consultants, PACs, media expertise, and grassroots training programs for political supporters.

The right's strategists, funders, organizers and activists have modeled the creation of an effective movement infrastructure. By attending to movement-building, they have created a juggernaut- an overwhelming force that has swept the right to power and swept away liberal reformism in 15 short years.

In the early 1990s Beth Schulman, Associate Publisher of in *These Times* magazine, circulated a memorandum that discussed the difference in funding patterns of progressive funders and right-wing funders. She pointed out that the right-wing funders invested in the building blocks or skeletal structure of their movement—such as publications, research centers, think tanks, and academic fellowships and chairs designated for rightist scholars, campus organizations, and youth groups (Schulman 1992; Bleifuss 1995).

Liberal and progressive foundations, on the other hand, were not underwriting movement-building, but instead were funding good works that promised to assure better social conditions and promote equality and tolerance. Much of this funding could be classified as humanitarian aid, which was needed in the face of the social service cuts of the Reagan/Bush years. Unable to turn a deaf ear to need and suffering, liberal and progressive funders lacked the discipline and single-mindedness of the right's funders. The result is that the right got greater political mileage for each dollar invested because the movement it underwrote was focused on a strategic plan for seizing power.

Thus, in the case of a particular right-wing issue, such as the liberalism of higher education or the increasing effectiveness of the gay rights movement, the right had in place all the components needed to launch a full-scale campaign to press the issue. Local single-issue organizations could tap into the resources of national right-wing legal firms, research centers, publishing houses, funders, and membership organizations. This allowed the firepower of an entire movement to assist the political work of the smallest grassroots right-wing effort.

One of the most effective roles of the right-wing movement infrastructure has been its role in knitting together secular social and economic conservatives and conservative religious activists. These two groups might have existed side-by-side without a conscious effort to coordinate and integrate their work. By combining forces through the networks and coalitions of the right, the impact of each sector has increased dramatically. United, the secular and religious right have seized power; separately, that would have been unlikely.

Related to movement infrastructure is the need for strategic planning. Without clear analysis, defined goals, and developed strategies, even the strongest movement will spin its wheels without actually capturing power. Two academics who write about the right's strategic planning are sociologist Seymour Martin Lipset and his critic, Michael Rogin, political scientist at UC/Berkeley. Lipset identified three sectors that contribute to right-wing success: Republican politicians, their core constituency of upper-income conservatives, and the lower-middle- and working-class adherents of backlash movements. Writing in the late 1960s and early 1970s, Lipset focused much of his attention on working class rightists. As a result, the role of Republican politicians and upper-income conservatives in the US right was long overlooked in academic circles.

Michael Rogin has corrected this oversight by using "resource mobilization theory." in case studies that have examined Joseph McCarthy, George Wallace, and political behavior in Orange County, California, Rogin has highlighted the role of political elites (Republican Party activists and office-holders in this case) and "cause activists," right-wing activists whose organizational base is outside the Party, but whose political goal is control of the Party. This is a crucial aspect of the success of the right wing of the Republican Party in taking over the Party. The "cause activists" are not harnessed by Party unity, or even Party loyalty. The Republican Party is simply a vehicle for the right's goals—the most appropriate and sensible vehicle, but one that is itself in need of right-wing reform.

In a search for new electoral cleavages to exploit within the Democratic Party, the right's Republican partisans saw the potential of the social issues, including racial tensions, as a source of division within Democratic ranks. A strategy of luring socially conservative Democrats away from the Democratic Party, which dates to the 1960s and is known as the Southern Strategy, has accomplished several overlapping goals: The growth of the power of the Republican Party, the diversion of resources to Republicans through control of policy-making decisions that affect the distribution of wealth, and the weakening of such political opponents as Democrats and left-leaning independent voters.

These goals were achieved not simply because of a spontaneous expression of backlash social sentiments, racial resentments, or economic anger. They were accomplished by capturing decision-making positions (winning political office), mobilizing resources (getting control of bureaucracies), and swaying public opinion (activating political ideologues through a network of organizations, publications, churches, research organizations, grassroots groups, national coalitions, conferences, TV and radio, voter education, and activist training). Because the right's movement is not led by Republican office-holders, the movement is not always system-supporting. It is often system-opposing, as New Right and Christian Right leaders ignore or confront Republicans deemed insufficiently loyal to the movement (Diamond 1995).

The role of the federal government in promoting or squelching a growing social movement is fluid and opportunistic. The government can be either a passive judge of competing movements and interests, or an active participant that promotes or inhibits them. The government can channel resources, confer legitimacy, and provide leadership for a social movement (Lo 1982). In the current right-wing movement, government power has been hotly contended- an acknowledgment of the crucial role that it can play as an asset or a roadblock for a movement.

Government also has its own independent interests, primarily those of self-preservation and preservation of the status quo. In some cases those needs may call for expanded rights for some groups, the promotion of greater tolerance, or strengthening of one or another disadvantaged group. In most cases, however, government interest lies with those holders of power whose interests it most strongly represents. In the case of the right, when right-wing activism is so extreme that it is directed at the overthrow of the government or the massive disruption of the status quo, government represses that sector.

(This is the case when the Bureau of Alcohol, Tobacco and Firearms (BATF) has attacked right-wing enclaves that have stockpiled weapons, right-wing tax protesters who have defied the IRS, or far-right movement activists who have engaged in illegal activity.)

For the most part, the right's movement-building has been financed by elites outside government, who have bankrolled a movement infrastructure that is openly hostile to government power in its New Deal form. Elites inside government have often (unsuccessfully) opposed the right's rapid ascension.

Conclusions

The current electoral and cultural success of the right has not occurred in a vacuum, but during a specific historical period in which five overlapping and reinforcing factors have converged to create a hospitable environment. These factors are driving the political and social direction of the country relentlessly to the right.

This analysis can help us to understand the challenge we face in responding to the dangerous movement known as the New Right, the Christian Right and the new Republicans. It is discouraging that many of the factors discussed above— especially economic contraction, social backlash, and the strength of the right's political infrastructure—mitigate against liberal reformist social change. That does not mean, however, that there is no hope. What is needed is a clear appreciation of both the danger we now face, and the potential for positive change that exists despite that danger.

The reactionary forces of this historical moment will not be stopped simply by progressives working harder. The engine of reaction must first be slowed in order to create breathing room for liberalism and the left. This requires a massive campaign of public education to expose the right's hidden agendas and actual motivations. There must also be careful documentation of the consequences of right-wing policies. Simultaneously, progressives need to develop new leadership and new ideas (Levitas et al 1995).

The most important quality in developing new ideas may be the ability to listen with new ears to the concerns, fears, hopes, and aspirations of the traditional constituencies of the left—low-income people, people who suffer from discrimination (especially racism and sexism), and working people on whose backs the profits of a rapacious capitalism are built. Historically, liberals and progressives have been better at advocacy than at listening. While the left and liberals have accomplished a great many reforms, the right has been more successful at creating a simple message that wins support by encapsulating frustrations and directing them toward unpopular scapegoats.

This is a powerful marketing formula that has been used in the past to bring ultra-right movements to power, most notably in Germany in the 1930s. It is a technique that thrives in a setting of economic hard times for working people. It rests on a movement infrastructure that can organize aggressively to spread the message and win recruits. And it thrives when progressives, reformers, humanists, and liberal religious people underestimate the threat they face or are too weak or unorganized to hold the line.

Religious liberals will have a crucial role to play in the restructuring of the liberal/left coalition. The punitive and vengeful brand of Christian fundamentalism that now dominates the Religious Right must be confronted by those whose religious beliefs lead to humane, socially conscious public policy.

Further, the strategists of liberal and progressive social change must admit the failure of their message and their policies to hold the loyalty of the average voter. With that admission must come a self-criticism that is honest, thorough, and seeks input from not only those who stayed with liberalism, but also those who have rejected it. Failed revolutionary movements in other countries are sometimes criticized by progressives for failing to examine adequately the reasons for their loss of popular support. No less should be done in the face of our own failure, if the rebuilding is to avoid the shortcomings of the past.

6

DRIFTING RIGHT AND GOING WRONG[1]

An overview of the US political Right

Chip Berlet and Jean V. Hardisty

Our country is in the midst of the longest period of Right-wing reaction against movements seeking equality, social justice, and economic fairness since the period of Reconstruction in the South following the Civil War. We picture hooded Ku Klux Klan nightriders carrying torches and lighting crosses when we think of this late 19th-century turmoil. We tend to forget the societal institutions and systems that also played a role in creating oppression for Blacks and preserving privilege for Whites.

Now, in the early twenty-first century, the attacks on social and economic justice predominantly take the form of state and national legislation passed by mainstream politicians. The Right-wing backlash today is targeted at a subtler "enemy." It is no longer simply African Americans who are portrayed as less than deserving citizens. Today the electoral Right uses an allegedly "colorblind" template to identify those who are outside acceptable norms of morality and family values. So, it is welfare "queens," lesbians, and gay men of all races, and "illegal aliens" (to name just a few) who are, by virtue of their identity, living an un-American life. In fact, anyone who is not Christian is suspect, especially Muslims. Jews are accepted as allies to the extent that they sign onto the Right's agenda. Meanwhile, virulently antisemitic extreme Right groups, including the neonazis, continue to advocate for White supremacy, promoting their agenda by recruiting young people to a vision of an idyllic "White America."

Those who want to successfully challenge the Right's policies need to understand that not all sectors of the US Right are alike. There are multiple networks of

1   A version of this chapter first appeared in early 2003 in the *National Council of Jewish Women Journal,* Winter 2002, pp. 8–11. It was rewritten later in 2003 as an effort to explain what was happening to a broader audience than we usually addressed.

Copyright 2003, National Council of Jewish Women, used by permission, all rights reserved. This version copyright 2019 by the Estate of Jean V. Hardisty and Chip Berlet. All rights reserved. Used by permission of the authors.

organizations and funders with differing and sometimes competing agendas. Different ideas and methods are used in various Right-wing social and political movements. No one organization "controls" the political Right. No single deep-pocket funder is "behind" the Right. Some large organizations are important, but many others appear to be more influential than they really are.

Traditional Republican Party conservatism is composed of several sectors, including corporate conservatives, moderate conservatives, libertarians, and neoconservatives. In addition, the political Right includes other sectors such as the Christian Right, the Patriot movement, and the extreme Right. Critics need to sharpen their focus and examine the details. It is not fair to equate the Ku Klux Klan with the Christian Right. It is fair to criticize anti-democratic aspects of both movements.

The Christian Right, for example, has no qualms about denouncing the Klan and other groups on the extreme Right that promote naked White supremacy and antisemitism, or that use aggressive intimidation or insurgent violence. A few zealots in the Christian Right use violence to oppose abortion, but Christian Right activists overwhelmingly work for reforms through legislation and support for candidates for public office. Some of these reforms, however, would deny certain civil rights protections to people who step outside heterosexual monogamy. The Christian Right urges women to adopt "traditional" roles that are secondary and submissive to men. Calls to make this country a Christian nation implicitly promote the idea that Jews and other non-Christians are second-class citizens. Much of Christian Right ideology privileges the culture of White northern Europeans at the expense of diversity and a pluralistic model of democracy. So while the ultraconservative Christian Right and the extreme Right are separate movements, they pull the society in the same direction, even while remaining critical of each other's groups, leaders, and plans.

Meanwhile, the Patriot movement occupies a middle ground between the Christian Right and the extreme Right. The Patriot movement represents a type of Right-wing populism that periodically surfaces on the US political landscape. Its most visible recent aspect was the armed "citizens militias" that flourished in the mid-1990s. The militia movement now has largely collapsed, but there is still a flourishing Patriot subculture with groups such as the John Birch Society and the website www.freerepublic.com serving as typical examples. People in the Patriot movement see the world through the lens of conspiracy, believing the government to be controlled by secret elites and fearing tyrannical government repression. Many deny the bigoted antisemitic aspect of their conspiracism or the White supremacist lineage of their bogus "constitutionalist" states' rights legal arguments. Some early militia leaders came out of extreme Right hate groups, and often tried to mask their bigotry to attract a larger audience.

Pat Buchanan is a key figure in this Patriot sector, where his brand of xenophobic nationalism finds an enthusiastic audience. Patriot leaders take fears over the economy, corporate globalization, and downsizing and focus them onto scapegoats, ranging from immigrants and people of color to the United Nations. Many in the militias, for example, blame their slipping social and economic status on an alleged government conspiracy to build a global New World Order. Sometimes people in the Patriot movement try to recruit from progressive groups involved in anti-war or anti-globalization organizing.

Participants in the Christian Right represent a different demographic group. They are often upwardly mobile suburbanites who are members of conservative Protestant evangelical, charismatic, or fundamentalist churches. These churches are growing rapidly across the country, while moderate or liberal Protestant denominations such as the Presbyterian Church USA and the United Church of Christ are losing members in record numbers. Not all members of conservative Protestant churches are active in the Christian Right, but it is within these churches that people are recruited and mobilized into social movements and political campaigns.

Those that join Christian Right groups, such as Concerned Women for America, tend to get much of their information about politics and world events not from network television and daily newspapers but through media produced by the Christian Right—including magazines, radio programs, television evangelists, and direct mail. These sources frequently portray a world awash in sin, with liberals, feminists, peaceniks, homosexuals and other subversives undermining a godly America. The Christian Right is the largest social movement in the United States, and the biggest voting bloc in the Republican Party.

Within the Republican Party, the Christian Right competes with more secular, upstart free market libertarianism and button-down business conservatism for dominance. Activists from all three ideologies are appointed to federal and state agencies and join debates over public policy, swamping calls for progressive reforms. This can create confusion for proponents of affirmative action or humane welfare policies who find themselves defending their views against three different sets of negative arguments. A local school board can find its comprehensive sex education curriculum under attack from libertarians who claim it is a waste of tax dollars, conservatives who claim it is an inappropriate diversion from the core curriculum, and Christian Right activists who claim it is immoral.

A network of national and state-level conservative think tanks churn out educational and research materials for their activists and sympathetic politicians and journalists. This explains why campaigns over school vouchers, sentencing guidelines, union dues, and faith-based initiatives seem to sweep across the country in waves. The Right's intellectual infrastructure began to be built in earnest in the late 1970s and matured in the mid-1980s. Examples of national think tanks include the Heritage Foundation for business conservatives, the Cato Institute for libertarians, and the Free Congress Foundation for the Christian Right. Through the synergy of research, publications, and conferences a variety of ideas are debated, slogans sharpened, and campaigns launched. Conservative foundations and corporations have learned to fund strategically, while most centrist and progressive foundations are reluctant to fund movement-building, for instance the type of infrastructure of the type that has been so successful for the political Right.

In the 1950s academics popularized the idea that people who joined Right-wing (and Left-wing) social and political movements were a "lunatic fringe" of "extremists" who suffered from some psychological malady. But most scholars now see

Right-wing activists (and activists in general) as relatively average people, recruited by friends into groups that offer a reasonable-sounding plan to solve political, economic, cultural, or social problems. This is true even for some people who join the many small neonazi groups, and it is certainly true for those active in more mainstream Right-wing movements. Their recruitment of average concerned people is the result of a carefully planned campaign to restore the Right to dominance in the Republican Party and the country as a whole.

How did the political Right gain so much power? After World War II the political Right faced four major hurdles in building a successful movement: it was identified as a club for wealthy elitists; it was fractured by internal feuds; it was seen as a safe harbor for racists; and it tolerated a nest of conspiracy theorists, some of whom were antisemites.

In the mid-1950s, William F. Buckley, Jr and a group of his Old Right conservative intellectual allies set out to restore the image and power of the Right, using Buckley's magazine *National Review* as the vehicle for debate. Known as "fusionists," they were determined to roll back the social welfare policies of Roosevelt's New Deal at home by building a conservative coalition composed of economic libertarianism, social traditionalism, and militant anticommunism. Professor Jerome L. Himmelstein (1990) explained that "the core assumption that binds these three elements is the belief that American society on all levels has an organic order—harmonious, beneficent, and self-regulating—disturbed only by misguided ideas and policies, especially those propagated by a liberal elite in the government, the media, and the universities" The fusionists led by Buckley began speaking out against overt White supremacy and antisemitism, and ostracized the John Birch Society for its paranoid-sounding conspiracy theories.

In the late 1970s a group of conservative strategists who had been active in the failed 1964 Barry Goldwater presidential campaign began to formulate a "family values" agenda that held enormous appeal for traditionalist conservatives of the Republican Party and the burgeoning Christian evangelical population. The coalition really jelled in 1979, when Robert Billings of the National Christian Action Council invited rising televangelist Jerry Falwell to meet conservative organizers Paul Weyrich, Howard Phillips, Richard Viguerie, and Ed McAteer. They wanted to use abortion as a wedge issue to split social conservative traditionalists away from the Democratic Party. Falwell took their idea of a "Moral Majority," and turned into an organization. This emerging movement became known as the "New Right" and it built a conservative voting base, provided foot soldiers for what became known as the Culture War, and captured the Republican Party.

After the collapse of communism in the Soviet Union and Eastern Europe during Ronald Reagan's second Administration, militant anti-communists focused on opposing big government, bureaucratic regulations, liberal collectivism, and godless secular humanism here at home. This allowed the fusionist coalition to continue into the new millennium. The electoral political Right still seeks coalition among its different sectors but tolerates substantial disagreement over specific policy questions. For instance, libertarians often support abortion, gay, and immigrant rights and defend civil liberties, in opposition to many business conservatives and

Christian Right traditionalists. But libertarians will join with these other Right-wing sectors to support tax cuts and harsh punitive sentencing of criminals.

Simultaneously, a new partner in the conservative coalition emerged. Neo-conservatives were former liberals—who had supported the Cold War against communism—who then shifted their concern to what they saw as a rising threat of global terrorism. They tend to be strong supporters of aggressive Israeli policies in the Middle East, and suspicious of Islamic militants. They support global US military intervention that is both pre-emptive and unilateral and have significantly influenced U.S. foreign policy since the terror attacks of September 11, 2001.

Neoconservatives joined with the Christian Right to support "traditional" moral values—which translates to attacks on the feminist, reproductive rights, and GLBT movements. They seek to pack the state and federal court system, including the US Supreme Court, with appointees who share their ultra-conservative viewpoints.

Key to the success of the new conservative coalition of the 1980s and 1990s was the use of populist-sounding rhetoric to mobilize resentment among predominantly White middle class and working class constituencies, especially men. Playing on anger over the erosion of traditional privileges, along with more legitimate fears over economic and social crises, the political Right skillfully demonized target groups and promoted scapegoating stories about waves of criminal immigrants and lazy welfare queens—stories that usually carried a racist subtext. It replaced overt racist rhetoric with what Rightist leaders call a "colorblind" political agenda. They claim the legislation prompted by the Civil Rights Movement ended the need for government action against discrimination and racism, and then systematically oppose all government programs aimed at redressing the effects of ongoing institutional racism

Right-wing populist rhetoric masks the fact that changes in the tax code and other economic initiatives pursued by the Right in the 1980s and 1990s overwhelmingly benefited the wealthy and created vast disparities between the rich and poor. Yet these initiatives were presented as reforms to stop the "tax robbery" of average citizens by government bureaucrats labeled as corrupt and incompetent.

Tax cuts invariably defund those programs of the federal government that seek to help impoverished constituencies, enforce laws against discrimination, and protect the environment. At the same time, federal funds have been shifted to build a huge infrastructure for the military, and various "anti-terrorism" programs of "homeland security" that have seriously eroded civil liberties.

This history helps explain how the political Right rose to its position of power and now dominates policy debates. The ascendance of Right-wing political power over government policies may seem less dramatic than the vigilantism of the militias or the murderous terror of Extreme Right race hate groups, but it has resulted in a dramatic erosion of civil rights, civil liberties, and basic human rights for many people in our country. The sectors of the Right may work separately, but together they continue to pull the nation away from the goal of building a truly fair and equitable democratic society.

INTERLUDE C

Condi's dad and the lessons of war[1]

Chip Berlet

When I hear Condoleezza Rice, US National Security Adviser for President Bush, defending the war in Iraq, I think of her father denouncing the war in Vietnam. Condi's dad was a Dean in the college of liberal arts at the University of Denver in the early 1970s when I was editor of the student newspaper, the *Clarion*. His name was John Rice, but no student dared call him that. He was an imposing figure, and we all called him "Dean" Rice.

In her book *Bushwomen* (2004) Laura Flanders traces how as a college student, Condi Rice was groomed and recruited by Right-wing Republicans. Ms. Rice, speaking in 2012 at the Republican national political convention in Philadelphia, said that her father "was the first Republican I knew," and she claimed, "in America, with education and hard work, it really does not matter where you come from; it matters only where you are going" (Rice 2012).

That's not what I learned from Dean Rice. I took his class on the "Black Experience in America," and continued to attend his seminars with his encouragement. The seminar was built around a series of invited speakers who lectured in a public forum followed by classroom discussions.

That's where I met Fannie Lou Hamer, a Black voting rights activist from Sunflower County Mississippi, who led a challenge to the all-White Mississippi delegation to the 1964 Democrat Convention, which failed that year but succeeded in 1968. That's where I heard Dean Rice explain that he had always refused to register as a Democrat because that was the party of the bigots who had blocked his voter registration when he and his family lived in the South.

---

1 Originally posted on October 27, 2004, during the Iraq War. Some minor revisions and bracketed insertions have been made. Addition resources and references are online at https://tinyurl.com/condi-and-war.

Dean Rice may have been registered as a Republican up North, but he taught me about working for progressive social change and opposing institutional racism. He taught me that White people like me enjoyed privileges routinely denied to Blacks. He taught me that the proportion of Blacks serving in Vietnam was tied to economic and social policies at home. And he pointed out that along with this knowledge came an absolute moral imperative to act.

The seminar speakers invited by Dean Rice included a wide range of perspectives—from members of the US Civil Rights Commission, to exiled South African poet Dennis Brutus, to Louis Farrakhan explaining the teachings of Black Muslim Elijah Mohammed, to Lee Evans and John Carlos who at the time were organizing Black athletes to resist racism on the field and off. It was Carlos and teammate Tommie Smith who gained international attention when, after winning a race, they strode to the medals podium, and during the US National Anthem they gave the Black Power salute at the 1968 Olympics in Mexico City.

(As *Washington Post* reporter DeNeen L. Brown put it in a 2017 retrospective: "They didn't #TakeTheKnee. Instead they raised a fist.")

I still have a tape of the lecture by Andrew Young who was then a leader of the Southern Christian Leadership Conference. It was long ago, but I think I remember Condi as a teenager all dressed up playing the classical piano introduction to Young's speech. Condi was so smart and talented she was a bit scary. We all knew she was being groomed to go far, but we never suspected she would end up painting a public picture of her father that many of us would not recognize.

Dean Rice had high standards for all of us; and as his students we respected him enough to ask him to speak in May of 1971 at a campus memorial service for the students slain at Kent and Jackson State the previous year. Dean Rice eulogized the dead students as "young people who gave their lives for the cause of freedom and for the cause of eliminating useless war." He read the names of those from the university community who had died in Vietnam. He spoke of the atrocities. Then he challenged us all: "When tomorrow comes will you be the perpetuators of war or of peace? Are you the generation to bring to America a lasting peace? Or did your brothers and sisters at Kent and Jackson State die in vain?"

Jim Heltsley, who taught in the Speech and Communications department, was deeply moved by the speech delivered by Dean Rice. That day he sent a large envelope to me containing a letter to the editor. Heltsley wrote: "After listening to Dean Rice and others speak of the 'senseless' war and of the atrocities committed there and within our own country, I shook with silent frustration ... I wanted to shout that it is all of us that are guilty-we who sit there and do nothing" (Heltsley 1971).

> I sat there in the sun looking at a one-eyed veteran and felt the place where my left elbow used to be-it was torn off by shrapnel in Korea in that infamous 'police action'. There must have been older faculty members present who felt the tearing sensation of bullets" in the Second World War. But here we sit and accuse others of not doing anything ... we are all responsible-in particular we who should be expert witnesses!

Heltsley wrote that he did not have the courage to be arrested in protesting the war, but that in the envelope was something he could do. Enclosed were his four Korean War medals he was rejecting, including a Purple Heart. I thought about the medals and the message, and what I had learned from Dean Rice over the years. I thought about how my brother had stood up for his different set of principles and was serving in Vietnam while I sat safely at a desk on a college campus. We ran the letter from Heltsley as the front page of the University of Denver *Clarion*, with images of the medals laid across the bottom of the page (Clarion 1971).

The next morning, I decided to get arrested with other demonstrators in an act of civil disobedience to protest the war in Vietnam. Not long after that I dropped out of college to be an alternative journalist and human rights activist.

7

WHAT WE FACE IN THE YEAR 2000[1]

Chip Berlet and Matthew N. Lyons

Since the 1820s, repressive and Right-wing populist movements have played an almost continual role in US political life. Why? In the broadest terms, structural inequalities have continually fueled social, political, cultural, and economic tensions of one kind or another. These in turn have provided numerous openings for repressive populist movements to develop.

Second, the United States has experienced almost constant upheaval since its founding, between wars, conquest and expansion, mass immigration, industrial growth and change, economic cycles, geographic and social mobility, and anti-oppression struggles.

Third, as the country has expanded and developed (and given its decentralized political system), older elites based along the Atlantic seaboard and in the Northeast, have repeatedly been challenged by newer, outsider factions of the elite based in other regions (Davis 1986).

These outsiders have sometimes used anti-elite conspiracism to rally grassroots support. Fourth, the United States was one of the first countries to establish mass-based electoral politics—largely through the work of repressive populist movements themselves. In this context politicians quickly established a tradition of demagogic appeals to "the people" against "the establishment."

We should not dismiss Right-wing populists as paranoid or fanatical extremists. This explanation was popularized in the 1960s by centrist analysts denouncing what they called "extremists of the Left and Right" (see Online Resources: Centrist/Extremist Theories).

---

1   This chapter is adapted from the book *Right-Wing Populism in America: Too Close for Comfort* by Chip Berlet and Matthew N. Lyons, Guilford 2000.
      Copyright 2000 Guilford Press. Used by permission. All rights Reserved. Additional material and updates, including charts and slideshows, are curated by the authors online at http://www.rightwingpopulism.us/.

Nor should we romanticize them as "the people" resisting tyranny—we need to recognize these movements as both complex and dangerous: complex, because they speak to a combination of legitimate and selfish grievances; dangerous, because they channel people's hopes and fears into misguided rebellions that only serve to heighten inequality and oppression.

There are several issues we believe are central to understanding Right-wing populism:

- these are movements engaged in real power struggles;
- they target both elites and subordinate groups;
- people find a real sense of effectiveness and community within these movements.
- unfair social and economic relations fuel populist resentments, especially when mainstream politicians are indifferent to or ineffective in challenging this inequality;
- different demographic groups join Right-wing populist movements; and
- resentments can be mobilized using demonization, scapegoating, and conspiracism especially in a narrative package called producerism.

The resulting dynamics are complex, placing populist dissidents in a tug-of-war between the far-Right and Centrist politicians, and prompting situations that can generate both vigilante bullying and violence, as well as improper government surveillance and political repression.

Why do people join Right-wing populist movements? We can identify several general factors that seem significant, including:

- anxiety over social, cultural, and political change;
- fears of losing privilege and status, as traditional social hierarchies have been challenged and become more fragmented;
- a sense of disempowerment in the face of massive bureaucratic institutions, both public and private, over which ordinary people have little influence;
- economic hardships and dislocations connected to globalization and other factors;
- disillusionment with mainstream political choices; and
- the weakness or nonexistence of Leftist radical alternatives that speak effectively to many people's concerns.

Michael Omi and Howard Wynant have described "the collapse of the 'American Dream,'" under pressure from social liberation movements, economic disruptions and upheavals, and the apparent decline of US global power in the wake of setbacks such as the Vietnam War (Omi and Wynant 1986,121–122).

For many people drawn to Right-wing populist movements, this sense of a many-sided national crisis persists even today.

Holly Sklar (1995b) has written of "the Dying American Dream." Her analysis highlights soaring economic inequality, growing poverty, inadequate real wages, the disappearance of union jobs, global corporate restructuring, the shredding of social programs, the growth of prisons, and the shift toward "a cheaper, more disposable workforce of temporary workers, part-timers, and other 'contingent workers.'" These trends disproportionately hurt people of color, but they also affect large numbers of White people, who form the vast majority of Right-wing populism's supporters. Many workers find little in their lives that confirms headlines boasting of a booming economy or low unemployment. Sklar underscores that as "the American Dream has become more impossible for more people, scapegoating is being used to deflect blame from the economic system and channel anger to support reactionary political causes" (1995, 115) Democrats as well as Republicans, liberals as well as conservatives, have been complicit in this process (Sklar 1986, 1995a, 1995b). The effect of globalization on the economy is hardly an analysis limited to the Left. Consider this quote from Business Week (1995, 73).

the Darwinian demands of global competition have led to waves of corporate downsizing. Real median incomes haven't moved much for two decades, while the earnings gap between the richest and the poorest Americans has widened. This has heightened workers' economic insecurity and sown doubts about the future.

Other writers have noted the bankruptcy of conventional politics for addressing social problems. Conservative analyst Kevin Phillips (1992, 38–42) wrote: "the sad truth is that frustration politics has built to a possibly scary level precisely because of the unnerving weakness of the major parties and their prevailing philosophies." Phillips cited both Republicans and Democrats for "ineptness and miscalculation." After decrying liberal elitism and arrogance, Phillips condemned Republican politicians who have "periodically unleashed the anti-black and anti-Israel messages they now complain about in more blunt politicians as 'bigotry'"

According to Phillips, "If Patrick Buchanan is to be put in a 1930-something context, so should the second-rate conservatives and liberals responsible for the economic and social failures from which he and other outsiders have drawn so many angry votes." Phillips expanded on this point in 1993 and 1994.

For a growing portion of the population in the 1990s, neither the Democrats nor the Republicans offered hope for redress of grievances. This in part explains the Perot phenomenon and the Reform Party.

Which Right-wing populist themes attract which groups of supporters? Hans-Georg Betz (1995), in his study *Radical Right-Wing Populism in Western Europe*, noted one frequent theme was xenophobia and racist scapegoating of immigrants and asylum seekers in an electoral context. Betz's review of voting demographics in Europe reveals that Right-wing populist parties attracted a disproportionate number of men, persons employed in the private sector, and younger voters.

In terms of social base, three versions of Right-wing populism have emerged:

- a Hayekian libertarianism centered around "get the government off my back" economic libertarianism coupled with a rejection of mainstream political parties—more attractive to the upper middle class and small entrepreneurs (Himmelstein 1990; Lo 1995);

- movements based on white nationalism, xenophobia and ethnocentric mono-cultures—which appear to be more attractive to the lower middle class and wage workers (Betz 1995; Klatch 1987); and

- a third version of Right-wing populism unique to the United States has a social base of politically mobilized ultraconservative Christian evangelicals (Marsden 1991; Martin 1996; Kintz 1997; Brasher 1998; Diamond 1998).

Politically-active persons in the Christian Right are motivated primarily by cultural, social and religious concerns (Green 1993, 1996; Green, Guth, Smidt, and Kellstedt 1996). Women play a significant role in this sector (Klatch 1987; Brasher 1998); as do politically-conservative pastors (Guth, Green, Smidt, Kellstedt, and Poloma 1997). A *Washington Post* survey of Promise Keepers attending the Stand in the Gap rally in Washington, DC, showed most of them had solidly middle-class income levels (Morin and Wilson 1997). This squares with the finding by Green, Guth, and Hill (1993) that Christian Right activism from 1978 through 1988 was concentrated primarily in relatively prosperous suburban areas.

In contrast, it seems persons in the more secular Patriot movement are primarily motivated by economic and social concerns (Kaplan 1997; Kaplan and Bjørgo 1998; Van Dyke and Soule 2002) . The study by Deborah Kaplan (1998) found members of a Patriot group in California had good reasons to fear downward mobility: "Many of the adherents here did suffer reversals, ... as a direct result of corporate restructuring strategies. As many as 49.3 percent, compared to 28.0 percent in a national news survey, said they had been 'personally affected' by business downsizing."

These different constituencies unite behind candidates that attack the current regime since both constituencies identify an intrusive and incompetent government as the cause of their grievances. Evidence suggests a similar constituency for Right-wing populists in the United States (Business Week 1995, 80; Manza and Brooks 1999).

One irritating tendency that muddles many analyses is the conflation of social movements, political movements, voting blocs, political campaigns, coalitions, and topical projects. While they generally overlap, they are not identical (Diamond 1998, 41–43). And the explanations promulgated by centrist/extremist theory in the 1960s—that "these people are crazy"—does not work.

This is not to suggest that there are no psychological factors in any of these It is to observe that Right-wing populist claims are no more and no less irrational than conventional claims that presidential elections express the will of the people; or that economic health can be measured by the profits of multibillion-dollar corporations, or that US military interventions in Iraq, Afghanistan, Haiti, Somalia, Kosovo, or wherever are designed to promote democracy and human rights.

To mobilize a constituency, Right-wing populists, like other movement organizers, develop ways to frame their arguments and appeals in ways that attract people to their movement's agenda. Right-wing populists also develop narratives about themselves and their society: who's good and who's bad, who has power and who doesn't, who is one of us and who isn't. These narratives may be wrong, but they are important, and they reflect real conflicts, fears, and longings. They are a means by which millions of people make sense of their world and decide how to act on their perceptions.

Producerism

Producerism is one of the most basic frameworks for Right-wing populist narratives in the United States. Producerism posits a noble hard-working middle group constantly in conflict with lazy, malevolent, or sinful parasites at the top and bottom of the social order. The characters and details in this story have changed repeatedly, but its main outlines have remained the same for some 200 years.

Producerism, in the forms we have examined, reflects a national culture that has long glorified individual hard work as the key to success and upward mobility. This tradition set Henry Ford's antisemitic philosophy apart from Czarist Russia's *the Protocols of the Elders of Zion*, which was rooted in an ethos of rigid class deference and inherited rank. But US producerism also reflects the rigidities of a racial caste system and the interests of middle- and working-class Whites, concerned with defending their privileges over people of color, yet resenting the powerful elites above them.

Producerism has been interwoven with other narratives in the Right-wing populist storybook, such as apocalyptic themes about an End Times battle between good and evil. Apocalypticism reflects the influence of Bible-believing Christianity—not only within the Right, but also as a major force shaping US politics and culture since the colonial period. Apocalyptic biblical narratives have also shaped both religious and secular fears of betrayal by political leaders plotting a repressive global regime. In recent decades, the theme of defending the traditional family against immoral, elitist feminists and homosexuals has also taken on a new centrality. Far from being irrational, this reflects a predictable effort to bolster heterosexual male power and privilege in the face of major movements demanding equality.

Heroes of "the real people"

Most people in Right-wing populist movements don't get up in the morning and say to themselves, "I'm going to victimize some oppressed groups today to get more power and privilege." What they are more likely to say is, "I want to get my fair share." They embrace narratives that portray themselves as victims and that depict the people they target as either more powerful than they are, being given an unfair advantage, or being immoral. This was true in 1676, when Nathaniel Bacon declared that a corrupt governor was unfairly favoring Indians against English settlers. It was true in the 1990s, when Right-wing populists demanded an end to "racial discrimination against white people" and "no special rights for homosexuals." Such claims are a form of scapegoating in defense of social inequality.

Right-wing and repressive populist movements relate to the established order in contradictory ways. They challenge us to go beyond binary models of power and resistance. It is oversimplified and wrong to treat such movements simply as attack dogs for bigoted elites. It is also a serious mistake to gloss over these movements' oppressive politics just because they challenge certain kinds of elite interests. and the reverse is also true: it is a serious mistake to gloss over the established order's oppressive politics—as Centrist/extremist theory does—just because Right-wing populists want to impose something that could be worse.

It is the dynamic interplay between the Right and the Center, and between Right-wing populist insurgency and established institutions, that is particularly dangerous. For example, President Clinton often responded to Republican attacks largely by embracing Right-wing positions, in a pattern that Democratic politicians have followed repeatedly.

State repression and Right-wing populism

Right-wing populists have scored major successes in helping to shift the political spectrum to the Right, and this influence must be combated. But actual Christian theocracy or Aryanist fascism in the United States is purely hypothetical, whereas a political system dominated by enormously wealthy elites is real—in fact, it is what we live under now. Rightists promote nightmare visions of the death penalty to help reinforce patriarchal families, or the formation of a "racially pure" White Christian republic; meanwhile, in our existing society, millions of women face sexual assault or domestic violence daily, and millions of people of color are relegated to rural and inner-city areas of rampant unemployment, poverty, violence, and state repression.

The growth of state repression is not simply a function of Right-wing initiatives. It is fundamentally a mechanism for political and economic elites to protect their own power. The Cold War produced a consensus among liberals, conservatives, reactionaries, and fascists on the need for a national security state to crush threats from the Left both inside and outside the United States. This consensus was challenged in the 1960s and 1970s, as many liberals, under pressure from the Left, criticized and sought to limit the most glaring abusive and illegal practices by government agencies. During the following years, ultraconservative organizations played a pivotal role in helping the security establishment circumvent such limits by shifting certain operations into private channels.

Since the 1970s, well-publicized Rightist-backed initiatives—the War on Drugs, crackdowns against "illegal aliens," and campaigns against "terrorism"— have been used to promote massive expansion of the security establishment, as well as serious attacks on civil liberties, especially against people of color. At the same time, the repressive apparatus has also grown through quieter measures such as expanded identification systems, increased ties between police and community organizations, and greater coordination between local, state, federal, and international police bodies.

During the 1990s, government forces also used the growth of Right-wing paramilitarism—such as the armed militias—as a rationale for further expanding state repression, which in turn fueled greater Right-wing insurgency. This is a vicious cycle in which each side scapegoats the other—what Girard (1986) calls mimetic scapegoating.

Here it is not simply the Right, or forces outside the Right, but also elite-sponsored opposition to the Right, that feeds authoritarian tendencies. To an alarming extent, liberal and even Leftist antiracists and antifascists—following centrist/extremist theory—have contributed to this vicious cycle by denouncing only Right-wing paramilitarism while ignoring the much more powerful repressive forces of the state itself—or worse, by directly urging a government crackdown as the way to fight the Right. Government abuse of power to silence dissent should be opposed regardless of the target group's political pedigree. History reveals, however, that while the state's repressive apparatus will sometimes go after Right-wing insurgents, in the long run its main targets are oppressed groups and the Left.

Centrist/extremist theory glorifies the US political system as democratic and glosses over its oppressive, antidemocratic features. It suggests that "irrational" dissidents of the Left and the Right are to blame for stirring up trouble. It implies that when Leftists organize to demand equality and human rights it is the disruptive moral equivalent of Right-wing campaigns to defend inequality and privilege. Whose interests does this analytical model serve?

8

CULTURE, RELIGION, APOCALYPSE, AND US MIDDLE EAST FOREIGN POLICY[1]

Chip Berlet and Nikhil Aziz[2]

John of Patmos—so named because of the small Mediterranean island where he lived—was an early Christian prophet. His writings, sometimes called "the Apocalypse of John," form the book of "Revelation," the last chapter in the Christian Bible. The words apocalypse, prophecy, and revelation all share the same root in ancient languages—a word that in its simplest form means unveiling that which is hidden.

Before Christianity, Zoroastrians wove apocalyptic themes into their spiritual tapestry; as did messianic Jews who were looking for signs of the Messiah—a great leader and redeemer—prophesied in their religious texts. These were mentioned in

1   Published in 2003, this chapter was an effort to explain the complicated relationships of societal forces named in the title. In most cases the mainstream corporate media has failed to educate voters about the millions of Americans who are devout Christians who read prophesies in the Bible as providing a script governing appropriate action in the contemporary political sphere. These folks are neither stupid nor crazy—as far too many Democratic Party fundraising efforts suggest.

   Originally written for an online magazine covering the Middle East, the publication's website has disappeared into the electronic ether. This original text lives on at Right-Web with permission. Right-Web itself is worth a peak at for substantial articles on US foreign policy coverage: https://tinyurl.com/mideast-apocalypse.

2   The coauthor of this chapter, Nikhil Aziz, attended the Road to Victory conference in Washington, DC, in November 2002. Distributed at the conference were materials from: Hands of Mercy, Messianic Times, Israel Alert, Christian Friends of Israeli Communities, Esteek of Israel, Galilee of the Nations, Holy Land Gifts, International Christian Embassy Jerusalem, Kesher Ministries, Magen David Adom, Maoz International, Messianic Jewish Alliance of America, Messianic Jewish Recording Artist & Evangelist, Messianic Jewish Resources, Messianic Liturgical Resources, Messianica, Middle Eastern Christian Coalition, One Israel Fund, Shop Holyland, The Remnant of Israel–Joseph's Storehouse, Ya Godda Pray.

the Christian Old Testament and formed the roots of the New Testament of the followers of a dark-skinned Jew named Jesus from Nazareth (see Online Resources: Apocalypticism).

Apocalyptic thinking—especially in the Christian Right—joins other factors that influence US Middle East policy, such as controlling global oil sources, assisting corporate-driven globalization, militaristic imperialism, and more. Why focus now on this one factor? Because the Christian Right is a powerful force shaping politics and culture in the United States, and they are the largest voting bloc in the Republican Party, so they can expect politicians to pay attention to their interests (Topic: Christian Right). That George W. Bush took his born-again religion seriously and applied it to his political decisions has been discussed widely (Austin 2003; Berkowitz 2003; Mansfield 2003; Rothschild 2003).

According to history professor Paul S. Boyer, author of *When Time Shall Be No More: Prophecy Belief in Modern American Culture* (1992) religious views in the United States have "always had an enormous, if indirect and under-recognized, role [in] shaping public policy." Boyer advises we pay attention to this hidden truth because of the "shadowy but vital way that belief in biblical prophecy is helping mold grass-roots attitudes toward current US foreign policy," especially in the Middle East (2003).

The apocalyptic style

Apocalyptic thinking involves the anticipation of a coming confrontation that will result in a substantial transformation of society on a global and historic scale. For some this is a huge bloody battle, while for others the transformation is peaceful (O'Leary 1994; Bromley 1997, 31–45; Wessinger 2000.

Apocalyptic views in the United States have deep roots. Some early Christian settlers saw the establishment of what became the United States as a fulfilment of Biblical prophecy. They believed the nation they were building needed to be defended against the subversive machinations of a literal Satan and his evil allies (Boyer 1992).

Starting in the colonial period—and as contemporary as today's headlines—the apocalyptic style has shaped public policy in the United States. The Battle Hymn of the Republic during the Civil War was an apocalyptic anthem in which Christians sang that their "eyes have seen the glory of the coming of the Lord." and that idea was plucked right out of the pages of Revelation (Berlet 1998a, 1998b, 2004, 2005a, 2005b, 2008).

There are many ways to read the complex and colorful visions in Revelation. The official Catholic position is that Revelation should be read as prophetic allegory and metaphor, and that Catholics should not be watching the clock for Christ's return. Within Protestantism, the range of apocalyptic views is vast, with most mainline denominations also downplaying the significance of Biblical apocalyptic prophecy.

In Revelation, God tells John of Patmos that one sign of the End Times are a series of "Tribulations" including wars, disease, famine, greed, and widespread sinful immorality. In the mid-1800s, theologian John Nelson Darby said he had decoded the timeline in which God preordained specific historical epochs or dispensations, including the final dispensation in which the End Times occurred (Boyer 1992, 80–112).

In this timeline, devout Christians are "raptured" up into heavenly protection before the Tribulations begin. Then the sinful are punished and Jesus Christ returns to rule over his loyal flock for one thousand years—a millennium. This combination of pretribulationist and premillennialist views can encourage passivity, but there are interpretations that encourage religious and political activism as well.

In the early 1900s, a group of theological conservatives defended premillennial dispensationalism, while denouncing mainline Protestant denominations. They complained that the leaders of the Presbyterians and Baptists (and to a lesser extent Methodists and Episcopalians), were drifting away from church fundamentals and compromising with modern science, popular culture, and liberalism. Thus was born the religious movement called "fundamentalism" (Marsden 1982, 1991; Ammerman 1991; Armstrong, 2000.

After World War II, a large group of theologically conservative Protestants who rejected the closed and rigid style of the fundamentalists emerged as what are now called "evangelicals." Some evangelicals who directly experience the presence of the Holy Spirit as part of a conversion experience describe it as being "born again."

According to a 2017 study by the Public Religion Research Institute: "White Christians, 81 percent of the population in 1976, now account for less than half the public—43 percent of Americans identify as white Christians, and 30 percent as white Protestants" (Winston 2017).

A significant proportion of evangelicals believe that Satan meddles in world politics and promotes sinfulness and strife (Boyer 1992). Author Hal Lindsey drew a huge audience of fundamentalists and evangelicals with a series of books starting in the 1970s claiming that the countdown clock of the End Times had begun to tick with the founding of the state of Israel in the Middle East, an event that was portrayed a fulfilment of biblical prophecy (Lindsey 1983).

For some Protestant evangelicals and fundamentalists, the text in Revelation is read as a timetable and script for the End Times that will include a massive battle between God and Satan on the plains of Armageddon, which today are located in Israel. A handful of Catholics also read Revelation in this way. When preachers tell them to look for the "signs of the Times" they look for signs that the End Times have begun. If they have, their activities—both religious and political—must change dramatically.

These Christians believe that in the End Times, an agent of Satan will appear as an actual world political leader who tricks devout Christians into helping build a one-world government and a one-world religion. This figure is called the Antichrist, and true Christians must resist him to protect their soul. They also must reject the Antichrist's "Mark of the Beast," represented by the number 666, which some fear is hidden in supermarket bar codes, security codes in paper currency, computer software, or tiny implantable microchips. They must fight cosmic evil in the secular world through moral persuasion, political activism, confrontation, and sometimes even violence.

As Frances FitzGerald explained in 1985:

> …elements of premillennialist thinking seem to exist in vague and diffuse form quite generally in the United States. Fundamentalist theology, for example, dictates that God and the Devil are everywhere immanent; thus, politics is not simply the collision of differing self-interests but the expression of a transcendent power struggle between the forces of good and the forces of evil … If the United States is the "Christian nation," then the Soviet Union must be the "evil empire."
>
> *(FitzGerald 1985, 106)*

A destructive tendency that can emerge from this belief system is the search for who is the Antichrist building a global "new world order;" what is the religion of the Antichrist, and what group of people are the agents of the Antichrist? According to Robert C. Fuller (1985, 5), "Today, fundamentalist Christian writers see the Antichrist in such enemies as the Muslim world, feminism, rock music, and secular humanism. The threat of the Antichrist's imminent takeover of the world's economy has been traced to the formation of the European Economic Community, the Susan B. Anthony dollar … and the introduction of universal product codes." Some Protestant apocalyptics in the United States still claim the Vatican is controlled by the Devil, for example the essay "Conclusive Proof from the Bible that the Pope is the Antichrist" (Pacific Institute 2019).

Examples of how this type of dualistic apocalypticism has influenced public policy include the colonial witch-hunts in New England; attacks on Catholics in the 1800s; claims that Jews controlled the media, banks, and colleges that spread beginning in the early 1900s; the Palmer Raids against immigrants in 1919 and 1920; the anti-communist witch-hunts of the 1950s; and 1990s conspiracy theories about a secret homosexual agenda. While this type of demonizing or dualistic apocalypticism is rooted in a religious tradition, it has morphed into a secular style as well, with examples in popular culture ranging from the movie "Apocalypse Now!" to television series including "the X-Files," and "Buffy the Vampire Slayer" (Berlet 1998b).

Belief in apocalyptic prophecy is widespread in the US (Boyer 1992). During the first Gulf War, 14 percent of one CNN national poll thought it was the beginning of Armageddon, and "American bookstores were experiencing a run on books about prophecy and the end of the world" (Lamy 1996, 155). In 1993, some 20 percent of those polled in the United States thought the second coming of Christ would occur near the year 2000 (Strozier and Flynn 1997).

Some premillennial dispensationalists believe they will be raptured into a safe heavenly embrace before the violent Tribulations. So why are so many of them actively involved in secular politics? Why not then just wait passively for the end? The answer lies in a variety of creative theological justifications (Harding 1994, 57–78) One of the assertions that mobilizes evangelicals into political activism is that truly devout and loyal to Biblical teachings, true Christians must obey God's command to take "dominion" over the earth.

This emerges after Protestant philosopher Francis A. Schaeffer and theologian Cornelius van Till, urged a more "muscular" and interventionist form of Christianity that became popular in the late 1970s. They influenced Christian Right activists such as Jerry Falwell, Tim LaHaye, and Pat Robertson—Christian Right leaders who took these theological ideas, added conspiracism and demonization, then spread the message that "Spiritual Warfare" was needed to cleanse society of the sinister influence of secular humanism (Diamond 1989).

Falwell went on to launch the Moral Majority and claimed that Jews and Christians were locked in a struggle with a violent Islam founded by the "terrorist" Muhammad (McKay 2005).

LaHaye became co-author of the *Left Behind* series of apocalyptic novels that portray Israel as under attack by the forces of the Antichrist (LaHaye and Jenkins 1995) One heroic mission by the Christian protagonists in the book series is the assassination of the former head of the United Nations who is revealed as the Antichrist himself (LaHaye and Jenkins 1995, vol. 6, 408–411). The series sold over 50 million copies. Pat Robertson went on to establish the Christian Coalition.

The Christian coalition, Israel, and the Aliyah

Three religious traditions—Judaism, Christianity, and Islam—see their prophetic history rooted not just in the Middle East, not just in Jerusalem, but also on a specific hilltop (Gorenberg 2000).

For Jews, the hilltop is called the Temple Mount, where the sacred Temple of Solomon once stood commemorating the site where God asked the prophet Abraham to sacrifice his son Isaac—and where God stayed Abraham's hand because he had shown his loyalty. The first two temples were destroyed, and it is a common element of Jewish religious tradition that Jews must return to Jerusalem (the land of Zion) and rebuild the third Temple of Solomon at which time the Ark—long lost—will be found. The Day of Judgment for Jews also involves Jerusalem. The Western Wall supporting the hillside is a place of prayer for observant Jews, and Aish HaTorah (2019) maintains a 24-hour live webcam view of the prayers by observant Jews.

The hilltop to Muslims is the Haram Al-Sharif (the Noble Sanctuary), and it is the site of one of Islam's holiest shrines—the Dome of the Rock—which encloses the rock from which the Prophet Muhammad ascended to heaven. This is also called the Al-Sakhrah Mosque. The larger Al-Aqsa Mosque is also on the hilltop, as are a number of smaller prayer rooms, domes, and minarets. Some Muslims believe there will be events that take place on Haram Al-Sharif that signal the Islamic End Times. These end times include the return of Jesus who is considered a major prophet by Muslims (Cook 1996, 2001, 2002; Berlet 2001; Rashid 2001; Rosenfeld 2001; Wessinger 2001; Tibi 2002; Gorenberg 2003). Muslims also have apocalyptic beliefs about the importance of the site, and they vary from passive and patient to militant and violent (see Online Resources: Muslim Apocalyptic).

For some apocalyptic Christians, the return of Jesus requires that Jews return to Israel (the ingathering or *Aliyah*), and rebuild the third Temple of Solomon on the hilltop Jews call the Temple Mount and Muslims call the Noble Sanctuary. Rebuilding the Temple of Solomon would violate the sanctity—and most likely destroy—the Islamic religious shrines now located on the hilltop. Some messianic Jews and apocalyptic Christians believe rebuilding the Temple of Solomon should take place anyway and this is a key (but not the only) factor in the growth of a movement called Christian Zionism.

Apocalyptic, millennialist, and dispensationalist thinking has greatly influenced Pat Robertson and other Christian Evangelical Rightists including Jerry Falwell, John Hagee, and Joyce Meyer. This explains both their activist interest in US foreign policy generally, and in particular, their positions on the Middle East. It is especially evident in their unqualified support for Israel and Islamophobic opposition to Palestinian self-determination. The result of this is a movement called Christian Zionism, which is also related to Christian Right support for the US war against Afghanistan and Iraq, and the general US presence in the Middle East. At the same time, Christian Right support for Israel does not mean an unequivocal embrace of Jews. Anti-Jewish as well as anti-Islamic and anti-Arab themes have been a common stream running through historic Christian Right ideology and activism.

Christian Right support for Israel comes in many forms from lobbying Congress and the Administration to adopt pro-Israel policies, intervening in the foreign policy debate on the Palestine-Israel issue, and funding the immigration of Eastern European Jews to Israel. The funding of Jewish immigration to Israel is in keeping with Christian Evangelical/Fundamentalist belief that the second coming of Christ is preceded by the Aliyah, and the rebuilding of the Third Temple in Jerusalem. This is also why most Christian Rightists oppose Palestinian statehood and the removal of Jewish settlements from the West Bank and the Gaza Strip—because God promised all of the Biblical land of Canaan to the Israelites.

A major display of the Christian Right's support for Israel was the 2002 Road to Victory Conference organized by the Christian Coalition, which was quite unlike any previous Road to Victory conference (author Aziz observed this and other things as he attended the Road to Victory conference in Washington DC in November 2002 where he collected documents).

The keynote speaker was Ehud Olmert, then mayor of Jerusalem, who was invited to address the Solidarity with Israel rally. The galaxy of Right-wing stars appearing at the conference either in person or through video included, former House Majority Leader Dick Armey (R-TX), former chair of the foreign relations committee Senator Jesse Helms (R-NC), Lt Col Oliver North, Alan Keyes, former Alabama Chief Justice Roy Moore, and former Israeli Prime Minister Benjamin Netanyahu.

Pat Robertson told the Solidarity with Israel rally:

"We should not ask (Israel) to withdraw (from the occupied territories)—we should stand with them and fight." … Robertson, who said his support for Israel is long-standing, cited the Book of Genesis, in which God granted Abraham and his descendants the ancient land of Canaan, now believed to be modern Israel.

(Horwitz 2013)

The report added that the "Solidarity with Israel rally … is just one element of a broader program called 'Praying for Jerusalem.' The campaign aimed to recruit 1 million Christians in 100,000 evangelical churches for a mass prayer for Jerusalem, as well as to promote Christian tourism and purchase of Israeli products" (Kumar 2002; Religion News Service 2003)

The Road to Victory conference exhibit hall (usually filled with Christian Evangelical ministries and organizations) also had a large number of conservative Jewish groups and Christian tourism groups. This included: The Israel Ministry of Tourism; the Manassas, VA based Christians for Israel USA which has an "Exobus" project that takes Jews from Eastern Europe and the former USSR to Israel; the Front Royal, VA based Church and Israel which runs the Christian Aliyah Network that also helps Jews to migrate to Israel; the Jerusalem based Bridges for Peace, "a Bible-believing Christian organization supporting Israel," which publishes *Dispatch from Jerusalem* and has a range of programs including migration and aid.

In addition, there were groups with more obviously Zionist agendas such as the Shawnee Mission, KS based National Unity Coalition for Israel which claims to be a coalition of 200 Jewish and Christian groups who "stand staunchly in support of a safe and secure Israel;" the New York based Americans for a Safe Israel which publishes *Outpost* and rejects Land for Peace instead supporting "Peace for Peace;" and the Washington, DC based hawkishly pro-Israel Jewish Institute for National Security Affairs, which publishes *Security Affairs*.

Distributed at the conference were materials from: Hands of Mercy, Messianic Times, Israel Alert, Christian Friends of Israeli Communities, Esteek of Israel, Galilee of the Nations, Holy Land Gifts, International Christian Embassy Jerusalem, Kesher Ministries, Magen David Adom, Maoz International, Messianic Jewish Alliance of America, Messianic Jewish Recording Artist & Evangelist, Messianic Jewish Resources, Messianic Liturgical Resources, Messianica, Middle Eastern Christian Coalition, One Israel Fund, Shop Holyland, the Remnant of Israel—Joseph's Storehouse, and Ya Godda Pray.

Most Christian Zionists support any action of the Israeli government and dismiss the rights of Palestinians (Berkowitz 2003) This is objected to from within various sectors of Christianity, especially mainline Protestant denominations (Hafften 2003; Whitlatch 2003) While some Jewish leaders such as Abraham Foxman of the Anti-Defamation League welcome Christian Zionist support for Israel, others are unhappy with the arrangement (Wagner 1998; Levitas 2003).

Rabbi David Saperstein, the director of the Religious Action Center of Reform Judaism, cautions that "If, as a reflection of their End Times theology, the message of the Christian Right to U.S. policymakers is 'don't be involved in getting the parties to the negotiating table,' then they certainly are going to be an impediment to the peace process, and that isn't helpful" (quoted in Levitas 2003).

Gershom Gorenberg points out that for Christian Zionists, Jews are actors in a play where the final curtain forces them to either convert to Christianity or die in a blaze of fire sent by God. Gorenberg has also pointed out the intolerance in the "Left Behind" series of fictional accounts of the End Times: "Intolerance: The Bestseller" (quoted in Levitas 2003).

Gorenberg (2012) writes that:

> Having spent years researching the Christian right's tie to Israel – listening to leading "Christian Zionists," reading their sermons and examining the links of some to Israeli extremists—
>
> I have to conclude that this is a strangely exploitative relationship. Accepting the embrace of conservative evangelicals poses problems of principle for Jews and Israel, in return for an illusory short-term payoff.
>
> Jews would do better to follow the Hebrew maxim "Respect him and suspect him," maintaining a polite distance and publicly delineating their differences from the Christian right, even while at times supporting the same policy steps.

Progressive Jewish groups warn that by forming a coalition with Christian Zionists, the domestic agenda of the Christian Right is given support. Received at Political Research Associates from the group Jewish Women Watching was an undated postcard titled "Strange Bedfellows," that listed troubling statements by Christian Right leaders Pat Robertson, Jerry Falwell, and Ralph Reed. On the back was pasted a condom, with the slogan "Practice Safe Politics," and the warning: "This condom will not protect you from the real intentions of the Christian right wing … abstinence from strange bedfellows is advised".

Christian Zionism can easily spill over into religious bigotry against Muslims. As scholar Boyer warned in 2003, "anti-Islamic rhetoric is at fever pitch today." One source of this Islamophobic bigotry is the glossy magazine *Midnight Call: The Prophetic Voice for the Endtimes*. Recent promotional mailings from Midnight Call included letters headlined: "the Prophetic Return to Israel:" "Islam, Israel and the USA;" and "Revealing the Hidden Truth about the Middle East." the latter is an advertisement for the book *Saddam's Mystery Babylon: Revealing the Hidden Agenda of the most Sinister Entity in the Bible*. While bashing Arabs and Muslims as possible agents of the Antichrist is common in this sector of Christian Fundamentalism, special warnings are issued against global peace efforts by the European Union and the United Nations—seen as part of the Antichrist's plan for a "New World Order" and one-world government.

Messianic militarism

Matthew Rothschild, editor of the *Progressive Magazine*, has dubbed the Bush Administration foreign policy "messianic militarism" (2003). This tendency is not unique to the Bush administration, but echoes the history of dualistic apocalypticism and a demonizing form of anticommunism that dominated U.S. culture for most of the 20th century (Kovel 1994; Berlet and Lyons 2000, 88–91).

When Ronald Reagan declared the Soviet Union was the "evil empire" and launched a massive funding of the military in the early 1980s, his actions were based on apocalyptic claims from both the Christian Right and a new movement built by hawkish Cold War ex-liberals dubbed "neoconservatism" (Husain 2003).

With the election of George W. Bush, the apocalyptic predictions of the neoconservative militarists gained even more support, especially when they produced the Team B reports. Khurram Husain in the *Bulletin of the Atomic Scientists* argues that their "claims were all drawn from worst-case scenarios. But the Team B reports are more significant for the thinking they reveal. The authors made projections of Soviet stockpiles and built up a picture of a Soviet Union bent on dominating the world based on wild speculation" (Husain 2003).

With the collapse of communism in Europe, the United States was re-framed as the defender of global civilization against the heathens and barbarians in "rogue states" where terrorism festered. This drew from an even earlier apocalyptic frame than anticommunism—a worldview that was an extension of the earliest Christian millennial visions which came to the US "from the original, English-speaking heartland, itself grafted on the crusades and the voyages of discovery" (Husain 2003).

According to Kees van der Pijl (2003), a European scholar, "Today, the missionary ideology constructed around the civilisation/barbarity dichotomy must satisfy the tastes of a Western public ... because every hegemonic strategy has to build on the available foundation of attitudes and dispositions in the wider population if it is to be effective." Therefore in the current Bush administration, "the End of History/Axis of Evil line of thinking ... argues that for the world to reach its definitive form in terms of civilisation ... [it is necessary to] neutralise the states 'mired in history' as potential rabble-rousers, the 'rogue states' beyond the pale" (van der Pijl 2003).

It is this dualistic apocalyptic vision that is shared by sectors of the Christian Right and the militarist hawks in the neoconservative movement. This coalition of "messianic militarism" eclipses the power of other sectors that helped elect Bush: The more moderate corporate internationalists; the anti-interventionist libertarians; and the paleoconservatives—so named because of their allegiance to the isolationism, unilateralism, and xenophobia of the Old Right.

Revelation and resolution

It is important to avoid stereotyping all evangelicals as backward, ignorant, uneducated, socially marginal, ultraconservative, fanatical, or dualistic. Some of the most theologically conservative Christian groups who embrace apocalyptic scenarios have long been involved in working for peace, social justice, and economic fairness. While many White evangelicals vote Republican, most do not vote (like most citizens), and some are independents or Democrats. More than 90 percent of Black evangelicals vote Democratic (Berlet 2003).

Glib phrases such as "religious political extremist" and "radical religious right" may make great applause lines for liberal or secular politicos; but they make it far more difficult to have a serious public conversation about the appropriate ground rules for the intersection of spiritual belief and political activism.

The problem is not religion, nor evangelicalism, nor fundamentalism, but when any belief system—spiritual or secular—employs dualism and demonization to cast their opponents as wholly evil while casting themselves as wholly good. The problem is when a bully justifies aggressive action with the cloak of the greater good, Manifest Destiny, or God's will. If we as a nation wish to steer our political leaders away from generating a global apocalypse of the violent confrontational variety, then we need to ensure that a vigorous policy debate on these matters is a priority.

INTERLUDE D

Taking Tea Partiers seriously[1]

Chip Berlet

It is 2009 and I am at a meeting at a Fuddruckers restaurant in Boise, Idaho, where the antler chandeliers and snowshoe wall decorations seem right at home. These are the patriotic men and women of the Idaho Liberty Agenda, a group that emerged from the 2008 Presidential campaign of Right-wing libertarian gadfly Ron Paul. Two Idaho state representatives are here to discuss proposed legislation.

But no one is making threats against Obama, and no one is waving bizarrely worded placards. Folks looking for the local meeting of car buffs keep opening the door to the Liberty Agenda meeting before being directed to a second meeting room. It's hard to tell the two groups apart.

Attending a Patriot meeting is like having your cable-access channel video of a PTA meeting crossed with audio from an old "Twilight Zone" television rerun. The people clearly seem quite sane and act like other folks in the restaurant. They are not clinically deranged, but their discourse is awash in paranoid-sounding conspiracy theories.

Idaho State Representative Steven Thayn is aware that many on the left think that "anyone who believes what we believe must be a Rightwing extremist kook." According to Thayn, all he is proposing is that we "need to retool the system" and "balance the budget." Of course, to Thayn, this "retooling" would include slashing

---

1   Travelling through several states in the Midwest and Rocky Mountain region, and northeast, I discovered that many who joined the Tea Party movement had legitimate complaints despite garbled language and a Right-wing political orientation.

This chapter is copyright 2010 *The Progressive* magazine, all rights reserved. https://progressive.org/magazine/taking-tea-partiers-seriously-d2/. Some revisions have been made. Special thanks to my friend and the publisher, Norman Stockwell. A scholarly treatment of the topic appears as Chip Berlet (2011), "Taking Tea Parties Seriously: Corporate Globalization, Populism, and Resentment," in *Perspectives on Global Development and Technology*, Brill Publishing.

taxes and essentially abolishing most government social services. Thayn, in his second term, is at the meeting with State Representative Phil Hart, also in his second term. Both are stalwarts of the Idaho Republican Party.

The group of Right-wing populists seems somewhat banal, but hardly directionless. The folks at the Idaho Liberty Agenda meeting are considering the group's legislative agenda and mobilizing supporters to attend local committee meetings of the state Republican Party. They are gearing up for the 2010 off-year national Congressional elections. They are angry, but neither crazy nor stupid. There are similar meetings happening across the country.

Republican election strategists are networking the "tea partiers." Reporters found that in "at least twenty-one states, local homegrown Tea Party groups are already recruiting precinct leaders" for the 2010 elections (Brant-Zawadzki and Teo).

Meanwhile, inside the beltway that encircles Washington, D.C. like a fence around a playpen, liberal pundits, Democratic Party strategists, and hired-gun fundraisers describe the growing movement of Right-wing populists as "radical right," "crackpots," or "wing-nuts." They are the "lunatic fringe" of the self-destructing Republican Party. These are just ignorant "rednecks" and "Bible-thumpers." So, just keep sending those checks to the Democratic Party and everything will be fine in the 2010 and 2012 elections.

It helps to recognize that much of what steams the Tea Party contingent is legitimate. They see their jobs vanish in front of their eyes as Wall Street gets trillions. They see their wages stagnate. They worry that their children will be even less well off than they are. They sense that Washington doesn't really care about them. On top of that, many are distraught about seeing their sons and daughters coming home in wheelchairs or body bags.

The anger is real and increasing among White working people. If we dismiss them all, we not only slight the genuine grievances they have, we also push them into the welcoming arms of actual and dangerous far-Rightists. With no one appearing to champion their cause, they line up with the anti-Obama crowd, and they stir in some of their social worries about gay marriage and abortion, dark-skinned immigrants, and a black man in the White House. A few in their midst project their frustration, anger, and rage into acts of violence.

If you drive several hundred miles northeast over the mountains from that Boise, Idaho, meeting of the Liberty Agenda you reach Helena, Montana, in about nine hours of twisting travel. The long distances between major cities and relative sparseness of population allows libertarians and other slivered political tendencies to flourish. Travis McAdam leads a tour of the Montana Human Rights Network offices in a converted downtown Helena bank building not far from the state capitol. On the guest tour, the staff likes to drag open a huge vestigial vault door to reveal a set of battered filing cabinets.

The Religious Right still has great influence in the Montana Republican Party and in the state itself, says McAdam, the executive director of the human rights group. He notes that in the past, "when the Religious Right loses a national election, they refocus on the states." McAdam thinks it is predictable that the

"Religious Right will be fighting tooth and nail to maintain the political power" they have in the Republican Party, not only in the states, but also as a way to regain national influence.

"Democrats need to start addressing the long-term effects of this rightwing populist upsurge," says McAdam. "A lot of people out here are getting their political education through the tea parties, so even when the Tea Party movement itself collapses, it will leave behind many new recruits for other rightwing groups."

McAdam and his researchers have found that the Ron Paul libertarians, the Christian Right, and well-established ultraconservative groups such as the John Birch Society are all competing to inherit the Tea Party recruits in Montana and form them into a conservative political movement. Indications are that this is happening nationwide. At the same time in Montana and some other states, it is clear that the Tea Party and town hall protesters are also being recruited by white supremacist and organized racist groups.

The activities of the Militia of Montana and the government standoff with the Montana Freemen garnered national headlines in the 1990s when armed units emerged from the broader "Patriot" movement during the early years of the Clinton Administration. Their ideas are "resurfacing at what are considered more mainstream meetings here in Montana," McAdam says. "We hear talk about the one world government and black helicopters, and now these traditional anti-government conspiracy theories are incorporating new talking points related to, among other things, the swine flu vaccination and the private prison industry."

On the ultra-Right, there is a plan among organized racists to encourage white people to move to Montana and build a segregated "separatist" homeland. "We even heard one racist leader suggest that conspiracy theories about Obama and the government are a soft way to get people interested in becoming active in building a white homeland here," says McAdam. The white racists are well aware of McAdam. On the racist Stormfront website, a post suggested that "Travis McAdam can move his sorry butt to South Africa and enjoy his negro overlords which he loves so much. Wonder if he'd cry for freedom then?"

Montana illustrates how Right-wing organizing can stretch from the Republican Party out to organized white supremacist groups. "We call that moving from the margins to the mainstream," says McAdam.

Veteran human rights organizers are pushing back against the inside-the-beltway spin that dismisses the Right-wing populists as a marginal lunatic fringe whose only danger is to the electoral fortunes of the Republican Party. The organizers out here say their communities and constituents are experiencing debilitating effects from the backwash of increasing anger and scapegoating.

Pramila Jayapal is the founder and executive director of One America, a statewide human rights group based in Seattle. "We stood up after 9/11 and did some effective organizing," she says. "We registered 24,000 new immigrant citizens. We worked with the governor and other political leaders and made some real gains."

The office of One America looks out on a multi-ethnic community that is predominantly pan-Asian, and packed with mom-and-pop restaurants and other small stores struggling to survive in hard economic times. Some storefronts are empty. Jayapal graciously shares her lunch of sushi while being interviewed. "You asked me about the condition on the ground now, out in our communities? The situation is much worse," says Jayapal. "Even if we have made small gains, it feels like there is a constant push to the political Right." She pauses. "People are so unhappy … the stories are so sad." Then she smiles. "Good organizing is about changing politics and policies, and we have the moral high ground."

Abdullahi Jama, senior community organizer with One America, echoes Jayapal's sentiments. "We have built a dialogue with conservatives in this state about immigration, but we see ultra-conservative think tanks and so-called experts constantly trying to create a clash between immigrants and law enforcement," says Jama. "The Somali community here ends up being portrayed as terrorists by people using arguments that we see as baseless conspiracy theories." Nonetheless, Jama, like Jayapal, is optimistic about their grassroots organizing efforts and their ability to reach out to white communities and reduce tensions.

Marielena Hincapié, executive director of the National Immigration Law Center based in Los Angeles says these "rightwing activists are creating a climate of fear in immigrant communities." She understands that the economic downturn has added to that climate. "Right now, there is high unemployment and a lack of an adequate social safety net for all working class people in the United States," She says, "and the fear and anxiety about our economic situation is cynically being used by anti-immigrant politicians and strategists and trumpeted by right-wing commentators." This anger among White working people is fanned by Fox News, talk radio, and other media.

The "lies and distortions about immigrants coming from these right-wing movements are based in racism and xenophobia," she warns, and "these forms of bigotry are spreading way beyond the boundaries of the conservatives themselves." Hincapié says progressives need to take the Right-wing populist anger seriously, understand the underlying economic concerns they have, and vigorously counter their organizing efforts rather than just dismiss them.

This type of savvy progressive organizing, however, is hampered by constant demonizing rhetoric coming from the Democrats and their liberal allies, rhetoric that portrays the majority of Americans who are angry at the government as crazies and fools. Outside the beltway, this type of snide nastiness increases the percentage of doors slammed in the face of progressive grassroots organizers trying to reach out to broader audiences.

We need to be wary of the way Centrists in both the Republican and Democratic Parties distort and confine the political dialogue. In their model, they are a noble and heroic Center defending society from the "extremists" of the Left and Right. By using terms like "extremism" and trivializing dissident ideas as dangerous or crackpot, Centrists are defending the status quo. They create the impression that dissident organizers are simply the advance guard for political insurgency, violence in the streets, and terrorism. The term "Radical Religious Right," for example, is designed by Democrats to get liberals to lump together the Christian Right with armed neonazi terrorists. Flip this model over, and the term "extremism" is used by Centrists to dismiss progressives as scary utopian radical troublemakers secretly building bombs in our basements. The "Centrist-extremist" model is also used by law enforcement to justify spying on dissident groups on the Left and Right.

The application of "Centrist-extremist" theory reinforces an elitist view of democracy and suggests that only certain people are capable of participation in "serious" policy debates. It also implies that policy debates confined only to ideas validated by the political "Center" should be taken seriously in civil society. Progressives, therefore, should be careful about using the term "extremism" or "extremist" as a label for political ideas or action they oppose. The model favored by Centrists marginalizes "extremists of the right and left" and thus undercuts progressive ideas for the fundamental reordering of priorities in the United States. The Centrist vs. extremist model also encourages the idea that those who oppose "extremism" are in no way complicit with maintaining systems, institutions, or structures of unfair power and privilege.

Art Heitzer, a Wisconsin attorney long active in progressive struggles, attended the National Lawyers Guild convention panel in Seattle late last year where Marielena Hincapié of NILC spoke about the plight of immigrants. Heitzer recognizes there are a lot of white working-class people being targeted for recruitment by reactionary Right-wing populist forces, but is convinced that "many of them could be our allies in holding Obama accountable to his campaign promises." Polling over the past 30 years shows that when Democrats forcefully stress issues such as relieving poverty or seeking peace, some independents and Republican voters who oppose abortion or gay rights will vote for a Democratic Presidential candidate despite their continued allegiance to gender-based hot button issues. This makes the Democratic Party rush to the political Center, continued troop deployments, and retreat from abortion and gay rights even more morally reprehensible and politically misguided.

Authors from Jean Hardisty (*Mobilizing Resentment*) to Thomas Frank (*What's the Matter with Kansas?*) have explained the ways many white working people can be persuaded to vote against their economic self-interest. The trick is to use social issues: abortion, gay marriage, socialist-fascist health care czars, grandma … unplugged. These white voters are not clueless, though, since while voting against their economic self-interest they are actually defending their advantages and privileges as white Americans. For men, it also retains a traditional social hierarchy with men on top. This model of male-led family structure is embraced by many conservative white women, especially those in fundamentalist Christian churches.

But there is no social science evidence that people who join Right wing movements are any more or less crazy or ignorant than their neighbors. While some have psychological predilections for authoritarianism and tend to see the world in overly simplified "us" vs. "them" terms, the same predilections can be found on the political left. This is also true with belief in conspiracy theories. Two serious demographic studies of the membership of the John Birch Society, demonstrate that Birchers are generally above average in income, education, and social status.

Fundraising and spin-doctoring is not organizing. Republicans have repeatedly won elections by out-organizing Democrats through face-to-face mobilizations and direct contacts with voters regarding favored issues. At the same time, Republicans over the past thirty years generally have been better at logistically supporting voter registration and Election Day turnout. Labor unions still play an important role, as do other special interest groups, including women, people of color, immigrants, and youth. It was excitement over the Obama campaign, especially among youth, that mobilized a successful grassroots registration and voter turnout effort in 2008. It is unlikely, given Obama's falling voter satisfaction ratings, that this mobilization for Democrats will be repeated in the 2010 election.

The shotgun wedding of the Palin wing of the Republican Party with Right-wing populists, the Christian Right, and economic libertarians could assist Republicans in further rolling back the social safety net and other progressive gains of the last seventy-five years. Are you ready for a Republican Presidential ticket in 2012 featuring Sarah Palin and Lou Dobbs? That certainly would be going rogue.

But no matter how the electoral political battles turn out, the trivialization of Right-wing populism must stop. It is toxic to democracy in a general sense. And it also results in an increasingly hostile environment for immigrants, people of color, Muslims, Arabs, reproductive rights activists, and lesbians, gays, bisexuals, and transgendered persons.

When Centrist liberals toss smug and dismissive names at the current Right-wing populist revolt, they make it more difficult for progressive organizers to reach out to unconvinced people who see their neighbors (and perhaps themselves) unfairly labeled as ignorant, stupid, or crazy.

The only way to counter the resurgent Right is to rebuild militant progressive movements and raise a ruckus. Then, even as we rally our base, we have a chance of convincing some on the Right that what we stand for will actually help them. But we can't get there by name-calling.

9

RUNNING AGAINST SODOM AND OSAMA[1]

The Christian Right, values voters, and the Culture Wars in 2006

Chip Berlet and Pam Chamberlain

With its eye on the 2006 mid-term elections, a coalition of Christian Right groups has launched a national campaign against same sex marriage featuring nasty, alarmist, and often bigoted rhetoric that demonizes gay men and lesbians. Speakers at various recent electoral mobilization events have warned of sinister forces threatening America from without and within. The external threat is said to be from Islamic terrorists and "Islamofascists," who embrace a culture of death as symbolized by the attacks on 9/11. The same culture of death poses an internal threat through gay rights, abortion, and pornography. Godly Christians must confront these threats in order to protect families, and especially children.

These sets of beliefs are not new, but there are times when they are submerged into the Christian Right subculture, and there are times when they surface as part of a public campaign. Although leaders of the Christian Right almost universally deny it, the goal of this revived public campaign is to elect Republicans to office in 2006, 2008, and beyond. The enemy being denounced is sometimes generic: gays, liberals, secularists, the Left-leaning media, Hollywood; and sometimes specific: Ted Kennedy, Nancy Pelosi, Rosie O'Donnell, the ACLU; but the actual target is the Democratic Party and its candidates. (This list was compiled by the authors from statements made at the Values Voters Summit in Washington, DC, September 21–24, 2006, which they attended.)

If they could help achieve firm Republican control of both houses of Congress and the White House, Christian Right strategists envision the appointment of proper conservative federal judges to replace aging liberal "activist" ones. They

1   This chapter benefited from the suggestions and advice given by a number of colleagues, including S. Wojciech Sokolowski, Cynthia Burack and Max Blumenthal, as well as Rob Boston of American United for Separation of Church and State, Sean Cahill of the National Gay and Lesbian Task Force Policy Institute, Peter Montgomery of People for the American Way, and Adele Stan of the *American Prospect*.

foresee this victory resulting in the eventual banning of same sex marriage, the rollback of gay rights, and the outlawing of abortion. The ultimate goal for many in this aggressive *dominionist* effort is to "restore" America as a Christian nation (Clarkson 1995, 2001, 2005; Berlet 2006, 2008).

Polls show that most Americans—indeed most Christians—seldom rank abortion, gay rights, and other social issues high on their list of priorities (Jones and Cox 2006).

When Christian evangelical "values voters" think about values, they don't limit themselves to gay rights and abortion; they also think about such issues as the economy, education, health care, poverty, and the environment. In terms of foreign policy, all Christians are pulled in two directions by different theological emphases on military strength and the pursuit of peace. So too, theological considerations apply when Christian evangelical voters evaluate particular candidates on a range of issues. Not all evangelicals are conservative politically or theologically; and some evangelicals who are theologically conservative (or even fundamentalist) are politically liberal or progressive.

This is easier to understand when looking at the difference in voting patterns between White Christian evangelical voters and Black Christian evangelical voters. More than 90 percent of Black evangelical voters have picked Democrats in recent Presidential elections. Many are opposed to same sex marriage and abortion, but their other values—the economy, social justice, health care—outweigh the gender-related social issues.

Be this as it may, highly-motivated core groups of predominantly White evangelical voters mobilized around social issues by a coalition of the Christian Right and the Republican Party can tip the vote tally in a handful of key states. There is a Culture War in America, but most voters are non-combatants. It is a guerilla war in which Christian Right institutions help win national elections for Republican candidates through micro-targeted grassroots mobilizations of voters. To be precise, there is compelling statistical evidence that the Christian Right is able, in *some elections*, to shift a *small but decisive number* of White Christian evangelical voters *in specific states* towards the Republican Party (Green and Silk 2005; Layman and Green 2006).

We suggest that in this election cycle, Christian Right strategists have selected certain social issues with care, foregrounding those that resonate with conservative evangelical "values voters;" and are micro-targeting those voters in key states. Highly respected demographer John C. Green explains, "White evangelicals are the most likely to have social issue priorities." The way voters concerned about values lean in any specific election after weighing social and economic issues "may simply be differences in values prompted in large measure by campaigns where the GOP stresses morality with success and the Democrats fail to stress the economy effectively" (authors' interview with Green October 10, 2006).

In 2004, there was even evidence that in some states, Black evangelical "values voters" were pulled into the voting booth for Republicans through this strategy. The same small trend may be occurring with Hispanic voters (Teixeira 2005; Abrajano, Alvarez, and Nagler, 2005; Cusack 2005).

This report takes you inside recent Christian Right electoral mobilization events to explore the messages and strategies of a new coalition that is claiming leadership of the Christian Right; explains how their micro-targeted election mobilizations work; and explains why the Christian Right will continue to play a major role in US political and cultural life for decades to come.

What Culture War?

Some scholars and journalists dismiss the idea of a Culture War that pits Christian dominionists against secularists, while others consider it a legitimate area of study (Denton 2005a, 2005b; Pew Forum on Religion & Public Life 2004; Campbell and Monson 2005; Green, Rozell and Wilcox 2006).

Others suggest that "values voters" span the political spectrum, and thus may not be a critical factor in future elections (Banks 2006).

One extensive recent poll found that "Social issues such as abortion and same sex marriage rank last in importance to the vast majority of Americans when deciding how to vote" (Jones and Cox 2006).

The poll also established that:

> An overwhelming majority of Americans, including at least three-quarters of every major religious tradition, say issues like poverty and health care are more important than hot-button social issues.
>
> When people think about "voting their values," more people think of the honesty, integrity, and responsibility of the candidate than any other values.
>
> Americans overwhelmingly agree that too many religious leaders focus on abortion and gay rights without addressing more important issues such as loving our neighbors and caring for the poor.

In the lead up to the 2006 election, the White House has been said to be worried that Republican voters might not be motivated enough to go to the polls (Allen and Carney 2006). There have been reports of declining support for the Republicans within evangelical ranks. Some Christian Right leaders have grumbled that the Republicans have not delivered on enough of the promises made after the 2000 and 2004 elections when they helped elect George W. Bush (French 2006; Kromm 2006; Krugman 2006).

Can the Christian Right legitimately take credit for Bush's 2004 victory? Didn't the pundits declare false the initial reports that "Moral Values" voters were Christian Right activists who had swarmed to the polls for the Republicans? They did, and it is true that the initial reports of a broad national trend were wrong in making certain sweeping assumptions. Since 2004, however, sophisticated studies of the exit polls in past elections have revealed that in some states, the voters who said they were concerned about "moral values," and who were also conservative Christian evangelicals, did indeed vote in significantly higher numbers for Bush, and almost certainly helped provide a margin of victory in key states such as Ohio.

According to John C. Green and religion professor Mark Silk (2005) regional variations in how voters ranked their concerns over social issues demonstrate that "moral-values voters were more important to the president's victory than the national totals imply." And in Ohio especially, Christian evangelicals and "regular worship attenders and less regular attenders were both more likely to be Bush moral values voters." Green and Silk conclude that as "Moral Majority founder Jerry Falwell hoped, the coalition of the moral has expanded beyond evangelicals, but for the most part more in the evangelical heartland than elsewhere." This group of "religious folks were more likely to choose moral values in the Bush regions than in the Kerry regions."

In a more extensive study in the *British Journal of Political Science*, political scientist Geoffrey C. Layman and John C. Green (2006) found the following:

> [T]he usefulness of the culture wars thesis varies by policy, religious and political context. The culture wars strongly influence mass political behaviour when religious perspectives are logically related to policy issues, communal experiences encourage these connections and electoral actors emphasize and differentiate themselves on such matters. Outside of these contexts, the culture wars have little political impact … The culture wars are waged by limited religious troops on narrow policy fronts under special political leadership, and a broader cultural conflagration is just a rumour.

There may be no broad Culture War sweeping the country, but there is a very real guerilla Culture War in which Christian Right institutions help win elections for Republicans by targeting key states with grassroots mobilizations of voters. In 1991 the Christian Coalition described the strategy of mobilizing small but decisive numbers of voters as the "15 percent solution," referring to the share of voters generally needed to tip an election. Realizing that they do not have to convince a majority to agree to them, they focused on mobilizing enough Christian voters to make a difference (Goldin 1993).

Running against Sodom

Same sex marriage is the current hot button topic in which, through the Christian Right, "religious perspectives are logically related to policy issues" as Layman and Green put it. These topics vary over time across a range of conservative social issues, although the two main themes since the late 1970s have been anti-abortion and antigay. Since the early 1980s, after helping elect Ronald Reagan by using abortion as a wedge issue, Christian Right strategists have grazed across conservative social issues linked to "moral values." They carefully track what topic and what type of rhetoric raises more money in targeted direct mail campaigns, and what turns out voters to the polls. For example, Republican strategists will take a close look at the voting patterns in the eight states that will vote on marriage restrictions this November. In 2003 there was a similar antigay campaign launched, aimed at influencing the 2004 Presidential election (Kaplan 2004, 2005).

Antigay campaigns are a recurrent theme in the Christian Right, and have been used for electoral voter mobilizations before (Herman 1997) Christian Right leader James Dobson, founder and current chairman of the board of Focus on the Family, campaigned actively in 2004, citing the "assault on marriage" that he saw as being waged by those who supported same sex marriage. Republican strategist and Bush advisor Karl Rove was reported as making the mobilization of conservative Christian evangelicals a key priority for the campaign (Kirkpatrick 2004).

Given the initial uncertainty over the influence of the Christian Right in the 2004 elections, it was not clear if Rove would once again encourage a high visibility Christian Right pre-election campaign using social issues. We now know the Christian Right efforts in 2004 had an effect, and we know this tactic of demonizing same sex marriage is being employed once again.

The Christian Right's anti-gay strategy, framed as "an assault on the family," is directly aimed at electing Republican candidates in the 2006 mid-term elections. This same strategy could be used for the 2008 Presidential race, because it has worked before in concert with statewide ballot initiatives and candidate framing issues.

The decision about this will not be based on the overall outcome of the 2006 mid-term elections, but on sophisticated analyses by Republican strategists of exit polls and other data that will reveal whether or not the grassroots micro-target techniques were effective in specific states. If it turns out that antigay rhetoric pulled some conservative evangelicals into voting booths in targeted races, then the reliance on antigay rhetoric will be continued through 2008. If not, then other issues will be field tested to identify the most effective hot-button social issue.

Micro-targeting is the technique used by Republicans to mobilize grassroots voter participation on Election Day (Helman 2006).

As journalists Mike Allen and James Carney explained in 2006:

> Republicans hope to close the deal in tight races with a get-out-the-vote strategy that was developed in the wreckage of the 2000 presidential campaign. Bush's team was led then, as it is now, by Rove, Bush's political architect and now White House deputy chief of staff, and [Ken] Mehlman, then White House political-affairs director.
>
> The G.O.P. says their volunteer forces in '04 proved to be more effective than the paid workers contracted by Democrats, unions and Democrat-oriented fund-raising groups.

At the Christian Right's "Values Voter Summit" Washington Briefing held in Washington, DC, in late September 2006, several speakers openly touted the fact that the Christian Right had played a major role in electing Bush in 2004. It was clear from conversations with attendees that many felt the statewide initiatives to block same sex marriage had drawn many evangelical voters to the polls, and that the vote for Bush in some cases came along for the ride. Judge Charles W. Pickering, Sr, made this same point when he said that Bush might not have won Ohio if the Marriage Amendment had not been on the ballot. Pickering, who Bush unsuccessfully tried to appoint to the federal appeals bench in 2004, said there was a culture war in America, with the battle over the confirmation of federal judges a central front. One conference workshop (discussed in detail later in this chapter) was based on applying micro-targeting techniques to local churches.

State ballot initiatives are one way to generate grassroots interest in a national election. In the 2006 elections, according to the Associated Press:

> The fate of hundreds of ballot initiatives will be decided. Several states will vote on proposals to ban same-sex marriages and raise the minimum wage. Republicans hope the former will boost turnout in crucial congressional races, and Democrats have similar plans for the latter.
>
> *(Espo 2006)*

In the 2006 elections, eight states voted on marriage restrictions banning same sex marriage, and Republican strategists hope this will pull conservative voters to the polls. The states are Arizona, Colorado, Idaho, South Carolina, South Dakota, Tennessee, Virginia and Wisconsin.

Professor Mark Rozell, quoted in Religion News Service, said both the Republicans and the Democrats realize that moral values and religion help shape how elections turn out:

> "We have motivated groups, both on the right and the left, trying to mobilize their constituencies, in large part because they believe values matter but they also understand that the two political parties are very closely competitive in Congress right now," said Rozell, a professor of public policy at George Mason University in Fairfax, Va.
>
> "Affecting a few electoral outcomes could be the difference between Democratic and Republican party control."
>
> *(Rozell quoted in Banks 2006)*

In 2004, *The Nation* columnist Katha Pollitt (2004) warned progressives that they should not be complacent about values voters because the Christian Right has so far been unable to push its full agenda through a Republican-controlled Congress. That is "like saying the left got nothing from FDR because it didn't get socialism," Pollitt quipped. The Bush administration has placed representatives of the Christian Right throughout the Executive Branch, affecting social, economic, scientific, and foreign policy.

That the current Christian Right set of issues and frames might well have been crafted by Republican strategist Karl Rove is a reasonable suspicion, and whether or not Rove actually helped devise the strategy, it is congruent with what the White House sees as advantageous. Leaders of the Christian Right certainly have access to key Republican politicians in Washington, DC. Just prior to the 2006 midterm elections, James Dobson of Focus on the Family told the Values Voter Summit audience that he had just spent two weeks in the nation's capital meeting with Congressional leaders (authors' notes).

It is unlikely that many Democrats were on his dance card. MSNBC reported that Ralph Reed, "former executive director of the Christian Coalition and an unsuccessful candidate for lieutenant governor in Georgia … got 18 [White House] meetings, including two events with Bush, between 2001 and 2006" (MSNBC 2006

It would be easy to picture Rove as the mastermind of all of this, but although he is skillful, the strategy was formulated by key Right-wing strategists in the late 1970s in a multi-faceted plan that brought Ronald Reagan to office (Martin1996; Diamond 1998, Hardisty 1999).

Rove came up through the political institutions created in part by this network that built the New Right as a coalition that included the growing Christian Right. Sara Diamond points out that this overall strategy relies on loosely-structured projects, in which a specific set of institutions and leaders on the political Right agree to a handful of hot button issues on which to focus, and a few key frames through which issues are presented (Diamond 1998).

With this type of symbiotic project—linking a Christian Right social movement to a Republican political movement—the actual implementation requires no central coordination. Participating groups agree to be on the same page, but they get to write their own text, often using the rhetorical style of Right-wing populism (Berlet and Lyons 2000). Jean Hardisty refers to this process as "mobilizing resentment" (Hardisty 1999).

While the Christian Right likes to pretend this is not about partisan politics, the reality is quite different. Even the ultraconservative *Washington Times* reports the obvious as their reporter Amy Fagan (2006) explained:

> Mr. Dobson and Family Research Council President Tony Perkins sought to rally the troops for the midterm elections by reminding them that Republicans helped get two new conservative justices on the Supreme Court and that Democrats are still blocking legislation and President Bush's judicial nominations.
>
> Mr. Dobson evoked applause and cheers when he reminded the crowd that "we do have two new very, very exciting Supreme Court justices," referring to Chief Justice John G. Roberts Jr. and Justice Samuel A. Alito Jr.
>
> The crowd was urged not to be convinced of reports that Republicans will lose control of Congress.
>
> "Don't believe everything you're hearing out there," Mr Dobson said.

Rather, Dobson, Perkins and other Christian Right leaders reserved to themselves the Right to tell the attendees at the Values Voter Summit exactly what to believe.

The FRC action Values Voter Summit and Washington briefing

Built around the slogan "Family, Faith, and Freedom," the Washington Briefing: 2006 Values Voter Summit used the Culture War as a central theme. These sorts of Christian Right pre-election voter mobilization conferences used to be hosted by the Christian Coalition, with the title "Road to Victory." Now that the Christian Coalition has unraveled as a national group, a new coalition has stepped in to fill the void. The conference was coordinated by FRC Action, the political action arm of the Family Research Council, with Tony Perkins at the helm. Co-sponsors included the political action arms of three other Christian Right groups: Focus on the Family Action (Dr James Dobson), Americans United to Preserve Marriage (Gary Bauer), and American Family Association Action (Donald Wildmon). Most of these groups have close historical ties. Dobson's Focus on the Family created the FRC to lobby Congress. Gary Bauer ran the FRC from 1988–1999. The wild card in this coalition is Wildmon, whose American Family Association is located in Mississippi. Wildmon is known for his inflammatory anti-gay rhetoric and occasional detours into veiled antisemitism (Institute for First Amendment Studies 1989). Wildmon's participation pulls this coalition further to the right.

Part football pep rally, part church service, and part TV game show, the September 2006 event held in Washington, DC attracted over 1,700 Christian Right grass roots activists from 48 states. The audience, primarily conservative Protestant evangelicals, was a mix of heartland cultural warriors, grassroots Republican political activists, and local church staff, including ministers and lay ministry workers. They were rewarded for their attendance with a series of speeches from their leaders. In fact, one of the purposes of the event was to signal a passing of the torch, from older figures like James Dobson and New Right strategist Paul Weyrich to their successors, men like Tony Perkins and Alan Sears of the Alliance Defense Fund. The event also showcased 2008 Presidential hopefuls like governors Mitt Romney of Massachusetts and Mike Huckabee of Arkansas, and Virginia Senator George Allen, who had the chance to float some political trial balloons over the crowd.

A majority of attendees were White, with a sprinkling of African-Americans, many of them pastors. Only a tiny handful of Latinos or Latinas were present. There were roughly equal numbers of men and women in the audience, with somewhat fewer women onstage; yet the fact that there were women, and even a women's panel, is an ironic testament to the cultural shift leveraged by the feminist movement.

There were a few Catholics and Jews. If there were Muslims, secularists, or mainstream Christians present, they kept a low profile, with the exception of the tall, lanky Rev. Barry W. Lynn, executive director of Americans United for Separation of Church and State. A well-known critic of the Christian Right, Lynn walked through the crowd trailing event staff like a file of ducklings. And it was a crowd that hissed every time Lynn's name was mentioned; booed when the American Civil Liberties Union was trashed; and groaned at the mere mention of the city of San Francisco. The otherwise polite and attentive crowd was treated to one speech after another in the hotel ballroom, in a didactic style and hierarchical format typical of Religious Right rallies—tightly orchestrated logistically, skillfully crafted in framing and messaging. Top down/bottom sore ... even in upscale convention seats.

The visual aesthetic was slick, modern, and high tech, including two huge projection screens and a booming sound system. Two side stage areas were designed to mimic television news stage sets, one with stools for interviews, another with a table for panel discussions. The proceedings comfortably accommodated the over 100 members of the media with plenty of riser space at the back of the room for network and cable cameras, and even a bloggers table with high speed Internet connections. A "Radio Row" of live broadcasting of reports and interviews sent to Christian stations was set up on a dais in the exhibit space. Tables in the exhibit area sprouted audio CDs and DVD videos.

There were special pay-per-meal breakfasts and luncheons where focused pitches were made. There was a breakfast for pastors hosted by FRC Action, and a breakfast hosted by American United to Preserve Marriage. Day two of the meeting dawned with the Alliance Defense Fund (ADF) breakfast, where there was much food, little tolerance for same sex marriage, and no room to get in. An overflow crowd of 250 sat through what was essentially an extended advertisement for the Alliance Defense Fund, which seeks to position itself as the major adversary to the American Civil Liberties Union (ACLU). Another luncheon was designed to introduce Donald Wildmon and his Tupelo, MS-based American Family Association, but by a show of hands, the majority of diners were already on his mailing list. The four cosponsors positioned themselves as the unified national voice of the Christian Right.

"Family, Faith, & Freedom": To protect the children

Tony Perkins established the main frame of the event, using scare tactics when he said, "we are facing threats from within and from without" (Blumenthal 2006). Against these threats conference organizers promoted a variety of ideas under the event slogan: "Family, Faith, & Freedom." Although these three values seem benign, the framing strategy constructed by the FRC painted a dire picture in which same sex marriage and abortion are threatening America from within, while terrorism is threatening the family from without—a frame that points to the terrorist attacks on 9/11, while leaping over criticism over the war in Iraq, other specific military interventions and the economy.

Here is how it works:

- **Family** is most important societal unit, sanctioned by God, limited to "traditional" heterosexual forms and designed for the procreation and protection of children.
- **Faith** guides our lives, and defines our politics.
- **Freedom** requires eternal vigilance and support for the war on terror.

Let's review what specific speakers actually said, and what they *implied*. The two main thematic areas we will dissect are domestic, primarily gay rights but also abortion; and foreign policy, centered on the 9/11 terrorist attacks and "Islamic fascism." While a few scholars have studied the relationship between militant Islamic movements and neo-Fascism, the authors feel the use of the term "Islamo-Fascism" or Islamic Fascism in the context of the US Christian Right represents a form of bigoted political propaganda (Berlet 2003).

We'll examine in more detail the messages, frames, and their subtexts, to understand what resonates for supporters of these groups and, potentially, other "values voters."

Families at risk

Echoing many at the Summit, George Allen (R-VA), running in a close race to maintain his Senate seat, said, "The most important institution in our society is the family." Massachusetts Governor Mitt Romney announced that the "culture of America is under attack" by same sex marriage.

According to Romney:

> Now my state's Supreme Judicial Court, about a year ago, struck a blow against that family unit, in my view. It said that our Constitution, written long ago by John Adams, requires people of the same gender to marry.
>
> Every child has a right to have a mother and a father ... the impact on children will be felt not just in a day or two or a year or two but over generations as we think about the development and nurturing of children.
>
> *(Appleman quoting Romney 2006)*

And as a way to explain his exclusive support of heterosexual marriage Tony Perkins said, "Marriage gets benefits because it benefits society" (Appleman quoting Romney 2006)

According to these speakers, same sex marriage is the major threat to the institution of the family. Gay men and lesbians threaten the family by raising children in homes without both a mother and a father. Gay adoptions and foster care are also unacceptable. "The ultimate child abuse is placing a child in a gay home," said Jennifer Giroux of Citizens for Community Values. Tony Perkins observed, "There's nothing in American politics today that brings people together than ... the defense of marriage."

Some speakers implied that just being gay is an insult to people with values and is the embodiment of evil. Two African-American pastors spoke about their views on homosexuality. Startling statements came from the Rev. Dwight McKissic of Cornerstone Baptist Church in Arlington, Texas. "I believe it's from the pit of hell itself that this movement is inspired, that it has a satanic anointment" (McKissic quoted in Boston 2006).

Citing a passage from the Book of Daniel, which states that the anti-Christ will have no desire for a woman, he asked rhetorically, "Could it be that the antichrist himself may be homosexual?" Linking his tirade to defense of the Christian family, McKissic told the crowd, "I don't think there is any issue more important than how we are going to define the family." He said that television shows portraying homosexuality in a positive light have put us "on the road to Sodom and Gomorrah," and "God's got another match … He didn't run out of matches" (McKissic quoted in Boston 2006).

Bishop Wellington Boone, from Norcross, GA, equated being gay with being weak on values: "Back in the days when I was a kid, and we see guys that don't stand strong on principle, we call them 'faggots.' We say you sissified out. You a sissy. That means you don't stand up for principles. God hadn't called us to be sissies, we're called upon to stand up, called up on a principled level" (authors' notes). Standing for the traditional family is therefore supporting Christian values.

The Summit maintained a much stronger focus on same sex marriage than it did on another topic that conservatives often cite as a threat to the family: abortion. Surprisingly, speakers did not often refer to abortion as a direct reason for voting. Instead they used it as way to talk about other issues, such as the opportunity for evangelism or their dissatisfaction with activist judges.

Georgette Forney, "abortion recovery" advocate, spoke about the Silent No More awareness campaign, which encourages women who regret having had abortions to speak out. She praised the many types of recovery programs as chance to practice evangelism, noting that they are all Christian based. "It is the opportunity to reach out and find people who are out there and don't know of God's love and meet them where they are in their pain," she said (authors' notes).

When Right-wing pundit Ann Coulter referenced abortion, she implied that the killing of seven reproductive health providers was a restrained response to court rulings unfavorable to anti-abortion activists:

> For two decades after Roe, no abortion clinic doctors were killed. But immediately after Planned Parenthood v. Casey, after working within the system did not work, produced no results … for the first time an abortion doctor was killed. A few more abortion clinic workers were killed in the next few years. I'm not justifying it, but I understand when you take democracy away from people, some of them will react violently. The total number of deaths attributable to Roe were seven abortion clinic workers and 40 million unborn babies.
>
> *(authors' notes)*

These critiques of abortion were met politely but without the enthusiasm and energy the anti-gay comments were able to generate.

Faith under fire

A common theme of the conference was the centrality of Christian values in American culture. "Christians create a core of conviction in this society," said Tony Snow, White House press secretary (authors' notes).

According to many speakers the ability to practice one's religion in the United States is being threatened by secularist movements. Panelists and a special exhibit booth addressed the alleged "War on Christmas," which refers to disputes over the boundaries of bringing the religious aspects of the holiday into the classroom and shopping mall. References to IRS examinations of church political practices and other enforcements of the separation of church and state were seen as attempts to limit religious expression.

Judging from the strength of the attendees' applause, many felt their ability to express their faith in everyday life was being threatened by secular forces. They were, therefore, appreciative of speakers who acknowledged their faith and its link to political power.

Bishop Wellington Boone asked, "How can someone who doesn't feel a need for God lead me?" It is the Christian's duty to participate in the democratic process. When Mike Pence (R-IN) reminded the audience that "God placed the miracle of democracy on these shores," he asked the audience to translate "timeless principles into timely action" by voting (authors' notes).

Freedom at risk

At the Values Voters Summit, defending freedom meant supporting the war on terror. Overlooking the enormous problems in Iraq and Afghanistan, speakers encouraged the crowd to rally against a common enemy, terrorists, wherever they are found. In an astonishing declaration that provoked loud applause, author and radio host William Bennett said, "When four Americans are burned, torched, stomped on, and hung and the city cheers, you take out the city. You level Fallujah." He suggested the country's leadership has sometimes been too tentative. "The discussion that is taking place, it is culturally weak ... We are probably going to have to talk more about the more we have to do to win this third world war. These should be the terms of discussion ... You're either on offense or you're on defense. And right now, the good guys are too much on defense." Quoting Alexander Hamilton, Bennett said, "When the government and the military appear anywhere in the world, they should appear like Hercules ... America, along with the rest of civilization, in this war, is our mission" (Wilson 2006).

James Dobson, of Focus on the Family, said of George W. Bush "When it comes to the war on terror, he gets it" (Brown 2006). Dobson told the crowd that they should face the fact that millions of Muslims want to kill Americans (James 2006; Fagan 2006). "When the point of negotiation is that the other person wants to kill you, there's not a whole lot to talk about. We're in a war, and it's time that we recognized it" (Brown 2006). According to a report in Agape Press, Wildmon's news outlet, in a neat linkage of freedom to family, "Dobson said he views the war on terror as a family issue because without security for today's children and those in future generations, there is no future for the family" (Brown 2006)

Gary Bauer, president of American Values and leader of Americans United to Preserve Marriage, described how passengers of United Flight 93 heroically ran toward the cockpit on 9/11. As a way to protect our freedoms he reminded the audience, "All you have to do is run to the voting booth" (Blumenthal 2006). Agape Press reports that Bauer suggested that "the left-wing appears to hate conservatives and George W. Bush more than they hate [al Qaeda], the Taliban, and Osama bin Laden" (Brown 2006). Ann Coulter picked up on this theme, suggesting that "the Democrats hate George Bush because he is fighting the war on terrorism." Tony Perkins linked liberal evildoers with Islamic militants (Blumenthal 2006).

Swimming in subtext

The event was overripe with subtle undertones of meaning. These subtext messages to the audience appeared designed to direct, motivate, and reassure the audience. Here is a sample:

Godly Christians must be involved in politics to take back America from the Godless secularists and liberals. Godly Christians must vote, and vote for candidates who win our approval and these candidates must come to us; we do not go to them begging. We may not always agree with the Republican leadership, but we need them on our side to win our cause. Aware of being criticized for being too partisan toward Republicans, Tony Perkins issued a statement regarding the conference claiming that, "The Washington Briefing … was not an opportunity for us to endorse candidates but rather an opportunity for candidates to endorse us and our values."

Our version of Christianity is correct, dominant, triumphant, defines the political center, and is politically powerful. Every other worldview is wrong, and unconnected to the real God. This is a struggle between good and evil. Our opponents are witting or unwitting agents of Satan. Former Florida Secretary of State Katherine Harris—famous for her role in the 2000 Florida Presidential election fiasco and now an elected U.S. Representative running for the Senate (Gumbel 2004)—planted herself firmly in the dominionist wing of the Christian Right (Harris 2006). At the final banquet of the conference, Harris emphasized the importance of the proper candidates winning in November, and suggested it was a battle against "principalities and powers." Many in the audience surely recognized this as a Biblical reference to "spiritual warfare"—in their view a struggle with the demonic agents of Satan (Arnold 1992; Diamond 1989). Just in case they missed the point, the emcee closed the banquet by reminding the audience that they were engaged in "spiritual warfare."

> Our faith, our moral superiority, and the fact we are persecuted by our opponents justify hatred of the enemy, and even violent resistance. Our God may be merciful, compassionate, and the God of justice; but our God is a zealous and vengeful God, and we are his agents on earth. Sin invokes punishment. This worldview emerged from several speakers. Colin Hanna, President of Let Freedom Ring, a 501 (c) (4) anti-immigration group, reinforced

his interpretation of this dual nature of a Christian God when he said that mercy and justice must be blended in public policy. He described amnesty for undocumented immigrants as "sin without consequences" and that "Amnesty is therefore not Christian."

We need a Christian counter-culture to overcome the depravity of secularized modern life. One of the most secularized arenas for evangelicals has been Hollywood. For instance, Donald Wildmon's AFA was founded to address immorality in the entertainment industry. At the Summit, an especially high energy panel, "Hollywood in the Heartland," introduced the audience to the work being done by Christian film producers and the alternate infrastructure that will support this counter-culture. Ted Baehr, who runs the Biblically based film review service, MovieGuide, highlighted the work he and others have undertaken to steer Christians towards more acceptable, family friendly popular culture. Rev, Tommy Tenney previewed his new film, a reworking of the story of Esther, "One Night with the King," and the audience learned that Hollywood has specific Christian movie studios, like FoxFaith.

We will win, because God is on our side.

Mid-term election partisanship

The Values Voter Summit was clearly part of a larger plan by the Christian Right to help elect Republican candidates to office in the midterm election. The highly visible event was staged to position the Christian Right as a viable electoral player with a powerful self-image. The Christian Right sees itself as still on ascendancy in US, but it feels the need to work hard to hold onto the power it has and to make future gains. Part of this involves staging local events around the country

Just prior to the midterm elections, Focus on the Family Action also ran three "Stand for the Family" political action "rallies designed to educate and motivate pro-family conservative Christians in three states where there are important races on November's ballot": Pennsylvania, Minnesota, and Tennessee (Winn 2006; Staff Reports CitizenLink 2006; Stollings 2006). On September 20, 2006, Max Blumenthal, reported:

> A day before appearing at the summit in Washington, Dobson held a stadium-sized get-out-the-vote jamboree in Pittsburgh, disguised as a supposedly non-partisan "Stand for the Family" rally, on behalf of one of his staunchest backers, Senator Rick Santorum, who trails his Democratic opponent, State Treasurer Bob Casey Jr. There, Dobson took to the podium to warn wavering "value voters": "Whether or not the Republicans deserve the power they were given, the alternatives are downright frightening."

Tony Perkins, Family Research Council President, was emcee for the evening, held because "the values vote is crucial this November because of the internal and external threats facing our nation." According to Perkins, "It's important for Christians to vote because that's how we register our opinions by who we vote into office. People who either reflect our values, or people who abhor our values" (Stollings 2006).

Dobson invited Christians to the event stating that the main issues for 2006 are preserving the family, protecting children and pursuing peace through strength. "We're here to do something about the dangers and threats that are out there" (Stollings 2006). The other two rallies were held in St. Paul, Minnesota October 3rd and Nashville, Tennessee October 16th (Stollings 2006). Although smaller than originally hoped by organizers, they still drew thousands of committed activists in each state.

Conclusions

The durability of the Christian Right

The strategy laid out at the Values Voter Summit and Liberty Sunday is for Christian Right activists to fly under the media radar and contact potential voters in the evangelical community who are already inclined to vote Republican, and motivate them to actually go to the polls on Election Day 2006 in order to preserve Republican control of Congress. The Christian Right—and Rove—hope that by micro-targeting constituencies in specific key states, they can make the difference. The bait they are using in this election is the issue of same sex marriage, both through a rhetorical framing approach and the use of statewide ballot initiatives. As of a few weeks before the election, public opinion seems to favor Democratic gains, however the Republican voter mobilization techniques could be effective in the typically lower-turnout midterm elections. There is no way to know at this point if that strategy will be successful.

Every few years—following an electoral defeat of Republicans, the collapse of a Christian Right organization, or the expose of a leader's shady past, the death of the Christian Right is announced in the media. Reports of its death have been, as they say, greatly exaggerated. The Christian Right will survive and remain a powerful factor in US social, cultural, and political life. That is because the Christian Right is a large and durable social movement, with a complex and diverse set of autonomous institutions that are linked to political campaigns through the Republican Party. The rising or falling fortunes of the Republican Party in any election cycle do not control participation in the Christian Right as a social movement. If one set of tactics fails, others will be field tested by skilled Christian Right leaders. Many of today's tactics have been in use for decades. Win or lose, skilled Christian Right activists will emerge from the 2006 midterm elections with stronger grassroots organizations and longer lists of names of potential recruits.

Fissures and wedges

Progressive social change activists can't win the Culture War, because it is a guerilla action, with the central frames established by the Christian Right. George Lakoff correctly points out that if you stay within the frame established by your opponent, you are more likely to lose the debate (Lakoff 2002, 2004).

New frames can be developed by progressives that stress wedges in the current configuration of the coalition that emerged with the New Right. Possible fissures, or cracks in the cement that binds sectors of the political Right together, do exist: The Christian Right, as one sector of the US Right, shares some positions with other conservative political interests.

- **Neoconservatives**: The Christian Right has been building a coalition with the Neocons around the anti-terrorist (and anti-Islamic) aspects of the "clash of civilizations" thesis, but some neoconservatives are nervous about the anti-modernist theocratic aspirations of some Christian Right leaders. In addition, some in the Christian Right are growing tired of war in the Middle East, their Holy Land.
- **Conservative business interests:** Calvinism and capitalism have long been partners, but the way some in the Christian Right chastise unrestrained materialism makes some business entrepreneurs nervous.
- **Libertarians:** the Christian Right can agree with economic libertarians on lowering taxes and government regulations and raising individual initiative and responsibility; but most libertarians want the Christian Right out of their bedrooms.

By reframing the debates and shifting the political terrain on which these debates occur, progressives can engage the multitude of Christian evangelical voters who are not consolidated around the issues outlined by the Christian Right. This recognizes that the Christian Right is a powerful force on the political and social scene, but that it is not nearly as powerful as it would have us believe.

An effective progressive response

The Christian Right, although significant, is not a monolithic force and has its own internal issues. The leaders of the Christian Right sometimes argue for policy positions that make their own followers uncomfortable. This is especially true in terms of the quest for dominionism. While some Christian Right leaders envision a theocratic Christian nation, few rank and pew evangelicals allied with the Christian Right want a theocracy, much less a fascistic one.

Although they would love us to believe they represent all Christians, in reality the Christian Right does not speak for all Christians or even all evangelicals. The idea of God is too big to shackle to narrow minds.

The Christian Right is a primarily a White subset of evangelicals who embrace fundamentalist or dominionist beliefs and are currently being mobilized around certain issues framed as "values." Many evangelicals, however, do not hold identical values to the ones touted at the Values Voters Summit or at Liberty Sunday. They may see God on their side, but sometimes they can be persuaded to vote in favor of issues important to progressives.

Certain groups of White evangelicals can be seen as potential swing voters, depending on the issues and how they are framed. For instance, the Summit called for support for Bush's War on Terror based on patriotism and Christian principles; but the growing dissatisfaction with the war in Iraq across all segments of the population can become a wedge, which could be framed in effective ways to counter the arguments of the Christian Right.

The Christian Right has already attempted to lure Black and Latino evangelical Protestants with their campaign against same sex marriage and abortion. But these groups also share similar concerns as progressives on a variety of issues. Progressives of all races, and holding various beliefs, can and must reach out to all these groups.

Using phrases such as "religious political extremist," "radical religious right," "Christofascism," or "The American Taliban" therefore, is counterproductive, because many evangelicals, not to mention Christians or religious people in general, find these terms offensive.

A shared respect for the Constitution could be one unifying principle. If progressives want to defend the Constitution, we must learn the religious beliefs of those evangelicals who dominate the Christian Right, treat these folks respectfully, and yet engage them in a critical public conversation over the appropriate boundaries for civic political debate set by the founders and framers of our nation.

Demonizing rhetoric from the Left not only pushes evangelicals away from the Democratic Party, but also pushes them out of potential partnerships around progressive issues. And from a progressive standpoint, the issue is not electing Democrats, but holding all politicians accountable for advancing social and economic justice.

10

THE RISE OF DOMINIONISM

Remaking America as a Christian nation

Frederick Clarkson[1]

In June of 2001, Roy Moore, the Chief Justice of the Alabama Supreme Court, installed a two-and-one-half-ton granite monument to the Ten Commandments in the state courthouse in Montgomery. Moore knew it was a deeply symbolic act. He was saying that God's laws are the foundation of the nation; and of all our laws. Or at least, they ought to be (Clarkson 2004). The monument (wags call it "Roy's rock") was installed under cover of night—but Moore had a camera crew from Rev D. James Kennedy's Coral Ridge Ministries on hand to record the historic event. Kennedy then sold videos of the installation as a fundraiser for Moore's legal defense. They knew he would need it. The story of Roy's rock epitomizes the rise of what many call "Dominionism." It is a story of how notions of "Biblical law" as an alternative to traditional, secular ideas of constitutional law are edging into mainstream American politics.

What is Christian dominionism?

Most Americans first heard about Christian "dominionism" during the 2008 Presidential election when Sarah Palin was picked as the vice-presidential candidate for the Republican Party. Palin appeared to be the first major political party candidate for national office who had been obviously influenced by dominionist thought.

Dominionism comes in "hard" and "soft" varieties, with the "hard" or theocratic dominionists emerging from a religious trend that arose in the 1970s. Dominionism—in its "softest" form the belief that "America is a Christian Nation," and that Christians need to re-assert control over political and cultural institutions—has been

---

1   Editor's note: the author is one of the most sophisticated reporters on the Christian Right and as a person of faith tries to treat the subject with respect while raising serious criticisms.

on the rise for a long time. Too many critics of Right-wing politics use the term "dominionism" to falsely claim that all conservative Christians want to eliminate separation of church and state.

The seminal form of Hard dominionism is Christian Reconstructionism, which seeks to replace secular governance, and subsequently the U.S. Constitution, with a political and judicial system based on Old Testament Law, or Mosaic Law. Not all dominionists embrace this view, though most dominionists look back to the early years of the American colonies to argue that before the Constitution, "the United States was originally envisioned as a society based on Biblical law" (Berlet 2004).

The terms "theocrat" and "theocracy," are openly embraced by few. They are terms used by outside observers to understand a complex, dynamic, and historic trend. So for people trying to figure out if a conservative politician, organization, or religious leader is "dominionist," I notice three characteristics that bridge both the hard and the soft kind.

- Dominionists celebrate Christian nationalism, in that they believe that the United States once was, and should once again be, a Christian nation. In this way, they deny the Enlightenment roots of American democracy.
- Dominionists promote religious supremacy, insofar as they generally do not respect the equality of other religions, or even other versions of Christianity.
- Dominionists endorse theocratic visions, insofar as they believe that the Ten Commandments, or "biblical law," should be the foundation of American law, and that the US Constitution should be seen as a vehicle for implementing Biblical principles.

Pieces of dominionism spill out in the day-to-day words and activities of our nation's leaders all the time. Former Senate Majority Leader Bill Frist (R–TN) routinely hosted tours of the Capitol for constituents, Congressmembers and their staffs—led by Christian nationalist propagandist David Barton. President George W. Bush claimed during one of his presidential campaign debates with John Kerry that the United States was founded as a Christian nation. Former House Majority Leader Tom DeLay (R–TX) said the United States should be governed under Biblical law.

A dominionist—Sen Sam Brownback (R–KS)—was a hopeful for the Republican presidential nomination for 2008, while other dominionists were challenging the GOP through the Constitution Party, the third largest party in the nation. Moore himself unsuccessfully challenged a business-oriented incumbent in the GOP gubernatorial primary in Alabama for 2006.

Hard dominionists like Moore take these ideas to their extremes. They want to rewrite or replace or supplement the Constitution and Bill of Rights to codify elements of Biblical law. Soft dominionists like Brownback, on the other hand, propose a form of Christian nationalism that stops short of a codified legal theocracy. They may embrace a flat tax of 10 percent whose origins they place in the Bible. They also are comfortable with little or no separation of church and state, seeing the secular state as eroding the place of the church in society.

Dominionism is therefore a broad political tendency—consisting of both hard and soft branches—organized through religiously based social movements that seek power primarily through the electoral system. Dominionists work in coalitions with other religious and secular groups that primarily are active inside the Republican Party. They seek to build the Kingdom of God in the here and now.

The three-shared dominionist characteristics of religious supremacy, Christian nationalism, and theocratic visions were on vivid display in the politics of Moore's ally, the late D. James Kennedy., the prominent author and Christian broadcaster. In early 2005, Kennedy displayed Roy's rock at his annual political conference, "Reclaiming America for Christ" held at his church, Coral Ridge Ministries, in Ft. Lauderdale, Florida. "For more than 900 other Christians from across the United States," reported the *Christian Science Monitor*, "the monument stood as a potent symbol of their hopes for changing the course of the nation" (Lampman 2005).

> … in material given to conference attendees, [Kennedy] wrote:
>
> "As the vice-regents of God, we are to bring His truth and His will to bear on every sphere of our world and our society. We are to exercise godly dominion and influence over our neighborhoods, our schools, our government … our entertainment media, our news media, our scientific endeavors— in short, over every aspect and institution of human society."
>
> *(Kennedy quoted in Lampman 2005)*

Kennedy, the *Monitor* noted, "regularly calls the United States a Christian nation that should be governed by Christians. He has created a Center for Christian Statesmanship in Washington that seeks to evangelize members of Congress and their staffs, and to counsel conservative Christian officeholders." The *Monitor* story showed Kennedy manifesting all three characteristics of a dominionist: he was a Christian nationalist; he was a religious supremacist; and his politics were decidedly theocratic. But of the three characteristics, Kennedy would embrace the first, but would probably demur on the second and definitely denied the third.

Moore and the separation of Church and State

The notion we often hear in public these days—of the supposed suppression of Christian expression by an alleged secular humanist conspiracy—stems largely from the works of Reconstructionist theologian R. J. Rushdoony and those of the Reconstructionist-influenced writer, Francis Schaefer. Christian Right leaders Tim LaHaye, Jerry Falwell, and Pat Robertson also echo these claims.

The charge can be heard across the decades in Christian Right claims that "secular humanism" is being taught in the public schools and that Christians are "persecuted" in America. A variation of this claim was made by soft dominionist, Dr Richard Land, a leader of the Southern Baptist Convention. "the greatest threat to religious freedom in America," Land declared, "are secular fundamentalists who want to ghettoize religious faith and make the wall of separation between church and state a prison wall keeping religious voices out of political discourse" (Thompson 2005).

Virginia Reconstructionist Rev Byron Snapp maintained, "religious pluralism is a myth. At no point in Scripture do we read that God teaches, supports, or condones pluralism. to support pluralism is to recognize all religions as equal" (quotes from Cantor 1994). Religious equality is, of course, exactly what the U.S. Constitution requires (Clarkson 1997). It is because this is so, in part, that there is such a desperate push for what Rushdoony called "Christian revisionism" of history.

Arguably, Moore is emerging as the leading Christian Reconstructionist politician in America. So, let's return to the story of Roy's rock. Moore was once an obscure Alabama county judge. He gained notoriety when the American Civil Liberties Union sued because he insisted on hanging a hand-carved Ten Commandments plaque in his courtroom and opening the proceedings with a prayer. While the case was ultimately dismissed because the plaintiff lacked standing to sue, Roy Moore became a nationally known as the "Ten Commandments Judge." Moore, then aged 58, turned his notoriety into election as Chief Justice of the Alabama Supreme Court in November 2000. Six months after his inauguration, he installed his famous monument. The ruling by Federal District Court Judge Myron H. Thompson in the inevitable lawsuit, declared that the display constituted "a religious sanctuary, within the walls of a courthouse." He ordered Moore to remove it; Moore refused, and he was ultimately removed from the bench (Clarkson 2004).

Judge Thompson was additionally troubled by Moore's partnership with D. James Kennedy. He wrote that it "can be viewed as a joint venture between the Chief Justice and Coral Ridge, as both parties have a direct interest in its continued presence in the rotunda. ... In a very real way, then, it could be argued that Coral Ridge's religious activity is being sponsored and financially supported by the Chief Justice's installation of the monument as a government official."

Moore became a *cause celebre* and a popular speaker at major gatherings of such organizations as the Christian Coalition and Eagle Forum. He was courted to head the national ticket of the overtly theocratic Constitution Party in 2004 and he headlined state party conventions while being publicly coy about his intentions. He ultimately decided not to run. (He was probably a stalking horse for his friend and financial backer, Maryland attorney Michael Peroutka, who appeared with Moore, and ultimately got the Party's nomination for president that year, despite being a political unknown).

Moore and his attorney Herb Titus (vice-presidential candidate of the Constitution Party in 1996) drafted the Constitution Restoration Act, which would allow local, state and federal officials to acknowledge "God as the sovereign source of law, liberty, or government" and prevent the US Supreme Court from gagging them. Sen Richard Shelby (R–AL), Sen Sam Brownback (R–KS), and Rep Robert Aderholt (R–AL) signed on as the bill's main sponsors, and announced its introduction at a press conference in Montgomery, Alabama in February 2004.

That same day, a conference sponsored by Moore's Foundation for Moral Law drew a Who's Who of dominionists and dominionist-influenced Christian Rightists, including Howard Philips, Herb Titus, John Eidsmoe, Phyllis Schlafly, Alan Keyes and representatives from such leading Christian Right organization as Coral Ridge Ministries, Focus on the Family, Concerned Women for America, and Eagle Forum. One of the featured speakers was Rev. Joseph Morecraft, from Cobb County Georgia, a leader of the theocratic Christian Reconstructionist movement (Morecraft 2004).

Both the House and Senate held hearings on the bill in 2004, and it was reintroduced in 2005. As of September 2005 it had eight GOP cosponsors in the Senate and 43 in the House. It is a classic and pioneering "court stripping" bill, seeking to strip the Supreme Court of its power of oversight. The clear presumption of the bill was that God's law is, once was, and should always have been the cornerstone of law and jurisprudence in the United States. While the bill never progressed out of committee, the depth of support for a bill of such profound consequence is one fair measure of how far the even most overt dominionist agenda has come.

The rhetoric of Roy Moore and other Christian Right leaders notwithstanding, the framers of the US Constitution explicitly rejected the idea of a Christian Nation. Seeking to inoculate the new nation against the religious persecution and warfare that had wracked Europe for a millennium, the framers made America the first nation in the history of the world founded without the blessing of an official god, church or religion. They were leaving behind local theocracies that had governed the colonies for the previous 150 years in which only white propertied men who were members of the correct, established sect were able to vote and hold public office. One of the formative experiences of the young James Madison was witnessing the beating and jailing of Baptist preacher who preached—it was against the law in Anglican Virginia.

Madison went on to become the principal author of both the Constitution and the First Amendment. Among the many historical issues faced by dominionists who embrace Christian nationalism and seek to revise history in support of their contemporary political aims, one is so clear and insurmountable that it is routinely ignored: Article 6 of the Constitution bans religious tests for holding public office—no more swearing of Christian oaths. By extension, this meant that one's religious orientation became irrelevant to one's status as a citizen. It was this right to believe differently, that set into motion the disestablishment of the state churches—and set the stage for every advance in civil and human rights that followed.

Crafting a slate of candidates

Moore had evidently set out to provoke a confrontation with the federal courts over the Ten Commandments monument—one he was destined to lose, much as Alabama Governor George Wallace lost in his defense of legal segregation 40 years before.

Moore took his show on the road, speaking about his alternative view of American history and law at major and minor Christian Right conventions around the country, and displaying the monument. It was typically cordoned off with velvet ropes and viewed with reverence, awe, and rubber necking.

Moore leveraged this notoriety beyond the lecture tour into a campaign for governor of Alabama. Moore was even given a (long) shot at winning the June 2006 GOP primary against the incumbent business oriented GOP governor Bob Riley (Moore lost), the *Atlantic Monthly* reported Moore was assembling "an entire slate of candidates to run under his auspices in the Republican primary ... Moore has, in effect established a splinter sect of religious conservatives bent on taking over the Republican Party, and his reach extends to every corner of the state." This had establishment types in both parties worried: "in style if not in substance," the article concluded, "Moore's religious populism is a lineal descendant of the race-baiting that propelled Wallace to the statehouse a generation ago" (Green 2005).

Christian Reconstructionism

While D. James Kennedy appeared to represent "soft dominionism," he was a borderline case. Some of what Kennedy, Moore and their allies pursued struck me as hard dominionist, and by this, I mean rooted in Christian Reconstructionism, a theology that arose out of conservative Presbyterianism in the 1970s. It asserts that contemporary application of the laws of Old Testament Israel should be the basis for reconstructing society towards the Kingdom of God on earth.

The seminal thinker of Christian Reconstructionism the late Rev R. J. Rushdoony, argued that the Bible is to be the governing text for all areas of life, art, education, health care, government, family life, law and so on. They have formulated a "biblical worldview" and "biblical principles" to inform and govern their lives and their politics. Reconstructionist theologian David Chilton succinctly described this view: "the Christian goal for the world is the universal development of Biblical theocratic republics, in which every area of life is redeemed and placed under the Lordship of Jesus Christ and the rule of God's Law" (Clarkson 1997, 78).

It has been difficult for many Americans to accept the idea that a theocratic movement could be afoot, let alone gain much influence in modern America, but Robert Billings, one of the founders of the Moral Majority once said, "if it weren't for [Rushdoony's] books, none of us would be here" (Cantor 1994).

This does not, of course, mean that everyone influenced by Rushdoony's work is a Reconstructionist. Rather, as Billings indicated, it provided a catalyst and an ideological center of gravity for the wider movement of ideas that have percolated throughout evangelical Christianity, and parts of mainline Protestantism and Catholicism for the past three decades. Rushdoony was also the first to detail what a Biblical society should look like and therefore, whether one agreed with him or not, his work became the standard by which many dominionists measure themselves.

The original and defining text of Reconstructionism, is Rushdoony's 1973 opus, *the Institutes of Biblical Law*—an 800-page explanation of the Ten Commandments, the Biblical "case law" that derives from them and their application today. "The only true order," he wrote, "is founded on Biblical Law. All law is religious in nature, and every non-Biblical law-order represents an anti-Christian religion." In brief, he continues, "every law-order is a state of war against the enemies of that order, and all law is a form of warfare" (Clarkson 1997, 79).

The Vallecito, California headquartered Chalcedon Foundation, the think tank under whose auspices Rushdoony did most of his writing, celebrated its 40th anniversary with a conference on his life and work. Interestingly, the Foundation's journal, *Chalcedon Report,* also reported that Roy Moore's Foundation for Moral Law was preparing "to hold seminars that will teach judges, lawyers, and law students about Biblical Law as the basis of America's laws and Constitution." "There is a lot more being written and said about this than there was a few years ago," Moore told *Chalcedon Report.* "The truth that's been cut off for so long is being brought out into the open, and it will prevail" (Duigon 2005).

Conclusions

The sudden rise of a Christian Right agenda in many states and the federal government has taken many by surprise. It may be tempting to see Roy Moore as an exception, but his rise is reviving old coalitions. In 2004, his former spokesman and legal advisor, Tom Parker, was elected as an Associate Justice of the Alabama Supreme Court. At Parker's request, US Supreme Court Justice Clarence Thomas traveled to Montgomery to swear him in. Ex-justice Moore then also swore him in. "the Chief's courage to stand for principle over personal position inspired me and animated voters during my campaign for the Alabama Supreme Court" said Parker. "So, I have been doubly blessed to have been sworn into office by two heroes of the judiciary" (Clarkson 1997, 79).

But Parker's politics has additional roots in the politics of the Wallace era. He has longstanding ties to neo-confederate organizations such as the Council of Conservative Citizens and the white supremacist League of the South and calls his home "Ft. Dixie" (Beirich and Potok 2004).

While Alabama has its distinctive politics, we can also see dominionist politics in the mix of the aggressive efforts to restrict access to abortion and to deny equal rights to gays and lesbians—and in the efforts to teach creationism and its variant "intelligent design" in the public schools.

Naturally, people look for explanations for how it has come to this. There are many factors for this trend, just like any other important trend in history. But many Americans, regardless of their political orientation, seem genuinely baffled and obsessed about one or another factor in the rise to power of the Christian Right: They look to issues of funding, mass media, megachurches, dominionism, and so on. It is all of these and more. However, following the logic of Occam's Razor, that the best explanation is usually the simplest, I offer this: The Christian Right social movement, fueled by the growing influence of dominionist ideology, gained political influence because it was sufficiently well organized and willing to struggle for power. And now they are exercising it.

While most dominionists would say they favor the US Constitution, and merely seek to restore it to the original intentions of the founders, in fact, their views are profoundly anti-democratic. The dominionist worldview is not one based on the rights of the individual as we have come to know them, but on their particular notions of biblical law. Among the political models admired by the likes of D. James Kennedy, Pat Robertson, and Reconstructionist writer Gary North is the Massachusetts Bay Colony, a government ruled by the intensely Calvinist Protestant sect, Puritanism. In the dominionist worldview, the biblically incorrect (and those of other religious views) should be second-class citizens at best. While few would admit to the clear theocratic implications of Christian nationalism, dominionism in the short run necessarily means reducing or eliminating the legal standing of those who do not share their views.

11

EXPORTING RIGHT-WING CHRISTIANITY[1]

Jean V. Hardisty and Chip Berlet

In this chapter, we examine one anti-human rights sector; Right-wing US-based Christians, especially evangelicals and Pentecostals—known in the US as the Christian Right. Newly empowered politically, it is increasingly becoming an international force working to oppose gay rights, women's rights, and other symptoms of modernity. By promoting traditionalism in other countries, it is exporting "the culture wars."

Conservative US evangelical churches have broadened a long tradition of international missionary work, intended to convert and "save" individuals, to include political work related to a Right-wing political agenda. The resulting assault on human rights is alarming.

In thinking and writing about the Christian Right, we are careful not to conflate its work and agenda with that of religious bodies in general. Our brush must not be broad or simplistic. Only if we have accurate information and a thorough understanding of the best means of defending human rights will our liberal, reformist, and progressive work succeed.

A profile of Right-wing Christianity in the United States

Although Conservative evangelical Christianity has always been a presence within US Christianity, it has, since the mid-1960s, increased its presence and influence in

1   This chapter was privately funded by a major foundation that wished to remain anonymous. We worked on the project doing research and data collection for over one month. The resulting report was circulated to nonprofit and advocacy groups internationally. As Jean's health began to fail, she decided to post it online at her personal website. I never learned the name of the funder.

Updated information on globalizing Christian and Hindu nationalism, and this trends' intersection with religious nationalists and religious supremacists in the United States, Russia, India, and Brazil, is online at https://www.researchforprogress.us/topic/47284/.

the political sphere, especially within the Republican Party. As conservative Christians have demanded a place at the political table, the lines between church and state have blurred. The strongest vehicle for this growing influence has been what are known as the "social issues"—including reproductive rights, gay rights, homeschooling, and marriage and divorce.

The US Christian Right is actually a spectrum of ideological and spiritual profiles. But across all sectors there is a focus on the "Culture Wars," officially acknowledged in US national politics by Right-wing Republican candidate Patrick J. Buchanan in his 1992 "Culture Wars" address to the Republican National Convention. In the transcript below we can see the rhetoric of Right-wing populism in service to a claim that liberals are conspiring against God and country. In throwing his support behind the nomination of President George W. Bush for a second term, Buchanan said:

> There is a religious war going on in this country. It is a cultural war, as critical to the kind of nation we shall be as the Cold War itself. For this war is for the soul of America. And in that struggle for the soul of America, Clinton is on the other side, and George Bush is on our side ... [W]e must take back our cities, and take back our culture, and take back our country
>
> *(Buchanan 1992)*

Buchanan invokes the Culture War frame to support specific Right-wing ideological positions on the economy, gender roles, and White racial solidarity. The Culture War also involves a conservative critique of multiculturalism and "political correctness" (Messer-Davidow 1993, 40–80; 1994, 26–41; Scatamburlo 1998; D.L. Schultz 1993).

Much of this ideological substance is compatible with conservative evangelicalism and Pentecostalism and serves as common ground with international conservative Christians. Among Christian conservatives, the most Right-wing sectors (dominionism and reconstructionism) advocate a civil government based on the teachings of the Bible (Clarkson 1997, 2001, 2005; Berlet 2011).

Christian Reconstructionism is a totalitarian US Protestant Calvinist theology that seeks to impose on nations Old Testament Biblical Law, primarily from Leviticus. This includes maximum of the death penalty for adulterers, homosexuals, and recalcitrant children. Christian Reconstructionism is not related to the Jewish Reconstructionist movement (Hardisty and Berlet 2012). Dominionism is a broad umbrella term used by scholars to group Christian theo-political tendencies that seek formal Christian nationalism (Barron 1992; Berlet 2011).

In some cases, US conservative Christians have looked for success for their agenda by establishing a presence in global bodies, such as the United Nations, and in countries with sympathetic adherents. We saw this in the case of Beverly LaHaye's Concerned Women for America, which has established a presence at the United Nations. Another method of establishing an international presence is to do so electronically, as in the case of Rev James Dobson's Focus on the Family which, during the 1980s and 1990s, established a global network of radio stations throughout Africa, Asia, and Latin America that broadcast his radio talk shows. Pastor Bill Hybels of Willow Creek Community Church holds annual electronic events, called Global Leadership Summits that claim to reach "into more than 200 cities in 70+ countries across the globe via videocast" (Hardisty and Berlet 2012). Another way is to hold international conferences on "Faith," "Families," "Leadership," and other conservative social themes (Hardisty and Berlet 2012).

Missionary work has been part of virtually every sector of US Christianity throughout the 20th Century. The Church of Jesus Christ of Latter-Day Saints (the Mormon church) are perhaps best known for its long-established missionary work, and the winning of souls for Christ is a long-standing work of Christian virtue. Its missionaries have been met with hostility, welcomed as enlighteners, and ignored as irrelevant. Some people have been converted as a result of this work.

But there was always a limitation in this type of missionary work: often its impact was local and people could ignore its teachings without sanction. As the Culture Wars heated up in the United States, with conservative Christian sectors enmeshed in the conflict, it became increasingly clear, in the US and internationally, that conservative Christian positions on the social issues are best "lobbied" at a national level.

With this understanding—and increasing political standing in the US—conservative Christian organizations have gone into the international arena with new sophistication and greater ambitions. We are now seeing a new form of Christian missionary work around the globe.

The current change from missionary work to political work

Sophisticated as that evangelical work has been, a new approach has strengthened the global reach of US-based Right-wing Christianity. Although local and regional evangelizing has been effective, it reaches only those who want to follow conservative Christian dictates. Far more effective is to legislate Christian-friendly laws that apply to all members of the nation state.

This thinking is now widespread among US Christian evangelicals, and African and Latin American nations have been their leading targets for organizing. They have exported the themes of the US "Culture Wars" that now characterize some international evangelical work. In addition to Christian organizations, a number of pastors of US megachurches, such as Rick Warren, Scott Lively, Joel Osteen, and Creflo Dollar, have actively courted African support for their agendas (Kaoma 2009).

Perhaps the best-known example is the proposed Ugandan law, "the Anti-Homosexuality Bill 2009," which was presented to Parliament on October 14, 2009. While it has not yet been passed into law in Uganda, the proposed law provides a good case study of the influence of Right-wing US evangelicalism in the affairs of African nations. Using the well-worn reasoning that homosexuality is a colonial import in Africa and will destroy the nation if left unopposed, Scott

Lively, President of Abiding Truth Ministries and a published Holocaust Revisionist author (Hardisty and Berlet 2012, fn.7).

Lively whipped up Ugandan resentment against homosexuality by holding a seminar in Kampala in May 2009, soon followed by the development of the legislation (Hardisty and Berlet 2012, fn.8).

Outside forces alone could not have done such dramatic political work. In the case of Uganda's anti-homosexuality bill, a major organizer of the anti-gay conference was Ugandan Stephen Langa of the Family Life Network in Kampala.

Since the end of colonialism, Christianity (especially evangelical and Pentecostal sectors), has grown exponentially across the global South. David Barrett and Todd Johnson (2004) found, for instance, that Protestantism in Africa has grown from 30 million in 1945 to 411 million by 2005 (Barrett and Johnson 2004, 28). Catholicism, on the other hand, has increased merely 1 percent, from 13 to 14 percent (Woodberry and Shah 2004, 49).

David Martin focusses on the Rise of Pentecostalism in the global South, noting that, whereas in the U.S. and Western Europe Pentecostalism is a subset of evangelicalism, it is its own religion in much of the global South. As such, it can mold itself to the local culture and can appeal to both "have-not" nationals and middle-class conservatives.

Increasingly, these conservative Christians in the global South are participating in politics. US evangelical and Pentecostal Christians would like to have an impact on that political work, by joining the local forces and by offering assistance and/or training. When such collaboration occurs, the resulting conservative political activism is felt primarily in the host country. But the US evangelical establishment benefits as its influence grows. A mutual goal of a "win" on the cultural issues is a boost to both the US Right and to its international allies.

Funding sources for international Right-wing Christian work

It is very hard to estimate the actual amount of money that US-based evangelical and Christian Right organizations spend on projects outside the United States. Identifying the funding of policy-related initiatives is even more difficult for a number of reasons:

Reporting requirements of the federal government are loose to begin with, allow churches to be very vague as to what details they must report, and are seldom enforced.

What an evangelical mission might label as "Humanitarian Aid" could, for example, include programs to reduce the spread of HIV/AIDS that stress abstinence from sexual activity and discourage the use of condoms—both considered failed approaches by most of the international public health community.

Very large churches, dubbed "mega-churches," can have thousands of members and the financial ability to raise funds to sponsor their own international projects with few if any governmental reporting requirements. The same is true with some smaller churches with parishioners who are very wealthy (Funding the Culture Wars 2005, 13).

According to Rev Kapya Kaoma, an Anglican priest from Zambia and a project director at Political Research Associates:

> Conservative funding to Africa is a new development. Historically, churches in Africa depended on financial aid from western mainline churches for most of their operations ... in the 1980s, IRD (Institute for Religion and Democracy) and other renewal movements attacked such U.S. churches as Marxist sympathizers.
>
> *(Kaoma 2009, 9)*

Homosexuality has proved a useful for the Right in driving a wedge in this relationship. The accusations of "support for terrorism" or "Marxist leanings" have also proved useful wedges (Williamson 2007).

When US Right-wing funders offer to replace the money formerly provided by mainline Protestant sources, it can be difficult for recipients to see the dangers of that money subtly shaping the agenda of the recipient religious bodies.

US human rights vs. global human rights

In the United States, the political Left often uses human rights as a reform framework. But it is seldom used in mainstream national policy discussions. When violations of human rights are discussed in the US media, it is usually in reference to torture, execution, and illegal imprisonment of political enemies in other countries. Globally (as discussed at the United Nations, for instance), human rights as a working framework demands individual and group rights in a setting of tolerance and non-violence. A progressive human rights perspective sees liberty, freedom, laws and rights as essential, and envisions justice as the goal (Hardisty and Berlet 2012, fn. 16).

Without such a framework, US reform efforts are often approached issue by issue. And further, when human rights is not consciously part of the definition of democracy, it can become defined simply as the equal right to vote and to own property.

Globally, reformers often apply the human rights framework to the pillaging of vulnerable communities by international corporations in pursuit of natural resources. Often, corporations manipulate local resentments and tribal rivalries, and even mobilize local militias to gain access to natural resources. US conservative Christianity is silent in criticism of these human rights violations because US conservative Christians often conflate Christian values drawn from the Bible with secular values drawn from ideological "Free Market" capitalism, itself influenced by a distinct form of Protestant Calvinism. This conflation opens the door to the use of religion (especially evangelical and Pentecostal Christianity) as a reliable ally of unregulated capitalism, even its most rapacious practices.

An example is the widespread practice in Nigeria of a Pentecostal practice known as "the gospel of Prosperity," a form of worship that promises riches in return for faithful Christian worship. In the US, the two largest Prosperity churches are Pastor Joel Osteen's Lakewood Ministries in Houston, Texas, and Creflo Dollar's Atlanta-based World Changers Church International, a part of Creflo Dollar Ministries. Both have large international practices and ambitions.

In Nigeria, enormous megachurches preach the gospel of Prosperity, prominently, Bishop David Oyedepo's Living Faith Church, which operates from a 565-acre headquarters called Canaanland. The parallel practice and similar size make the gospel of Prosperity megachurches perfect allies in international collaboration for mutual gain (Griswold 2010, 57–60).

Conservative Christians, whose Right-wing secular allies have been actively opposed to a human rights framework, include a major US organization, the Institute for Religion and Democracy (IRD) that works to crush liberal forces within U.S. Protestantism, including many that have pursued a human rights perspective. The IRD works at both the national and global levels and seeks allies internationally to oppose liberalism within Protestant denominations. Although a favorite IRD target is the Methodist Church, its best-known work has involved the effort to split the Anglican Congregation (in the US known as the Episcopal church) to prevent the entrance of gay priests and ministers into the clergy (Hassett 2007).

IRD also agitates against Muslim "extremism" and "terror." As IRD describes its work on its website:

> Today the worldwide community faces danger such as it has never known before. Radical Islamists are waging a war of violent terrorism, causing chaos and intimidation across the globe. In our writing and speaking, IRD's Religious Liberty Program highlights the connection between the situation of Christians in the Islamic world and the effect and influence of global jihad/radical Islam on Western civilization in order to both support our brothers and sisters in their ongoing struggle and to learn from their experience.
>
> We connect U.S. Christians and churches with their international partners through our religious liberty work, fostering reasoned, effective social witness on Christian persecution and other human rights issues.
>
> *(IRD website 2012)*

For supporters of human rights, the impact of conservative evangelical and Pentecostal Christians   both those working from the U.S. and those nationally based in Africa, Asia, the Middle East, Eastern Europe, and Latin America—is a major obstacle to the protection of minorities and the pursuit of democracy. Through attacks on gay rights, women's reproductive rights, and even environmentalism (which is seen as a "liberal hoax"), as well as the demonization of Islam and tolerance of non-Christian religions, many Right-wing evangelical and Pentecostal Christians stand firmly against democracy, equal rights, and religious freedom (Ranger 2008).

The global Roman Catholic anti-abortion network

When in 1973 the US Supreme Court overturned restrictive laws on abortion rights in the case Roe v. Wade, US anti-abortion groups such as Roman Catholic-based Human Life International, began a counter-campaign. In 2005, when the Ethiopian legislature legalized abortion, the Guttmacher Institute reported that opposition came from the Ethiopian Orthodox Church and the Roman Catholic Church, while the National Council of Islam did not issue any public statements. According to the report, "the most damaging and vocal opposition came from a group called the Christian Workers Union for Healthcare in Ethiopia which appeared to have been formed solely for the purpose of lobbying against liberalization of the criminal code on abortion" (Singh, Hussain, Bankole, and Sedgh 2009).

Human Life International has a long-term strategy for rolling back liberalized abortion laws such as the one in Ethiopia. It coordinates the group Seminarians for Life International and in its name, sends a newsletter "to the world's seminaries in six different languages." HLI hosts Summer Seminarian Institutes, including one in 2005 that trained African priests. Father Aloysius Mugisha, for example, graduated from the HLI seminarian program in Kenya and then launched "a new HLI affiliate in his current station in Ethiopia" (Human Life International 2011)

Mugisha is a missionary with the Apostles of Jesus, a relatively new missionary congregation founded in Uganda that is "sending out hundreds of priests in Africa and around the world" (Meaney 2010, 6).

According to the HLI report:

> When Fr. Aloysius was sent to Ethiopia by his religious superiors [in 2009] he saw how desperately they need pro-life missionaries and educational activities. He started the "Precious is Life Apostolate" and invited HLI to come for a speaking tour.
>
> *(Meaney 2010, 6)*

The report condemned the Ethiopian legislature for legalizing abortion in 2005, saying it "opened a floodgate of preborn baby killing" which it describes as "diabolical." The report claimed that "Ethiopia's seminarians and nuns are eager to receive HLI materials," and "condoms sink Ethiopia deeper into the AIDS crisis" (Meaney 2010, 1).

The Apostles of Jesus Missionaries, another anti-abortion Catholic group, today engages "in direct pastoral work in more than 60 apostolic communities in more than 30 dioceses in Uganda, Kenya, Tanzania, Sudan, South Africa, Djibouti and Ethiopia" (Apostles of Jesus 2011).

The mission that coordinates and fundraises for the Apostles of Jesus is based in the United States, with the Apostles of Jesus Mission Offices in the cities of Shenandoah and Northampton in Pennsylvania and with the Development Office in Catasauqua, Pennsylvania.

Concluding thoughts

The US is not the source of all Right-wing religious activity in the Global South. Nor is it uninvolved in the rise of a global Right-wing religious wave of cultural, economic, and social conservatism. The growing collaboration between the US religious Right and conservative Christians internationally benefits each, and both threaten the pursuit of human rights.

We urge you to study the presence of anti-human rights forces in your country, so that you and your allies closely monitor and regularly challenge their work.

During 30 years of studying the US Right, we have developed some rules of the road for activists challenging the Right that can apply as well to the Right internationally:

- Do not imagine Christianity or any other religion to be monolithic. Try to examine each situation with a researcher's dispassionate eye.
- Do not generalize and demonize the followers of Right-wing leaders. Their motives are complex, and it will do no good to denigrate or insult them.
- Remember that, while not all money is dirty money, enriching oneself with public funds should be exposed, even when the corrupt individual supports human rights goals.
- It can be enlightening and educational for people to learn the theological, ideological, financial, and valid critiques of the organizations that have attracted them. That may be new information for them.
- We believe that democracy thrives where people defend human rights and honor justice as a collective goal of society.

12

THE TEA PARTY MOMENT[1]

Abby Scher and Chip Berlet

"The whole country is going socialist, higher taxes, slowly losing your liberty. It's liberty or socialism. It's not both … Anytime you are taking from one group of people and giving to another, you are denying the rights of a group. Taking from the wealthy — you can't continue to take their money, give it to people who are less productive. What is part and parcel of the American spirit and what people don't understand is giving charity is not something you can demand from people."

(Nevada Tea Party activist and professional's wife)

What is the Tea Party moment? When relatively privileged people rise up with economic grievances and reactionary solutions, can they be called populist, a happy word that suggests action for "The People" against robber barons? How can it be populist when Beltway political entrepreneurs and economic royalists ally with local activists to shortcircuit weakened party structures in ways that elevate the role of big money in elections? Or is it a rebellion of elite individualists, secular and Christian, objecting to an administered society who want to be left alone; or of whites who feel Blacks and Latinos get all the benefits of government? What about the small numbers of working class supporters who feel unmoored from

---

1   Author Scher conducted field interviews in Nevada. Author Berlet conducted field interviews in Idaho, Massachusetts, Montana, Colorado, Ohio, and Washington. Portions of this chapter were adapted from material published in popular and online media including the *Progressive Magazine*, and the cited works of the co–authors listed in the online references. This text first appeared as "The Tea Party Moment" by Abby Scher and Chip Berlet in *Understanding the Tea Party Movement,* edited by Nella Van Dyke and David S. Meyer. Copyright 2014 by Ashgate Publishing Company, Burlington, VT. Used by permission. All Rights Reserved.

stable jobs and a predictable future, abandoned by government, and wondering why the big guys get the bailouts?

How about all of the above?

The rise of the Tea Party

The Tea Party movement gathered force starting in early 2009 with calls for reducing the $1.3 trillion federal budget deficit and stopping federal extensions of power to save the American auto industry and regulate health care. Egged on by beltway organizers, Fox News (particularly Glenn Beck whose Fox television show began airing in January of that year), talk radio, and far Right websites like WorldNet Daily, core activists called for further tax cuts on the rich to unleash economic growth, and also the rollback of the New Deal and Great Society safety net. During the 2008 campaign, Right-wing Christians had seen candidate Obama as a threatening Muslim or even as the Antichrist, an agent of Satan, who according to prophecy will come as a political leader looking like a man of peace. After his election that apocalyptic vision was secularized and embraced in other Right-wing quarters as the conspiratorial claim of the "birthers" that Obama was an imposter born outside of the United States (Berlet 2010).

Many spout populist slogans, but some ally and identify with parts of the monied elite like David Koch, the oil industries billionaire, who view the "free market" as a realm of freedom injured by government action and see a redistributive tax system as a form of theft. "Why would I want to raise taxes on the rich when I want to be rich?" asked one retired small business owner. The famed lack of formal structure among Tea Partiers only enlarges the power of their beltway allies in agenda setting.

The angry apocalyptic Tea Party mood fears the federal government's huge $1.3 trillion budget deficit presages America's collapse, and sees "Obamacare" as a communist folly that will destroy health care in this country. The Tea Party activists we interviewed believed big government is gobbling up the "free market" and destroying the businesses it needs to rely on for its tax base. The Keynesian idea that there are times when the government must invest in the economy and jobs if the private sector is stuck — or even former Federal Reserve Chairman Alan Greenspan's support for tax hikes to reduce the deficit — were dismissed as tired discredited theories, "socialist" or even class warfare. Embracing trickle–down economics like a life jacket, they saw cutting taxes as the only way to soothe the churning waters of an economy in trouble.

This is not the Silent Majority but a very vocal minority. More than 80 percent of Tea Party supporters oppose raising taxes on families making over $250,000, compared to the majority of all Americans who say raise taxes on the rich. In early August 2011, the specter of raising taxes on the rich galvanized the 70–plus strong Tea Party Caucus in Congress during the struggle over raising the debt limit, but you hear similar opposition to tax hikes on the wealthy in interviews at the grassroots.

While the Cato Institute, the Koch–funded libertarian think tank in Washington DC, and other Koch–funded beltway allies want to claim a libertarian free market loving coherence to the movement, many local Tea Partiers continue to support big government programs and just fear the feds have overreached, putting their own entitlements at risk. The small business owner we quoted who wants tax cuts for the wealthy also supports Medicare and Social Security, and thought media disinformation was to blame for statements to privatize the programs by Sharron Angle, his candidate of choice for Senate in his home state of Nevada in 2010.

Far from being a sanitized libertarianism, grievances of some white activists against racial minorities were visible from the start. One of the Tea Partiers' first acts following its takeover of the Nevada state Republican Party in 2010 was to block the GOP Latino caucus chair from participating in state party phone calls. The only pride recognized is the pride in being American. Any other ethnic identification is dismissed as racist.

Once we disentangle all the conservative strands of the movement, we can see the Tea Party moment as a perfect storm bringing together five major political and economic trends of the last 20 years. The Right-wing populism scapegoating minorities and "welfare cheats" is only one response to diverse trends.

First, rising economic inequality produces social and political isolation with some of the rich separating themselves from the rest of America (Massey 2007). They no longer see themselves as part of a civic community and have been powering a (legal) tax strike for the last 30 years or more. They have been funding efforts to promote their anti–tax ideology in both secular realms — seen in Jane Mayer's widely cited New Yorker article about David Koch (Mayer 2010) — but also in religious arenas. It is bearing fruit as regional elites and small business people are having their grievances shaped by this ideology. Didn't someone once say the ruling ideas of an age are those of the ruling class? Well there's a battle raging. The Tea Partiers side with this part of the ruling class who they see as fellow producers and often show racial resentment of immigrants and blacks, scapegoating them as "tax eaters" who are taking their money just like the ruling class resents their tax money going to the common good.

Second, the Right-wing insurgency is a sign of a legitimation crisis. This is when the public loses faith in the government's ability to accomplish anything, including fixing the economy. The government may be unable to deal with the problems of capitalism for any number of reasons: partisan gridlock, counterproductive ruling class control, or the overwhelming nature of the economic problem (Habermas 1975). New York Times reporters Kate Zernike and Megan Thee–Brenan (2010) interviewed economically insecure Tea Partiers who feel abandoned by government and figure government has already absented itself and proven to be unreliable in helping those who are not well off. So why give the government any more taxes or power? Larry M. Bartels (2008) tracked a similar sentiment even before the Tea Party emerged. He found that as Democratic and Republican officials alike failed to represent the views of their working class constituents, these voters stopped expecting the government to do so.

Third, the Christian Right increasingly embraces a free market ideology. Free market Christianity preexists the Tea Party of course, and is well studied (Kintz 1997, Moreton 2009). Postwar anticommunism was one crucible forging the link. Today, you see Christian free market ideas promoted by former Arkansas governor Mike Huckabee and Minnesota Congresswoman Michele Bachmann. The Heritage Foundation and today's Christian Right have been building ideology together since the 1990s (Meagher 2006) and it is bearing fruit, particularly since Glenn Beck used his Fox platform to popularize free market Christianity. Obscure Christian Right ideologues became regulars on the Glenn Beck show, like W. Cleon Skousen (the John Birch Society thinker who is now dead but whose books are high on Beck's reading list) and the Texas Republican and pseudo–historian David Barton (who argues Christian individualism undergirds the Constitution and promotes the free market)

Not that this linkage has everyone on the Right happy. Koch and his allies created libertarian institutions to try to create a free market base to the Republican Party that counters its reliance on conservative evangelicals. While the Koch–founded Americans for Prosperity has accommodated the social conservatives, other institutions like the Cato Institute and FreedomWorks appear less happy with conservative Christian elements powering parts of the Tea Party and promoting the anti–Muslim story line.

Fourth, some classes think they respond better to a "flexible" economy than others. They feel they don't need/don't benefit from the larger infrastructure of government that regulates the economy and creates a social safety net for retirees and those the economy leaves behind. It seemed like everyone interviewed in Nevada was a fairly privileged businessperson or retiree who sold their successful business. Some said they were ready to do without Social Security or Medicare for the sake of the country.

Fifth, party institutions are becoming less important, as big money backs individuals rather than a party, but also because Americans less and less identify with political parties. The powerful elements of political parties are no longer the party regulars or central committees but campaigns. Campaigns rely on big donors to deliver soundbites through big advertising buys, bypassing party regulars. This opens the way for Tea Party influence. The local Tea Party insurgents allied with beltway players to provide the grassroots power that party regulars generally provide. This was certainly true in Nevada; and the *New York Times'* Matt Bai (2010) documented the same dynamic in the campaign for the Delaware Senate seat in 2010 when the Tea Party candidate Christine O'Donnell defeated a moderate Republican congressman in the primary. But the lack of formal structure among Tea Partiers only enlarges the power of GOP oriented beltway organizations in agenda–setting in the movement.

Finally, the backlash against an administered society gives a libertarian edge to the movement. Bureaucratic efforts to rationalize an out of control economy and government bargaining with economic sectors can lead to complex and confusing reforms like the health care overhaul. While the political left opposes the complexity by supporting a government–sponsored single payer health care system, the Right casts its lot with large insurance companies.

Who are Tea Party supporters?

Despite the political resonance created by Tea Party campaigners, a September 2010 poll found only 11 percent of Americans identified with the Tea Party movement (Public Religion Research Institute 2010, Jones and Cox 2010). A massive A *New York Times*/CBS poll in April 2010 found that almost half of Tea Party supporters or close family member relied on Social Security or Medicare. They were more likely to be evangelical Christians (39 percent, versus 28 percent of all people interviewed). They skewed older, wealthier and more educated, with 20 percent in families earning more than $100,000 a year, compared to 14 percent of the general public. Sixty five percent were older than 45. And they were 90 percent white (Zernike and Thee–Brenan 2010).

It is a truly grassroots force with existing free market–championing organizations like Americans for Prosperity and FreedomWorks trying to channel it. Zernike and Thee–Brenan (based on the *New York Times* poll and interviews) write that many Tea Party supporters do not want to cut taxes or dismantle Social Security or Medicare, and instead are most concerned about the size of the deficit. Tea Party supporters also seem to fear the prospect of being "administered" by an over–reaching federal bureaucracy. The Tea Party activists and staffers, on the other hand, want to both cut taxes and dismantle Medicare and Social Security, unlike many Tea Party supporters. Nonetheless, the activist grassroots organizers, many of them older, get ideological training from youthful free marketeers working for the Beltway organizations.

Libertarians

Some of the beltway groups supporting local Tea Party activists, like Americans for Prosperity and FreedomWorks, seemed created in order to nurture a libertarian voting base so that the GOP would not be as dependent on Christian conservatives to win office. But now many Tea Partiers are showing Christian conservative colors — only about a quarter of those polled who align themselves with the Tea Party say they are libertarians while 75 percent call themselves conservative Christians — and the two groups are split (Montgomery 2012, Public Religion Research Institute 2011a). Americans for Prosperity keeps supporting the free market Christian conservatives who take up the Tea Party banner, ignoring their religious arguments, while FreedomWorks seems uncomfortable with religious Right Tea Partiers.

The Christian Right

Nearly half of Tea Party supporters said they were conservative Christians in polling by the Public Religion Research Institute (2011a). Two–thirds say abortion should be illegal. Fewer than 20 percent support gay marriage. Similarly, Tea Party supporters "tend to have conservative opinions not just about economic matters, but also about social issues such as abortion and same–sex marriage" (Clement and Green 2011).

Some 27 percent of registered voters "expressed agreement" with the Tea Party Movement. Tea Partiers, however, are much more likely than registered voters as a whole to say that their religion is the most important factor in determining their opinions on these social issues. And they draw disproportionate support from the ranks of white evangelical Protestants (Clement and Green 2011).

Both Christine O'Donnell in Delaware and Sharron Angle in Nevada are among the new breed of Right-wing Christian free marketeers that includes Mike Huckabee, the former Arkansas governor who supports a flat tax, Sarah Palin, and Michele Bachmann, the Minnesota Congresswoman who launched the House Tea Party Caucus.

O'Donnell and Angle were backed in their primaries by the antitax beltway group Club for Growth and Tea Party Express, a paper–thin front operated by Republican consultants in California (Burghart, D. and Zeskind, L. 2010, Brant–Zawadzki and Teo 2009).

Their Christian free market ideology shows the success of a 20–year strategy of free marketeers to blend their ideology with the Christian Right, so that the social conservatives who make up much of the voting base of the Republican Party would embrace low–tax, anti–New Deal politics of the economic conservatives. This made them compatible with the Tea Party moment and comfortable under its antigovernment umbrella. But, as the studies just quoted suggest, plenty of Tea Partiers did not embrace their conservative Christianity.

Analytical lenses

White racial antagonism

Tea partiers show greater racial grievance than white evangelicals as a whole (a group that includes some liberals). Fifty eight percent of Tea Partiers say minorities get too much government attention while the figure is 38 percent for white evangelicals (Public Religion Research Institute 2010). Other surveys by Public Religion Research Institute (2011b, 2011c) reveal Tea Partier opposition to diversity and immigration. Studies by Parker (2010) and Keil and Keil (2012) found significant racial antagonism towards Blacks and Latinos.

This fit our experiences in the field. In Nevada we met a few Asian American who were Tea Party supporters, and listened to a handful of African Americans visiting from out of state. Otherwise everyone was white. Most were retired, since Nevada, as the lowest taxed state in the nation, attracts a lot of retirees. In Ohio one Latino man carried a sign to a statehouse Tea Party rally noting his ethnicity and daring reporters to interview him. At a meeting in Idaho, everyone in the Fuddruckers restaurant private dining room looked white.

By using elaborate social science variable analysis, The Center for Social Inclusion (CSI) found a connection between economic issues, race, and voter support for Tea Party messages (2010) The CSI study demonstrated how economic stress and racism among whites is linked. CSI found that "in congressional districts facing economic stress, the Tea Party used economic insecurity and growing racial fears to win in majority–White districts." Yet in predominantly white "congressional districts not in foreclosure distress" voters tended not "to support Tea Party candidates. Race was correlated with Tea Party victory, but not class." In those districts that had "large numbers of people of color and high foreclosure rates" there were "few Tea Party candidate victories. According to the CSI report:

> The Tea Party's strategy of dividing voters along subtle, and not so subtle, references to race and ethnicity works in White economically distressed communities, but not necessarily White economically healthy communities or communities with sizable populations of color.

The purge of the Latino caucus from the Nevada Republican Party after the Tea Party takeover made racial grievance visible. Tibi Ellis, the head of the state's Latino caucus, was barred from participating in state party calls. "The extreme conservatives say, well we're all Americans we don't have to cater to any group, but we do—we have a veterans' coalition, a business coalition, a Jewish coalition …. If anything will show how radical this new leadership is, it's things like that. Nobody is calling me to the table to see what my community is doing."

Other members of the Tea Party reveal what Joseph Lowndes (2012) called "a strong desire for racial innocence." They affirm racial equality but overlook the practices that create inequality. And they assert a small government ethos that would explicitly leave the "less productive" behind.

Economic uncertainty

Clarence Lo (1995) has shown that the 1970s Anti–Tax Movement sprang from anger by White homeowners who resented state and federal initiatives to help poor and underemployed people—seen (inaccurately) as overwhelmingly composed of Black people and other people of color. The scapegoats were "faceless bureaucrats," "tax and spend Democrats," "utopian social engineers," and "liberal elites." Racism was clearly involved, but so was fear of falling down the economic ladder. The economic distress in populist movements can be measurably real, realistically anticipated, or a sense of relative deprivation that is a blend of concrete and imaginary fears (Berlet 2012).

In researching the Klan of the 1920s, Rory McVeigh (2009) argues that shifting power dynamics disrupting traditional hierarchies in economic, political, and social power relationship launch the processes by which Right-wing groups mobilize a mass base large enough to intrude into public debates in the larger society. The economic downturn of 2008 has left millions of people in the United States unemployed or underemployed. Even when still holding down a job, the mostly White, middle–class, Republican Tea Party activists are afraid of the possibility that their economic, political, or social status may drop—just as McVeigh theorizes (Berlet, 2010, 2012).

Past Right-wing populist movements have been accompanied by the perception that economic security was being threatened. This has been shown with the progressive Prairie populists of the 1880s, the Ku Klux Klan of the 1920s, and the Patriot and armed citizens militia movements of the 1990s (Van Dyke and Soule 2002, Kaplan 1998, Ostler 1993). In her study of the latter movements Gallaher (2002) found that these mostly male and white activists stand on a fault line because they:

> occupy conflicting social positions. On the one hand, their class positionality, which leaves them captive to the ebb and flow of the global market, creates the context for their oppression as workers. On the other, their dominant racial and gender positions oppress by virtue of their normativity, even if the individuals in question do not set out to do so (Gallaher 2002)

One issue that stumped analysts for decades was that the Ku Klux Klan in the 1920s built a mass movement that attracted millions of White followers from relatively mainstream segments of Protestant middle class at a time when the economy was not just roaring but booming. McVeigh reviewed Klan literature and found that members feared losing economic power at a time of national prosperity due to their experience of threatened competition from upwardly–mobile Catholics and Blacks (McVeigh 2009).

It apparently is the perception of losing power, privilege, and status in economic, political, and social spheres (race, religion, gender) that matters, not statistical economic indicators. This gives new life to slightly revised versions of earlier theories seeking to explain Right-wing movements such as Status Anxiety and Relative Deprivation (Tatlovich and Smith 2001, Gurr 1966). Even Hofstadter's (1965) theory of the Paranoid Style polishes up nicely if filtered through the lens of more recent scholarship on millenarian, millennial, and apocalyptic groups.

Struggles over political, economic, or social power can highlight one of more of these factors, and are especially energetic and angry when all three occur at the same time as was true in the United States when the Tea Party Movement formed.

Economic power, however, acts independently from social power, because as Tatalovich and Smith note: "values–not economics–lie at the heart of these disputes, and 'status' claims are inherited by tradition and custom rather than defined through market forces. Governments intervene in the marketplace to achieve distributive goals, but status equalization looks toward the erosion of (largely private–sector) social hierarchies. These social interactions are fundamentally dissimilar from economic transactions" (2001).

The Role of Conspiracism

Conspiracism as an analytical lens for movements appears episodically in American history. Robert Alan Goldberg (2001) explains:

For generations, Americans have entertained visions of vast conspiracies that target their religion, race, and nation. Salem witches, British ministers, Catholic priests, slaveholders, Wall Street bankers, Jews, Bolsheviks, and black militants, all in their turn and among many other suspects, have been cast in the plotters role.

David Brion Davis (1971) argues that social and political movements to counter the "threat of conspiratorial subversion" gained strength early on because the country was "born in revolution and based on the sovereignty of the people." He also observed that "crusades against subversion have never been the monopoly of a single social class or ideology, but have been readily appropriated by highly diverse groups." According to Goldberg "Conspiracism thrives when power is exercised at a distance by seemingly selfish groups zealous in their authority [and] all are susceptible to the prompting of conspiracy thinking, with class and gender lines offering no barriers." Furthermore, conspiracist belief "demands confrontation and breeds activism and social movement mobilization." (Goldberg 2001). In the past this has generated subversion panics and countersubversive social movements.

Many Tea Party supporters gain ideological training in the threat of liberal subversion from Glenn Beck, the loquacious Fox network star. Beck resuscitated old John Birch Society conspiracy writings to help make sense of the moment for many anxious Americans. Beck also teaches a fundamentalist view of the US Constitution that portrays it as a Christian individualist document undergirding the free market that has been distorted with liberal amendments like that supporting a progressive income tax.

"Most of us who left are indeed fiscal conservatives and ardent supporters of constitutional rights, so the 'Marxist' accusation is a reflection of the deep paranoia and delusion within the current CCRP leadership," said the former chairman of the Las Vegas area Clark County Republican Party (CCRP) after he stepped down. "If we have to purge the RINOs (Republicans in Name Only) from power before we purge the fascists in power, so be it," replied an unrepentant tea partier. This echoes claims made on the national level. "The secular–socialist machine represents as great a threat to America as Nazi Germany or the Soviet Union once did" Newt Gingrich wrote in his book *To Save America* (2010: 4).

The overheated rhetoric in the Tea Party about Obama, liberals, and socialists destroying the "American Way of Life" is a form of demonization not uncommon in the bare–fisted battles in political life throughout US history. Rogin (1987) refers to this in the public sphere as "episodes in political demonology." The demonization of an adversary involves well–established psychological processes (Lifton 1961, Noël 1994, Altemeyer 1996, Young–Bruehl 1996, Harrington 2004). This, however, does not imply any psychological dysfunction. Augusto (2009), who studied the use of rhetorical demonization in opposing abortion–focused groups, found, "the process by which one group cultivates a negative image of an opponent" actually "accounts for a great deal of the interaction between movements and counter–movements and plays an important role in how each side views itself and its opposition."

Tilly (1978) suggested spreading fears of a serious threat was an effective way to build a social movement. Since the 1960s Right-wing movement leaders have skillfully exploited fears in the middle class and working class that their economic, social, and political stock was falling (Frank 2004, Hardisty 1999, Kazin 1992, 1995, Ehrenreich 1989).

These apocalyptic warnings of impending doom are often part of a masculinist rhetorical strategy used to quickly mobilize action (Quinby 1999, 1997, 1994). But women embrace the demonization too. As the *Wall Street Journal* first reported, Sharron Angle was a member of the Right-wing Christian, gun–toting, anti-government, income–tax–hating Independent American Party of Nevada during the 1990s while serving on a local school board in the Reno area (Radnofsky 2010). A party that thinks Republicans are "too corrupt and socialistic," the state-wide party still fields candidates and has 60,000 people on its voter rolls. They echo larger Patriot Movement narratives warning archly of America losing its sover-eignty to a North American Union encompassing Mexico and Canada, and calling for public lands to be transferred to private control or the United Nations (Berlet 2009).

Conclusions

The first wave of books on the Tea Parties takes a variety of approaches to their examination of the Tea Parties. Jill Lepore provides an excellent corrective coun-terpoint to the Tea Partiers revisionist history of the United States, and discusses the Right-wing role in revising textbooks. Her main focus, however, is not the movement itself, although each chapter starts with a fascinating contemporary anecdote (2010, esp. 3–16). Skocpol and Williamson treat the Tea Party and its participants as an instrumental social movement, but spend little space placing the Tea Party in analytical historic perspective. Street and DiMaggio (2011) contend that the Tea Party is not a real social movement at all, but a pseudo–movement fiction created by elites. They refer to "false" populism (141–144).

Kate Zernike (2010), a journalist by trade, provides the most detailed picture of the Tea Party as a form of social movement populism in her book *Boiling Mad: Inside Tea Party America*. She cites Kazin (1995) on populism from the Right (Zernike 2010, 53–54); McGirr (2001) on 1960s anti–communism providing the basis for Tea Party anti–collectivism (Zernike 54–55); and Warren (1976) on "Middle American Radicals" (Zernike 57–58).

The value of using Right-wing populism to describe the Tea Parties—or using different terms such as White Citizenship Movement, Precariat, Middle American Radicals, Anti–Statist Populism, or White Nationalism—is debated by scholars, and discussed in an edited collection on the Tea Parties (Rosenthal and Trost 2012; see especially chapters by Berlet, Disch, Lowndes, and Postel).

While not all Tea Partiers are Right-wing populists, we identify the Tea Party movement as a form of "Right-wing populism" because we believe this termi-nology illuminates one of its most vital aspects. The ancient poet Hericlitus reminds us that "Everything changes and … you cannot step twice into the same stream;" yet when he calls it a stream, we know of the fluid entity to which he refers. Right-wing populist movements always appear in different guises at different moments and different places, yet they share certain basic similarities.

The internal GOP struggles for power will be playing out long after this volume goes to press. Exactly when the Tea Party moment will pass is unpredictable; but when it does, another Right-wing populist formation will start brewing.

13

FROM THE KKK TO DYLANN ROOF[1]

White nationalism infuses our political ideology

Chip Berlet

When Dylann Roof pulled a gun at a Bible study in Charleston, South Carolina on June 17, 2015, his shots rang through history to the roots of the ideology of White supremacy, which justified genocide of indigenous peoples and the enslavement of Black people from Africa. We deny this at our own risk.

Roof attacked the Emanuel African Methodist Episcopal Church, which by the early 1800s was at the center of Black resistance to slavery in Charleston, according to African-American history scholar Gerald Horne. Black people, Roof feared, threaten the existence of the White race. Events in the church's history play a role in Roof's fear. Inspired by a slave rebellion that began in 1791 in what is now Haiti, Emanuel parishioner Denmark Vesey of Charleston began organizing an insurrection against slavery, using the Charleston AME church as a base.

Roof might have been unaware of the specific history of "Mother Emmanuel," but he had immersed himself in a narrative that is deeply rooted in our nation's history, a narrative that takes into account the history of Charleston's historic congregation.

Roof told a participant in the Bible study, "I have to do it. You rape our women and you're taking over our country. And you have to go." Horne and

---

1   With growing alarm several us who studied White nationalism and the language of the Republican Party feared a continuation of violent acts prompted by the "scripted violence" rhetoric of racist demagogues. After the White Supremacist murders at the church in North Carolina I asked *The Washington Spectator* if I could write a heartfelt polemic rather than a dispassionate journalistic or scholarly study.

Copyright 2015, *The Washington Spectator*. Used with the permission of the publisher, all rights reserved. The author thanks his article editor and friend Lou Dubose. The Washington Spectator resides online at https://washingtonspectator.org/.

other social scientists believe Roof inherited the fear of murderous Blacks raping White women from a common historic narrative of White supremacy.

Horne says that after the bloody Haitian slave revolt, American newspapers were full of stories salaciously describing "marauding Blacks with sugar cane machetes hacking the White slave-owners to death." Regardless of their veracity, these stories informed a historic narrative that was seized upon by the founders and early members of the Ku Klux Klan.

After the Civil War, the Ku Klux Klan "was largely halted following federal legislation targeting Klan-perpetrated violence in the early 1870s," said *Klansville, U.S.A.* author David Cunningham in a PBS documentary. In 1905, Thomas Dixon, Jr., wrote *the Clansman: An Historical Romance of the Ku Klux Klan*, later turned into the silent film "the Birth of a Nation" in 1915. The White supremacist frame of Black men pillaging, raping, and murdering was returning to the mainstream.

Dylann Roof looked beyond our native anti-Black texts. His website was "the Last Rhodesian." Roof allied himself with the cause of Rhodesia because, according to the racist Right, the failed struggle in the 1960s to preserve African White nationalist societies, including Rhodesia and South Africa, was a warning about the communist conspiracy to use Black people to pave the way for totalitarian tyranny. This thesis was purveyed by the John Birch Society, whose historic and current conspiracy theories are utilized by Right-wing conspiracist pundit Glenn Beck. A decade before US Supreme Court Justice Clarence Thomas was appointed to the bench, Thomas joined racist conspiracy theorists when he became affiliated with the Lincoln Institute, a Right-wing think tank that embraced apartheid in South Africa as a bulwark against communism.

As the world is wired today, these White nationalist conspiracy theories are a click away. Jennifer Earl and Katrina Kimport, the co-authors of *Digitally Enabled Social Change: Activism in the Internet Age*, are among the first sociologists to have shown that the internet can mobilize people into social movement participation. Right-wing groups from the militia to the neo-Nazi movements were early adopters of online technology, even before the internet created a world wide web of unedited communications that brought racist and antisemitic (and now anti-Islamic) rhetoric into our homes.

Roger Griffin studied terrorism for the British government. His *Terrorist's Creed: Fanatical Violence and the Human Need for Meaning*, describes the phenomenon of "heroic doubling," which can turn a "normal" individual into someone who carries out acts of fanatical violence as a media-carried clarion call to arms to defend an idealized pure community under threat from a demonized "Other."

Roof was influenced by the Council of Conservative Citizens. The CofCC's racist rhetoric provides the most extreme versions of the demonization of Blacks and White liberals, while a more muted—sometimes coded—version of White supremacy is routinely broadcast on cable news and AM radio talk shows. The first Black president, Barack Obama, continued to provide a lightning rod for racist rhetoric even after he left office.

White nationalism infuses our political ideology as a nation—from our major political parties to the armed ultra-Right militants. We need to confront the color line that bestows on White people unfair advantages. We need to revoke that grant of privilege by working to correct the injustice that still stains our nation with the spilling of blood. As Dr King warned us, either we build community, or we will face chaos.

14

ROMNEY APPEALS TO WHITE TRIBALISM IN OHIO[1]

Arun Gupta and Michelle Fawcett

Bounding up to a podium, Romney was ready to proselytize. Thousands of faces turned toward him in the chilly evening air. Word was that Romney's conquest of Obama in the first debate had infused his robotic demeanor with passion. It was hard to see much evidence of that.

To polite applause, Romney blandly declared, "That's an Ohio welcome. Thank you, guys." He tried to rouse the audience with a counter to Obama campaign chants of "Four more years," and the crowd hesitantly recited "Four more weeks," their tone as flat as the surrounding farmland.

No matter. Romney dove into his stump speech. It was the gospel of lower taxes, freer trade, stronger military, and drill, baby, drill, and the audience was receptive. He hit all the buttons, "jobs," "small business," "compete," and "opportunities." Some specifics drew hearty cheers: "Get rid of the death tax," "get that pipeline in from Canada," and "our military must be second to none."

The crowd responded favorably because the ideas are presented simply and clearly. People are hurting, and Romney says he'll create more jobs and put more money in your pocket. His message is he won't do it through welfare, like Obama, but by encouraging American values like entrepreneurialism, strength, and self-sufficiency.

Author Thomas Frank (2004) calls this brand of politics "Pity the Billionaire … a revival crusade preaching the old-time religion of the free market." Frank argues the post-Obama resurgence of the Right is not about racism or culture wars, but a

1   The authors began by following the various events of the Occupy Wall Street move-
    ment in a cross-country tour during which they began to note the backlash building in
    the Right-wing of the Republican Party. Published on October 15, 2012

    This chapter first appeared in *The Progressive* magazine and was posted online on
    October 15, 2012. It is used here with the permission of *The Progressive* magazine and
    the publisher Norman Stockwell. Copyright 2012, *The Progressive* magazine, all rights
    reserved.

populist politics of resentment. The Right, he explains, has effectively defined the economic crisis as "a conspiracy of the big guys against the little," and their solution is "to work even more energetically for the laissez-faire utopia."

It's not either-or as Frank contends, however. The Right is invoking "producerism," telling Americans bruised by the downturn that your pain is due to social factors, which are presented as coded racial categories.

Political Research Associates, a group of scholars who study Right-wing movements, defines producerism as a call to "rally the virtuous 'producing classes' against evil 'parasites' at both the top and bottom of society." The concept stretches back to the Andrew Jackson era, and weaves "together intra-elite factionalism and lower-class whites' double-edged resentments." Today, the parasites at the top are liberals, bureaucrats, bankers, and union "bosses"; the ones below are "welfare queens," teachers, Muslims, and "illegal aliens." They are all taking money from the hard-working Americans in the middle.

By historical standards Romney should be a Walter Mondale, a candidate who has lost even before the race begins. But he is effectively utilizing the politics of White resentment because of Obama's dismal economic record. Tens of millions of low-wage workers feel their world is coming apart and they don't know whom to blame. to them, change may mean lower wages, fewer hours, no health care, or a lost home. Romney plays on fear by linking it to Obama. In Sidney he said, "the president seems to be changing America in ways we don't recognize," which elicited chants of "USA! USA! USA!"

It's not that the United States is inherently Right wing, as many commentators claim. In Ohio, autoworkers say there is almost universal support among their co-workers for Obama because the auto bailout saved their jobs. But the bailout affected less than 1 percent of all US jobs. In a recent poll the president has the support of only 35 percent of White working-class voters compared to Romney's 48 percent.

The Romney rally was stunningly White. Among the estimated 9,000 people, it was hard to find more than a handful who looked to be Black, Latino, or Asian. Attendees complained about welfare and high taxes destroying the country. Romney fed the resentment by claiming Obama was going to "raise the tax on savings," "put in place a more expensive death tax," and raise taxes on "a million" small businesses.

Democrats dismiss Romney as a snake-oil salesman. Joe Biden pointed out in the debate against Paul Ryan that the GOP counts billion-dollar hedge funds as small businesses. That's true, but it doesn't account for the popularity of their ideas. You see, the Republicans have turned small business into a catch-all group the way "working class" once served that function for the left.

According to the Federal Reserve Bank of Cleveland, the number of self-employed and employer firms—those with employees other than the owner—numbered 15.7 million in 2009. It's likely that most are kitchen table, garage or laptop operations, but that's beside the point. Republicans are courting millions of Americans whose livelihood depends on unswerving faith in the market.

Of the five people we talked to who told us their profession, four said they were a small-business owner. They did not seem to think of themselves as workers, but as frustrated entrepreneurs. When Romney says he's going to help small business expand and stop Obama from increasing taxes on small businesses they think he's speaking to them. They hope Romney will return the nation to its natural free-market state—free from regulations, bureaucrats and welfare—in which hard-working Americans like them achieve the success they deserve.

Why shouldn't they believe this rhetoric? The Democrats mimic the Right even when they control all of Washington. Obama says he will make business more competitive, cut taxes, sign trade deals, bomb the world into democracy and drill, frack and mine for energy. The Democrats' dilemma is they are in the pocket of Wall Street but need votes from groups that want the economic pie to be sliced more evenly. The result is liberals worship the same free-market god as conservatives but have no conviction about it.

Absent an alternative, many voters veer Right because they are reaching for the only lifeline they see. "Energy independence" and "a military second to none" are not just catch phrases. They provide millions of decent-paying jobs for the White working class.

This is not to say Romney voters always understand what they are voting for. Talking to some was like walking Through the Looking Glass, where backwards is forwards. Supporters repeatedly ascribed to Romney positions that are the exact opposite of what he advocates. Or they swallow lies about Obama that contradict their own experience. This suggests that racial identity often outweighs rational self-interest. Romney again made this a direct appeal, capping his speech by saying, "We're taking back America."

Ron Elmore, a small businessman who sells education supplies, preferred Romney because he would "get America going in the right direction again." Elmore said he was struggling to get by and believed Romney would help his business by increasing education funding.

Two 16-year-olds, Jennifer Poling and Caitie Johnson, called themselves Romney backers. Johnson said, "There's too many people today who depend on the government." Poling said her mother is a "hardcore Obama" supporter because Romney is against women's rights. Poling, though, shrugged off the Right's explicit anti-abortion politics, saying, "I don't think they [Congress] will let Romney pass any laws against abortion."

Jeff Doresch, who owns a small business detailing cars, was angry. "Obama is shutting us all down. He's destroying us with tax increases." When asked how his taxes had fared under Obama, Doresch responded, "They've stayed the same."

Eighteen-year-old Andy Egbert and 16-year-old cousin Troy Kloeppel's family owns 5,000 head of beef cattle. Egbert said, "Romney is going to make more jobs for the middle class instead of sending them overseas to China." Kloeppel supported Romney because he was opposed to welfare fraud: "It's a great system if it's not abused." Egbert chimed in, "A lot of people are lazy and are paid to do nothing."

Jason, a local soybean farmer, said, "I like everything about Romney." Why didn't he like about Obama? "No Obamacare," he said before quickly departing.

A businessman worth a couple hundred million dollars was telling a White audience that a president who is changing the country "in ways we don't recognize" was stealing their money for job-killing programs like Obamacare. In a warm-up talk, Ohio Governor John Kasich railed against "bureaucrats" and "California rules."

The audience knew what they meant. "We"—White America—are besieged by liberals using our tax dollars on undeserving poor, dark people. This attitude is often expressed as a crude or violent desire to eliminate the other, such as with the spate of "chair lynchings." At the rally one vendor hawked toilet paper with Obama's face on each sheet. Another sold buttons that read, "Forget your cats and dogs, spay and neuter your liberal." Jeff Doresch said, "With Obama, if there's another four years, it will be like when Hitler was here." A few hours west of Sidney, near Fort Wayne, Indiana, a highway billboard showed a picture of armed commandos with text that read, "the Navy SEALs removed one threat to America ... the voters must remove the other."

But it's not just about aggression. In his one effective moment, Romney painted a vision of a beloved, exclusionist community. He told a story about an American flag that went up in the Challenger, which was recovered intact after the shuttle exploded and that "was like electricity ... running through my arms" when he touched it. He turned the secular symbol into a holy one that embodies "who we are." Romney said, "We're a people given to great causes. We live our lives for things bigger than ourselves." That "who," was people in the military, "a single mom," "a dad taking on multiple jobs." Finally, he said, "We're taking America back."

There's little doubt that Romney will double down on decades of bipartisan policies that benefit plutocrats. But that's not what the audience in Sidney heard. Romney offered an easy-to-grasp explanation that spoke to their years of suffering, their unease with the present state of affairs and their anxiety about the future.

An election or two down the road the appeal to White tribalism may no longer work due to shifting demographics, but it could triumph this November.

15

"TRUMPING" DEMOCRACY[1]

Right-wing populism, fascism, and the case for action

Chip Berlet

The candidacy of Donald Trump has prompted a vigorous public debate over whether or not Trump is flirting with fascism. Some analysts suggest his political dance partner is leading him to the tune of Right-wing populism. Other analysts say Trump's marriage to fascism already has been consummated. Either way, Trump is stomping on the dance floor of democracy in a way that could collapse it into splinters. It's a "scary moment for those of us who seek to defend civil rights, civil liberties, and democracy itself," warns political analyst Noam Chomsky in an email sent in 2015.

Back in 2010 Chomsky started lecturing about the collapse of the Weimar Republic in Germany into the abyss of Hitler's totalitarian Nazism. There are parallels to our current political climate than need to be examined cautiously, even though conditions in the US are not nearly as bad as those faced by the Weimar Republic.

Is it fair to suggest Trump—neofascist or not—poses a danger to civil society itself, as occurred in Germany at the end of the Weimar Republic? A review of Trump's rhetoric makes this a legitimate question. Trump keeps gaining ground. As *New York Daily News* columnist Shaun King wrote in November 2015:

> For nearly six straight months, no matter how racist, sexist, anti-immigrant, or anti-Muslim Trump gets, he has maintained his lead in the polls. In fact, from all indications, it appears the more his public talk resembles that of a white supremacist, the more rabid and entrenched his support gets.

1 Published on December 12, 2015 after attending and viewing several Trump rallies and reading reports on Trump's rhetoric. I also spent many hours interviewing people in several states at bus stops and bars and fast-food restaurants and other non-traditional research locations in Massachusetts, New Hampshire, and Texas.

The examples of Trump's fascist-sounding rhetoric are numerous. In June, Trump tweeted, "I love the Mexican people, but Mexico is not our friend. They're killing us at the border and they're killing us on jobs and trade. FIGHT!" (Chowdhry 2015). In July Trump falsely asserted, "the Mexican Government is forcing their most unwanted people into the United States. They are, in many cases, criminals, drug dealers, rapists, etc." (Washington Post 2015a).

Trump's sexism was displayed at the Republican debate on August 6 when he was asked by Fox News reporter Megyn Kelly about referring to women as "fat pigs, dogs, slobs and disgusting animals." Trump later attacked Kelly on CNN, saying, "You could see there was blood coming out of her eyes. Blood coming out of her wherever." the *London Guardian* reported that the "insinuation that Kelly was menstruating crossed a line for organisers of the Red State Gathering, a conservative event featuring GOP presidential hopefuls." That group cancelled an appearance by Trump (Helmore and Jacobs 2015).

Forging ahead, Trump claimed in September that the United States had become the "dumping ground for the rest of the world" for undocumented immigrants and proposed rounding up and deporting some 11 million of them, including their children, who are U.S. citizens (Leopold 2015). In a series of rambling and contradictory statements, Trump called for widespread surveillance of Muslims and refugees in the United States and seemed to agree to the need for a federal database registering all Muslims, although he later backed off to say he was only considering it as a possibility. He confirmed that he wanted such a database for all Syrian refugees (Carroll 2015).

As Trump's viciousness ballooned, the corporate press shifted from portraying him as a carnival sideshow geek to recognizing that he posed a threat to civil society and even democracy itself (Stanley 2015). The media reported with palpable disgust when, during a press conference, Trump mocked the physical disability of *New York Times* seasoned political reporter Serge Kovaleski (Ryan 2015).

Amid mounting disruptions of his campaign rallies by anti-Trump activists, Trump began to mock them, tried to silence them, and even ask that they be forcibly removed. In one incident Trump appeared to approve of the physical attack on a Black Lives Matter protestor who interrupted a November rally in Birmingham, Alabama (Johnson and Jordan 2015). The Washington Post (2015b) reported that Trump yelled, "Get him the hell out of here … Throw him out," whereupon the protestor "fell to the ground and was surrounded by several white men who appeared to be kicking and punching him," while CNN filmed video (Mark and Diamond 2015). Trump later remarked on Fox News that "Maybe [the protester] should have been roughed up, because it was absolutely disgusting what he was doing" (CNN 2015). This was the same rally at which Trump announced to his cheering supporters, "I want surveillance of certain mosques" (Mark and Diamond 2015).

Trump's appeal to White nationalism became increasingly obvious. While Trump can't control who supports his candidacy, the *New Yorker's* Evan Osnos observed with disdain that even "the Daily Stormer, America's most popular neo-Nazi news site, had endorsed him for President" (Osnos 2015). Writing about Trump's nasty rhetoric, and the alarming welcome it has found during the Republican pre-primary media blitz, *American Prospect* journalist Adele M. Stan (2015) put it bluntly:

> What Trump is doing, via the media circus of which he has appointed himself ringmaster, is making the articulation of the basest bigotry acceptable in mainstream outlets, amplifying the many oppressive tropes and stereotypes of race and gender that already exist in more than adequate abundance.

A Weimar moment?

The Weimar period is crucial to understand because it was that precise moment in Germany's history when a broad united front, crossing traditional political boundaries to defend democracy, could have blocked the mass base of a Right-wing populist movement threatening to morph into a fascist juggernaut. Professor Peter Bookbinder at the University of Massachusetts in Boston has studied the Weimar Republic as it eroded into fascism in Germany. His collection of essays at the Facing History and Ourselves website, in a section entitled "the Fragility of Democracy," explores the moments when public interventions might have altered what happened in Europe (Bookbinder 2015a).

As Bookbinder told me, "right now our society is facing some of the same tensions as seen in the Weimar Republic. People didn't take seriously the threat to democracy when they could have; and when they did see the dangers it was too late" (Bookbinder 2015b). He continued:

> There are certainly some similarities to the rhetoric of the Weimar Period in Trump's speeches, but also in that of some other Republican candidates, and Trump especially seems to be playing to an audience of angry White men who have held a privileged status as a group, but now see their status being challenged by people who they see them as undeserving.
>
> *(Bookbinder 2015b)*

Some commentators now are referring to Trump as a fascist demagogue, and Bookbinder thinks "they have a point" since "Trump is a strange combination of a fascist demagogue and a late-night talk show host comedian. But we shouldn't laugh at him because his is dangerous. When I watch Trump, even his facial expressions have the character I associate with the fascist demagogue Adolf Hitler. Trump's crude humor also plays to some of the prejudices of many in his audiences" (Bookbinder 2015b).

Mass media, demagogues, and scripted violence

Perpetrators of ethnoviolence and attacks based on race, religion, or gender "often take their cues from what they hear in the media," wrote Robert Reich in a column on his website after the deadly attack on a Planned Parenthood clinic in Colorado Springs in November (Reich 2015). Reich, Secretary of Labor in the Clinton administration, warned that "the recent inclination of some politicians to use inflammatory rhetoric is contributing to a climate" in which fear of violence is real and growing among targeted groups (Reich 2015).

Now a professor at the University of California at Berkeley, Reich was shocked when Republican Presidential hopeful Carly Fiorina continued to allege "that Planned Parenthood is selling body parts of fetuses," even though the claim has been proven baseless. Fiorina isn't alone, Reich continued. Mike Huckabee calls it "sickening" that "we give these butchers money to harvest human organs," noted Reich. And after the Colorado shootings, Trump falsely claimed "some of these people from Planned Parenthood [are] talking about it like you're selling parts to a car." Much of Reich's column consists of a horrific list of physical attacks on facilities operated by Islamic groups and Planned Parenthood in recent months (Reich 2015).

While violence is often used by ultra-Right groups such as the Ku Klux Klan and various neonazi groups in the US, it is less common in conservative social and political movements. But Trump's use of alarming Right-wing populist rhetoric, aimed at mobilizing his predominantly White base, is changing that status quo. The conservative Right generally tries to avoid this obvious and threatening sort of inflammatory language. In the *Washington Spectator*, political analyst Rick Perlstein (2015), who has written several books about US conservatism, observed of Trump that, "Previous Republican leaders were sufficiently frightened by the daemonic anger that energized their constituencies that they avoided surrendering to it completely, even for political advantage."

The Nazis cultivated the idea of an apocalyptic battle between good and evil. This, coupled with claims of a Jewish financial conspiracy and a sense of national humiliation that demanded redress, helped mobilize the mass base for fascism among the electorate in Weimer Germany. and it also legitimized the violence that followed Hitler's rhetoric. Street fighting became rampant during the collapse of the Weimar Republic, as "Brownshirts" took to the streets to attack the targets singled out in Hitler's speeches as a "threat" to Germany.

Similarly, Trump's use of demagoguery aimed at scapegoated targets is laced with references to conspiracy theories involving President Obama—namely that he was not born in the United States. Tea Party conspiracists claim Obama is a secret Muslim and part of an evil plot. Trump also portrays Muslims in an apocalyptic framework, implying Muslims are a threat to the survival of the United States. Deborah Caldwell in *Fortune* suggests Trump has touched a chord precisely because "people find his apocalyptic rhetoric enticing and familiar—because America has end-times obsession deeply embedded in its national psyche" (2015). Conspiracism and apocalypticism are among the core components of Right-wing populism, along with demonization, scapegoating, and "producerism," which is the division of the population into "productive" members of society struggling against the "parasites" above and below who are subversive, sinful, or lazy (Berlet and Lyons 2000, 6–9).

In their study of how media manipulation for political ends can help incite genocide, Mark Frohardt and Jonathan Temin (2003) looked at "content intended to instill fear in a population," or "intended to create a sense among the population that conflict is inevitable." They point out that "media content helps shape an individual's view of the world and helps form the lens through which all issues are viewed." According to the authors:

> In Rwanda prior to the genocide a private radio station tried to instill fear of an imminent attack on Hutus by a Tutsi militia.
> In the months before [conflicts] in Serbia, state television attempted to create the impression that a World War II-style ethnic cleansing initiative against Serbs was in the works.
> Throughout the 1990s Georgian media outlets sought to portray ethnic minorities as threats to Georgia's hard-won independence.

Frohardt and Temin found that demagogues facilitated the likelihood of violence against specific demonized and scapegoated target groups by creating a widespread fear in the general population that serious—perhaps lethal–attacks on them were "imminent;" even though "there was only flimsy evidence provided to support" these false claims. They continued:

> When such reporting creates widespread fear, people are more amenable to the notion of taking preemptive action, which is how the actions later taken were characterized. Media were used to make people believe that "we must strike first in order to save ourselves." By creating fear the foundation for taking violent action through "self-defense" is laid.
>
> *(2003)*

Similar findings were reported by the International Development Research Centre of Canada in 2007 (Annan and Thompson 2007). Since the end of World War II, there have been studies demonstrating that demagogic rhetoric can produce what I and others refer to as "scripted violence." in this process the demagogue can claim there is no direct link between the inciting language and the violence of "random" perpetrators (Berlet 2014x).

Using the F-word—Why terminology matters

There are good reasons why Trump's statements cause our progressive antennae to wiggle. Trump's swaggering demeanor recalls that of Italian Fascist leader Benito Mussolini. Several journalists have suggested that Trump is using rhetoric like that used by Adolf Hitler in mobilizing Germans to support fascism. Some just call Trump an outright fascist (Berlet 2015c).

In doing so, however, some writers have fallen victim to a hoax quote on fascism wrongly attributed to Mussolini: "Fascism should more properly be called corporatism because it is the merger of state and corporate power" (Berlet 2015d). It's not clear where this fake quote originated, but it confuses Italian corporatist syndicalism with modern business corporations. The spelling is the only major similarity. Mussolini and his adviser, fascist philosopher Giovanni Gentile, consistently wrote that under fascist rule corporations (and all other sectors of society) must bend to the iron will of the fascist ruler (Mussolini with G. Gentile 1932, 1935a, 1935b).

Despite how loosely or inaccurately the terms are sometimes used, "fascism" and "totalitarianism" have very specific meanings. A totalitarian state is a central goal of fascist movements, including neofascism and neo-Nazism. Totalitarian states enforce total control over every aspect of a person's life—political, economic, social, and cultural—in order to reshape the individual and unify society. Totalitarianism is like authoritarianism on methamphetamines. Public debate and opposition are not tolerated. Core democratic systems are crushed. Dissidents are rounded up and sometimes executed. Political theorist and author Hannah Arendt argued that Nazism and Stalinism were the prime examples of totalitarian movements that gained state power (Arendt 1951, 1963). However frightening Trump's ascent might be to progressives, the candidate in 2015 is neither a neo-Fascist nor a totalitarian ideologue, but a Right-wing populist bully. The distinction matters for reasons that go beyond simple taxonomy. Calling Republicans fascist or totalitarian leads progressive organizers into a dead-end of crafting the wrong tactics and strategies for the moment in which we live.

Professor Roger Griffin is a world-class authority on the subject of fascism, and author of several books including *the Nature of Fascism* (1993). Griffin defines fascism as:

> …a revolutionary form of nationalism, one that sets out to be a political, social and ethical revolution, welding the "people" into a dynamic national community under new elites infused with heroic values. The core myth that inspires this project is that only a populist, trans-class movement of purifying, cathartic national rebirth (palingenesis) can stem the tide of decadence.
>
> *(1991, xi)*

Another expert, Emilio Gentile, author of *The Sacralization of Politics in Fascist Italy*, says fascism raises politics to the level of a sacred struggle seeking totalitarian control over society. It is "a mass movement with multiclass membership" that:

> …believes itself invested with a mission of national regeneration, considers itself in a state of war against political adversaries and aims at conquering a monopoly of political power by using terror, [electoral] politics, and deals with leading groups, to create a new regime that destroys [electoral] democracy.
>
> *(Gentile 1996)*

Despite Trump's campaign slogan—the promise to "Make America Great Again"—neither of these definitions describe his program, even though he appears to be getting close to neo-fascist rhetoric. Trump's obvious early mass appeal is built around Right-wing populism. Matthew N. Lyons and I explained the term in our book *Right-Wing Populism in America*:

> Populist movements can be on the right, the left, or in the center. They can be egalitarian or authoritarian, and can rely on decentralized networks or a charismatic leader. They can advocate new social and political relations or romanticize the past. Especially important for our purposes, populist movements can promote forms of antielitism that target either genuine structures of oppression or scapegoats alleged to be part of a secret conspiracy. and they can define "the people" in ways that are inclusive and challenge traditional hierarchies, or in ways that silence or demonize oppressed groups.
>
> *(Berlet and Lyons 2000, 4–5)*

Populism is confusing because it is at once an ideology, a strategic organizing frame, and a rhetorical narrative storyline that names friends and enemies. While Left-wing populism often organizes people around expanding economic fairness, Right-wing populism relies on prejudice and bigotry, demonization and scapegoating of an "Other," and fears of traitorous, subversive conspiracies.

Trump uses populist rhetoric to appeal to "the people," even as he campaigns on his status as an elitist member of the 1 percent. Margaret Canovan (1980), author of *Populism*, a key academic book on several populist variants, calls this "politicians' populism." Populism on the political Right is clearly a cynical scam, but one with a history of short-term success in political contests as the means of one set of elites unseating the faction of elites currently running the government. Italian philosopher Umberto Eco (1995) called this a "selective ... qualitative populism" and warned that there "is in our future a TV or Internet populism, in which the emotional response of a selected group of citizens can be presented and accepted as the Voice of the People." and now we have "Trumpism:" the use of Right-wing populism to mask the fascistic demonization of targeted groups.

Although they can look similar, Right-wing populism is distinct from fascism. As the University of Georgia's Cas Mudde, an internationally-recognized expert on global Right-wing movements, told the *Washington Post* in an article on Trump, "the key features of the populist radical Right ideology—nativism, authoritarianism, and populism—are not unrelated to mainstream ideologies and mass attitudes. In fact, they are best seen as a radicalization of mainstream values" (2015c). Mudde, author of *Populist Radical Right Parties in Europe* (2007) sees Trump's ideology and rhetoric as comparable to several European movements, particularly Geert Wilders' Party for Freedom in the Netherlands, Jean-Marie Le Pen's National Front in France, and the Danish People's Party. These Right-wing populist movements flirt with fascist themes, but are not full-blown neofascist movements, although they share many similarities in terms of exclusionary rhetoric, organic nationalism, and nativist bigotry.

The trickiest part is that many scholars now see Right-wing populism as a building block of neofascist movements. Fascism emerges from Right-wing populist mass movements when a faction of the 1 percent decides it is necessary to promote violence to regain control of a rapidly destabilizing nation facing a crisis. Fascism is the last resort of those in power trying to maintain control. Terminological distinctions matter because some of the strategies and tactics we craft while organizing against a Right-wing populist movement must be categorically different from organizing to block the rise of a totalitarian fascist state.

To challenge the waves of vicious anti-democratic attacks in the United States we must study the forces that have unleashed them as well as determine the exact moment in history in which we struggle against them. People's lives may depend on it. As fascism builds toward grabbing state power, the situation quickly unravels. Sporadic attacks and acts of terrorism against the named scapegoats become more frequent and widespread. People need to focus on organizing around physical self-defence. This is not that moment. Things are bad, but not as bad as when Weimar collapsed into the hands of Hitler and his thugs.

During a period of Right-wing populism, as we are experiencing now, the focus of organizing must be to defend the scapegoats targeted by demagogues like Trump. Millions of White people seem to be having panic attacks in the face of the changing racial demographics of our nation. Our task is to build citywide and even neighborhood coalitions to defend economic and social equality. The coalitions must be multi-issue and cross boundaries of race, gender, class, age, ability, and more.

Suzanne Pharr, author of *in the Time of the Right* (1995) talks about "divisions that kill." By keeping us divided, the defenders of the status quo have an easier time exploiting us. She suggests that in the current political climate, organizers must bring the discussion back to the neighborhood level. "We have to get people to talk about what duress they are experiencing and the losses their communities are experiencing. Then we need to talk about what has been stripped away from our community and family support systems." This is how we can reach out to our neighbors and convince them to "stop blaming poor people and people of color and start looking in the direction of the forces holding us down" (2015).

But be aware that the targeting by our Right-wing adversaries is opportunistic and can shift in an instant to reproductive rights, the LGBTQ community, the environment, or "tax and spend" liberals. Back in 1994 the main target of the Right was the gay community, and Right-wing strategists were using race as a wedge issue to get Black ministers to denounce the "Homosexual Agenda."

The current crop of Republican candidates includes several active with the Christian Right and their agenda to curtail reproductive rights, force gay people back into the closet, and make women handmaids to male supremacy. Meanwhile, Carly Fiorina makes wildly inaccurate statements about Planned Parenthood and Jeb Bush is beating the militarist war drums with a frenzied ad campaign. Behind these candidates are millions of dollars of donations from wealthy "Free Market" fanatics pushing "neoliberal" policies to gut government services and cut taxes for the rich.

No matter who becomes the Republican candidate for President in 2016, the damage is already being done, and it is increasingly harming a range of scapegoated targets. This is a new political and social moment. Republicans have used bigoted rhetoric in the past, but anger has grown as buying power and status have shrunk among many Whites. This is producing a more virulent strain of White nationalist nativism and masculinist rage.

Why are these people so angry?

The crowd listening to Trump's stump speech in Massachusetts this October cheered his attacks on Mexican immigrants. The supporters my partner and I spoke with were fed up with the status quo, suspicious of President Obama, and very much liked Trump's campaign slogan, "Make America Great Again." Great for whom? Cleary not everyone. Trump supporters are angry. They resemble the folks in the film Network, who were told by a raving demagogue to open their windows and shout: "I'M AS MAD AS HELL, AND I'M NOT GOING TO TAKE THIS ANYMORE!" (Lumet and Chayefsky 1976). This is the quintessential Right-wing populist primal scream. Who is kicking them down the ladder of success? Someone has to be blamed for turning their American Dream into a liberal, "politically correct" nightmare.

When Trump uses the phase "politically correct" he is using a concept re-engineered by the Right in the 1980s as a way to silence activists demanding equality for traditionally oppressed peoples and groups in the United States. This is similar to the propagandistic use of terms such as "radicalization" and "extremism" to demonize dissent on both the Left and the Right (Berlet 2011).

Trump's rhetorical propaganda is aimed at appealing to a growing base of angry and frustrated White middle and working-class people. In a script broadcast by Trump ad nauseam, he is telling them who to blame for their slipping economic, political, and social status. According to sociologist Rory McVeigh, people who join Right-wing movements tend to be convinced they are losing or about to lose status, power, or privilege in one or more of three civic arenas: economic, political, or social (2009).

We have seen exclusionary, repressive, or Right-wing populist movements in the United States before. President Andrew Jackson (1829–1837) was cheered as a champion of "the people" even as he kept Black people in chains and forced the Cherokee nation and other indigenous peoples out of their ancestral homelands to make room for White pioneers (Berlet and Lyons 2000, 40–46; Google Educational Resources 2017). After the Civil War, the Ku Klux Klan launched a murderous wave of violence against freed slaves and their supporters in the South (Chalmers 1965; Wade 1987; Trelease 1995). The large populist movements of the late 1890s began as an overwhelmingly progressive force, seeking economic fairness and curtailing the abuses of economic elites, but some supporters later turned their anger against Jews and Blacks (Dobratz and Shanks-Meile 1988).

The backlash against the Civil Rights movement of the 1960s frequently used populist-sounding conspiracist rhetoric, suggesting that communists and Jews were stirring up otherwise happy Black people to prepare the United States for a takeover by the Soviet Union (Nelson 1993; D. N. Smith 1996). The presidential campaigns of George Wallace and Pat Buchanan were built using clear and coded Right-wing populist appeals to a White nationalist base (Buchanan 1992; Carter 1995; Perlstein 2001, 2009, 2014). After the Democratic Party endorsed civil rights in the 1960s, many White people left the Democrats and began supporting the Republican Party. Social scientists found that in some counties in the South, a large and active presence of a Ku Klux Klan movement predicted a significant shift of voters from the Democratic Party to the Republican Party (McVeigh, Cunningham, and Farrell 2014; McVeigh 2014).

In more recent history, the rise of the Tea Party exemplified Right-wing populism, as an angry constituency was mobilized back in 2009 (Berlet 2014). The Tea Party idea originated with supporters of uber-libertarian Ron Paul, but the franchise was scooped up by conservative billionaires who funded training and rallies around the country. Over time Christian Right activists played a leading role in local Tea Party groups, shifting the focus to a toxic blend of nativist anti-immigrant and anti-Muslim rhetoric coupled with homophobia and antiabortion propaganda (Berlet 2014; Scher and Berlet 2014). By 2015 the Tea Party grassroots was heavily populated by White nationalists (Burghart and Zeskind 2015). This was Trump's voter base.

Folks who support the Tea Party and other Right-wing populist movements are responding to rhetoric that honors them as the bedrock of American society. These are primarily middle class and working class White people with a deep sense of patriotism who bought into the American dream of upward mobility. Now they feel betrayed. Trump and his Republican allies appeal to their emotions by naming scapegoats to blame for their sense of being displaced by "outsiders" and abandoned by their government (Scher and Berlet 2014).

Emotions matter in building social movements. The linkage of emotion and politics are at the heart of a forthcoming book by University of California, Berkeley, sociologist and author Arlie Hochschild (2016). In it, Hochschild reports on conversations with Tea Party members in the South, where the movement is strongest (Hochschild 2015a). Many she spoke with long doubted that Obama was American; even after the publication of his long-form birth certificate some still suspect that he is Muslim, and harbors ill will toward America. Hochschild also observes that this set of beliefs was widely shared among people who otherwise seemed reasonable, friendly, and accepting. How she wondered, could we explain this? (Hochschild 2015b).

Her premise is that all political belief:

> …is undergirded by emotion. Given the experiences we've undergone, we
> have deep feelings. These shape our "deep story." and this is an allegorical,
> collectively shared, "honor-focused," narrative storyline about what "feels

true." We take fact out of it, judgment out of it. A "deep story" says what happened to us from the point of view of how we feel about it.

(Hochschild 2015c)

The "deep story" of the Tea Party is that the American Dream has leveled off. Ninety percent of Americans between 1980 and 2012 received no rise in salary while dividends from a rising GDP rose dramatically for the top 10 percent (Economic Policy Institute 2014; Political Research Associates 2017).

Since the election of President Ronald Reagan in 1980, the 1 percent has enriched itself while pushing most of us into a downward spiral of exported jobs, lower wages, unsafe working conditions, and tax breaks for the wealthy. Government social services such as public health and food stamps have been slashed. Public works projects, from bridges to sewers, have been gutted. Shifting tax dollars to private charter schools has strangled public education, the keystone of democracy. This has been happening in communities of color for decades. Now it is front-page news because research shows it is devastating White working class and even middle-class communities (Chen 2015; Devega 2015).

Amid a rising gap between the rich and poor, the middle has been pressed out—especially blue-collar men, the bottom of the middle. Their search for other sources of "honor"—what Hochschild feels is an underlying crisis among Tea Party members—has also encountered resistance, and they have met with criticism, insult, and injury, from upper-middle class liberals who look down on them as "rednecks."

Most Tea Party supporters feel the government is allowing them to be shoved aside, displaced, dispossessed, and disrespected by newcomers, outsiders, and immigrants who they don't see as proper citizens (no matter their legal status).

Trump is popular among many Tea Party movement activists, although national leaders are remaining coy in terms of an endorsement (Miller 2015). The Tea Party and Trump conspiracy theories feed off each other and bolster a sense that there is a plot to disempower White people. Trump and other Republican candidates capture their hearts and minds by telling them their anger is justified and then point them at scapegoats rather than the institutions that have failed them. A culture permeated by the legacies of White supremacy leads the White middle and working class to blame their real downward mobility on people of color and "non-White" immigrants, and in that way reproduces both structural racism and the class-based power of the 1 percent.

Much of this rhetoric, like Trump's, began as a specific attack against Mexicans and Latinos, but it keeps expanding. There is a "Trump Effect increasingly sweeping through the country," warned immigrant rights activist Pablo Alvarado, Director for the National Day Labor Organizing Network (2015). For example, after the Paris attacks a number of Republican governors banned all refugees from entering their states (Oathout 2015). The Puente Human Rights Movement, a grassroots migrant justice organization based in Phoenix quickly responded with a statement declaring, "Scapegoating and xenophobia don't make us safer" (Oathout 2015).

But the attacks aren't only coming from the Republican Right. Democratic Senator Diane Feinstein, for example, is now criticizing immigrant-sheltering sanctuary cities (Coren 2015). The center of the entire political spectrum in the United States is being shifted to the Right. The political views of today's "centrist" Democrats resemble the views of many Republicans during the Nixon administration. White voters have been maneuvered into choosing White racial privilege over their own economic security. This explains the question asked in Tom Frank's (2004) book, *What's the Matter with Kansas?*

In 2015, the same mass base cheers Trump while he is "mobilizing resentment." That tactic, which Jean Hardisty explored in her 1999 book of the same name, is a long time part of Right-wing politics in the US. But now, as demographers predict that the majority of people in the US will be non-White by the middle of the century, the existing emotional response behind that resentment is getting stronger.

From analysis to action

The debate over what we should call Trump's vicious political movement should not stop us from organizing now to protect the people being demonized and scapegoated as targets of White rage. The current wave of Right-wing populism in the United States is breeding a backlash movement that will take creative and bold strategies and tactics as we organize to defend democracy and diversity in the public square.

Trump is a political performance artist portraying the psychological Id of the American Dream. He unleashes the fearful and angry feelings of people who live in a society run as a zero-sum game requiring the successful to climb up over those labeled as inferior. So as the old "Liberalism" consensus collapses from the center while the Right is on the rise, what do we do?

Our challenge is to expose the ideas and policies of Trump and his Republican cronies while competing for folks in their voting base who are legitimately concerned about their declining economic and social future. At the same time we need to put pressure on backsliding liberals who now have the space to abandon justice for unauthorized immigrants and other targets of Republican venom.

Activists need to build broad and diverse local coalitions that tactically address local issues while strategically linking them to national struggles. Building broad, inclusive, and egalitarian coalitions is hard. Bernice Johnson Reagon is a progressive scholar, singer, and activist. She helped found the women of color vocal group Sweet Honey in the Rock. Reagon advises that, when doing real coalition building, "Most of the time you feel threatened to the core, and if you don't, you're not really doing no coalescing" (Reagon 1983).

There are times when liberals and progressives can form alliances, but it can be frustrating. PRA's founder, Jean Hardisty, explained this in her essay "My On-Again, Off-Again Romance with Liberalism" (1996). At times when the Right is a growing threat and the Left is weak, she argued, "liberal reforms have to be defended. Now we are swimming against a tide that is thick with peril ... and like it or not" progressives must "work with liberals, as well as with any other Left-leaning sectors" in a "united front against the agenda of the Right." Also keep in mind the Right-wing backlash is a coalition that has fissures and cracks that can be wedged apart. We need to analyze and take advantage of the stress cracks in any Right-wing coalition while making sure in our coalition work these strains are openly discussed and resolved honestly and equitably.

The late human rights activist Audre Lorde once described herself "As a Black, lesbian, feminist, socialist, poet, mother of two including one boy and member of an interracial couple." Lorde explained that "I usually find myself part of some group in which the majority defines me as deviant, difficult, inferior or just plain "wrong" (1983). Lorde taught us that:

> From my membership in all of these groups I have learned that oppression and the intolerance of difference come in all shapes and sizes and colors and sexualities; and that among those of us who share the goals of liberation and a workable future for our children, there can be no hierarchies of oppression.

Race, class, and gender issues are all complex and related, and no single form of oppression trumps another. That's why the concept of intersectionality is so important. All systems of oppression need to be unraveled.

Currently focus is on the hierarchies of power and privilege that maintain a system of oppression on which this nation was founded: White nationalism. That's the core text and subtext of the Trump campaign rhetoric. At the center of our struggle today is the idea of a "White Race"—which in scientific terms is nonsense. But in terms of the struggle we face: "Whiteness" is at the center. There is a White Race in the minds of millions of Americans. Whiteness is a social, cultural, political, and economic fact.

Right now, we need to be organizing against Right-wing populist scapegoating, especially racist White nationalism and anti-immigrant xenophobia. White people need to reach across the political divide and engage White neighbors in conversations about how the nasty rhetoric is making it difficult to have serious discussions on how to fix what is broken. We all need to be engaging in struggles in our local communities, schools, workplaces—even on the supermarket checkout line.

Back in 2010 as the Tea Party Movement was first brewing, Chomsky raised the example of the Weimar period in Germany as a warning. At a meeting held by *Z Magazine*, Chomsky fielded questions on how the Left should organize against the racist, anti-immigrant, anti-Muslim, and antigay backlash arising out of the Tea Party (Chomsky 2010). "First of all," Chomsky said, "you need to understand it. They say to themselves 'We work hard, we're Christians, we're White ... and now They are taking it all away from US.'" Chomsky pointed out that, though often bigoted, these "feelings are genuine ... and they have to be dealt with."

Organizing must be "done in a way which doesn't frighten people," that doesn't "elicit their worst emotions and reactions."

Hochschild's sociological analyses and Chomsky's political analysis reinforce each other. Chomsky explained that we need to pay attention to the feelings of resentment which are "very understandable" from their point of view. You begin by recognizing that their anger "does have legitimate roots. People feel … seriously threatened … people's way of life is being taken away from them." It's not the immigrants who should be blamed, however, but the greed of the financial sector."

Chomsky reminded the activists that when organizing, "You don't want to brazenly flaunt in front of people your attacks on their values. … How this pans out depends on us." It is "our choice … Do we give up? or do we push for more freedom, more justice, more equality, more participation, more control over our own lives—all decent things?" the last question to Chomsky was how could progressive activists build a successful movement. He replied to the whole room, "We all know how … by education, by organizing, by activism."

Acknowledgement

Special thanks to professor Aaron Delwiche and students participating in the Lennox Seminar on Propaganda and Political Persuasion at Trinity University, San Antonio, Texas. For more resources, see https://www.researchforprogress.us/top ic/47845/trump-and-propaganda/.

16

REPUBLICAN IDEOLOGICAL SHIFT IN ELECTION 2016[1]

Alex DiBranco and Chip Berlet

In this chapter we examine how ideologies, meta-frames, frames, and narratives exert a powerful pull on the collective behavior of large groups of people. This not only primes these populations for mobilization into specific social movements and social movement organizations (SMOs), but also makes them receptive, in this case, to political campaign rhetoric. We do this by examining the role of four core ideological tendencies around which a number of Right-wing movements are clustered:

- White nationalism and White supremacism;
- Christian nationalism and Christian supremacism;
- heteropatriarchy, masculinism, and male supremacism; and
- producerism and neoliberalism

(We omit the ideology of Militarism, in part because in the context of the 2016 elections Militarism appears to cross party lines and involve Presidential hopefuls who are Democrats and Republicans. We also recognize the role of authoritarianism, but omit it as well because it exists across the political spectrum, especially in masculinist frames.)

By tracing the roots and branches of these ideological tendencies, we seek to clarify their power to mobilize often-temporary political and electoral power blocks from within pre-existing social movements and in spite of cleavages and tensions. One reason this works is that the heart of the Right-wing response to the Republican rhetoric is an emotional attachment to the promises of the "American Dream" (Manza and Brooks 2014; Hochschild 2016).

---

1   Adapted and expanded from a presentation made at a roundtable at the 2017 annual conference of the American Sociological Association. Copyright 2019, Alex DiBranco and Chip Berlet. Used by permission of the authors, all rights reserved.

We build our analytical framework on the idea that race, gender, and class are inextricably linked in the construction of systems of oppression. Buechler (2000) has observed that race, gender, and class are "omnipresent in the background of all forms of collective action" and have "institutional embeddedness within the social fabric at all levels." Buechler further argues that these distinct yet overlapping power structures need to be analyzed independently and jointly in order to "theorize the different, specific, underlying dynamics that distinguish one structure from another" (Buechler 2000, 105–107).

White nationalism

Though the United States is a founded on various forms of White nationalism, as a people, most of the White population is in denial regarding the historic record (Roediger 1991; Feagin and Vera 1995; Ignatiev 1995; Ferber 1998; Feagin 2001). Today, White nationalism, a form of racist nativism combining xenophobia with ultra-patriotism, infuses our political ideology as a nation—from major political parties to the armed ultra-Right (Higham 1992[1955]; Hofstadter 1965; Bennett 1995[1988]).

Nativists deny the suitability for citizenship (or even residency) of those suspected of being unable or unwilling to function as loyal and patriotic citizens. As "real citizens" with the only legitimate claim to the sovereign nation, nativists must protect the nation from "alien" intruders. The nativist litmus test can use race, country of origin, religion, language, loyalty to foreign regimes, or dissident political philosophy as grounds for rejection. In Europe, nativist movements were built around core ethnic, racial, and religious traits of peoples who formed early nation-states, which B.R.O Anderson (1983) refers to as "imagined communities." In the US, three branches of Nativism grew from roots planted prior to the Civil War—anti–radicalism, Anglo–Saxon racialism, and anti-Catholicism (Higham 1972, 3–11).

For decades, some human rights groups have suggested—intentionally or not—that White nationalism is practiced primarily by so-called "Extremist" groups, such as White supremacist organizations including the Ku Klux Klan (KKK) and neo-nazis who engage in "hate crimes." We do not find this to be an accurate or useful construct (Whitlock and Bronski 2015; Beyerstein 2015).

The nativist rhetoric directed toward immigrants today derives from the frame used by White nationalists (including the KKK) against Black Americans, warning of the danger posed by uncivilized people of color, the guise of opposition to "illegal immigration" providing more socially acceptable cover. White nationalist xenophobia is central to Donald Trump's message. Referring to Mexico, he said: "They're sending people that have lots of problems and they're bringing those problems with us. They're bringing drugs. They're bringing crime. They're rapists." Consider another quote from 2015: "I have to do it. You rape our women and you're taking over our country. And you have to go." Those are words attributed to White Supremacist Dylann Roof, speaking to the African-American congregants of Charleston's Emanuel African Methodist Episcopal (AME) Church. Roof then produced a handgun and began shooting the participants of a prayer group. In 2017, Roof was convicted on multiple murder and bias crime charges, and was sentenced to death at the recommendation of the jury.

According to African-American history scholar Gerald Horne, the American White supremacist narrative of men of color raping and killing, echoed in Roof's and Trump's rhetoric, was inspired by stories from white refugees fleeing the bloody 1791–1804 slave rebellion in what is now Haiti (Horne quoted in Berlet 2015). Soon American newspapers were full of stories salaciously describing "marauding blacks with sugar cane machetes hacking the white slave-owners to death." Regardless of their veracity, these stories informed a historic narrative that "inspired both slave revolts and a dangerous cycle of slave owner brutality," explains Horne. Inspired by this slave revolt, in 1822, Denmark Vesay of Charleston used the AME church as a base for organizing an unsuccessful insurrection against slavery (Flemming 2009; Fanning 2014). Roof probably was unaware of the specific details of the historically-Black "Mother Emmanuel" church, but he had immersed himself in a White racist narrative tied to Charleston's most famous congregation.

In the aftermath of the Civil War, the founders and early members of the KKK seized upon the frame of Black brutality and White supremacy. Though the formal group "was largely halted following federal legislation targeting Klan-perpetrated violence in the early 1870s," according to David Cunningham (2014), the repression of Black people continued in a variety of guises, from everyday reinforcement of segregation and the "color line," to vigilante violence such as lynching (Douglass 1881). Then in 1905, Thomas Dixon, Jr., wrote *The Clansman: An Historical Romance of the Ku Klux Klan*, later turned into the silent film *The Birth of a Nation*, inspiring a renewed wave of White supremacist violence.

By 1915, the White supremacist frame of Black men pillaging, raping, and murdering was returning to the mainstream, with KKK membership soon "numbering in the millions" (Cunningham 2014). When Klan activity declined again, White people continue to respond violently to Black attempts to change racist structures. In *Confronting the Color Line: The Broken Promise of the Civil Rights Movement in Chicago*, authors Alan B. Anderson and George W. Pickering (2007[1986]) document how an angry white mob physically attacked the Rev Martin Luther King upon his arrival in Chicago in 1966 to lead an open housing campaign, galvanizing a white backlash movement that continues today and echoes in the gunshots in Charleston.

Each time those with a White collective identity felt they were losing power, they embraced a formerly despised group and elevated them to the social status of White people, positioning Blackness as the stable antithesis for Whiteness with other races and ethnicities falling on a spectrum in between. From the late 1880s to 1900s, nativist ideology was spread by White Anglo-Saxon Protestants ("WASPs"), who did not consider the wave of immigrants from Eastern and Southern Europe to be White, including religion and "complexion" among their grounds for exclusion from the category (Fox 2012; Fox and Guglielmo 2012).

There was thus little outcry over the Palmer Raids in late 1919 and 1920, which deported thousands of Italian and Russian immigrants speciously accused of being anarchists or Bolsheviks (Post 1923). Only when White nationalists found them-selves losing numerical power under the existing definition would Eastern and Southern European immigrants become recognized as "White."

According to Zorbaugh "The processes of inclusion and exclusion shaped the formation of white racial identity unevenly but enabled impressive progress toward inclusion among whites of those groups" (1929).

Religion and nativism remained intertwined with the rise of Protestant Fundamentalism, excluding Catholics who were seen as under the control of the Pope and not loyal to America. However, with the shift in concern to "atheist" Communists later in the 20th century, Protestant Fundamentalists would begin the alliances with American Roman Catholics that would undergird the present-day Christian Right umbrella—eventually accepting Mormons as well, who nonetheless continue to hold a precarious outsider role in the coalition.

The problem in the 2016 election cycle is that White nationalism appears to have run out of those it is willing to re-categorize as "White." Sometime near 2050 our nation will be home to a majority of "non-White" people, including Black, Latinx, and Muslim populations. This reality stokes the racist, nativist, and xenophobic fears fanned by Trump and the Republicans.

While abortion and homosexuality were selected by strategists for the emerging Christian Right in the 1970s and 1980s as effective mobilizing issues, according to Randall Balmer, leaders including the late Paul Weyrich (co-founder of the Heri-tage Foundation) admitted that maintaining the tax status of segregated all-White Christian academies was "the primary issue that provided the glue to bind together the troops in the Religious Right." White evangelicals' support for Trump despite his weaker stance on abortion and homosexuality, and despite mainstream evan-gelical leaders' concerns about his family values, draws from the historical inter-twining of White nationalism and Christian conservatism (Viser 2015; Moore 2012).

The Family Research Council's Tony Perkins, who has compared gay rights to the Nazi genocides, explains Trump's appeal: "Here's a guy who is out there unfettered by the political correctness. He's not afraid to say what he thinks. That's attractive."

Much like the adoption of the phrase "religious liberty" in the 1970s to defend Bob Jones University's segregationist policies, conservative discussions of "political correctness" and "free speech" operate as coded language to mobilize the racist and xenophobic base while blocking critiques from the Left. Present-day covert White nationalism also speaks through denunciations of affirmative action as "reverse dis-crimination" and the insistence on their version of "colorblindness":

> King's vision of a colorblind America was about a future utopia. However, conservatives now think King's civil rights movement was an unmitigated success, that the nation is truly colorblind. That [President Obama] (whom they hate) is black is proof of such progress. Conservative colorblindness, then,

ignores the ways in which race continues to handicap a person's chances of success.

(Hartman 2013)

Christian nationalism

Christian nationalists seek to return to an idealized past America founded on devout Christian values. They believe in a revisionist history most prominently promoted by discredited historian David Barton, whose narrative of the Founding Fathers' intentions run contrary to the entirety of historical evidence. A narrative of victimization, in which Christian nationalists see themselves as under attack by secular forces, strengthens the movement by keeping the grassroots mobilized in a constant state of crisis. Trump does not talk about an explicitly "Christian" America, yet Christian nationalists hear that implicitly in his constant pledges to "Make America Great Again." At the Values Voter Summit, a major Christian Right gathering, Trump spoke to a common victimization narrative in pledging to return "merry Christmas" to stores using "happy holidays." This seemingly innocuous language change has been portrayed since 2004 as a "war on Christmas" (echoing an earlier campaign by the conspiracist John Birch Society in 1959), which can only make sense to those who believe that America is a Christian nation and this a direct attack stripping away its identity (M. Goldberg 2007, 162).

The Puritan's Calvinist concept of God's "elect" informed the glorification of America as a "city upon a hill," a beacon of Christian virtue to the rest of the world. Max Weber argued in *The Protestant Ethic and the Spirit of Capitalism* that Calvinism developed in symbiotic relationship with the rise of capitalist economies (1999[1930]). Calvin had asserted under the concept of predestination that only a few were already selected by God as the "elect" and thus headed to heaven, with most people—even most Christians—doomed to Hell.

In the US, most Calvinists stood Calvin on his head and believed that material signs of wealth were proof of that God had chosen you. Early "Calvinists justified their accumulation of wealth, even at the expense of others, on the grounds that they were somehow destined to prosper. It is no surprise that such notions still find resonance within the Christian Right," writes Sara Diamond (1995). Though for most the doctrine of predestination has fallen away, the equation of money with moral status remains, making a virtue of Trump's constant glorification of his own wealth.

Up until the late 1800s, most US Protestants tied the vision of an elect Christian American to their "postmillennial" belief in the apocalyptic End Times prophesied in the Bible (especially the book of Revelation). They believed that Jesus Christ would return only after Christians had converted enough people to establish a Godly Christian society purified and prepared for his triumphant arrival. Michael Northcott explains, "American postmillennial apocalypticism involves the claim that the American Republic, and in particular the free market combined with a form of marketised democracy, is the first appearance in history of a redeemed human society, a truly godly Kingdom" (2002). This is why the Protestants who sought the abolition of slavery in the mid-1800s would sing the Battle Hymn of the Republic, proclaiming, "Mine eyes have seen the glory of the coming of the Lord" (Howe 1862). This phrase meant that they saw the approaching End Times.

Since Postmillennialists believe that they must seize control of secular political intuitions *before* Jesus will return, this makes them committed to political action, but their numbers today are very small due to a revolution in the late 1800s within Protestant theology called "premillennial dispensationalism," the belief that Jesus Christ will return at the beginning of a millennium of godly rule (Marsden 1982; 1991; Ammerman 1998; Armstrong 2002).

When the socially conservative fundamentalist movement emerged after World War I—a backlash against mainline Protestant denominations for their truce with the Enlightenment, science, and evolution—it began to adopt a religious world-view called "premillennial dispensationalism."

Premillennialists, who make up the majority of U.S. fundamentalists and evangelicals, scan the Bible for signs that they believe will appear to indicate the approach of the End Times. Forty-one percent of Americans believe that by the year 2050, Jesus will have returned to take saved Christians to Heaven in the "Rapture" following a period of chaos and destruction that signals the coming End Times (Caldwell 2015).

Then the faithless and wicked left behind on earth will undergo a period of great "tribulations," which include God exterminating those who refuse to convert to Christianity, an interpretation of the End Times popularized by Right-wing Christian leader and best-selling co-author of the *Left Behind* series Tim LaHaye. This increases the urge to convert people to a "born again" form of Christianity and thus save souls before time literally runs out (Martin 1996).

Scorched by the ridicule for their opposition to evolution highlighted in the Scopes "Monkey Trial," many fundamentalists retreated from political and electoral participation until the 1950s, when the Reverend Billy Graham rallied them to resist the communist menace. During the same period, however, there were institution-building initiatives (Worthen 2013). Premillennialists often saw the burgeoning U.S. government apparatus, the spread of Soviet and Chinese communism, and the United Nations as part of the prophesied Antichrist system (Oldfield 2004). This helped bring them into Catholic William F. Buckley's emerging "Fusionist" conservative political coalition.

Premillennialists still remained largely withdrawn from politics until the late 1970s. In 1979, theologian Francis A. Schaeffer began showing his new film, comparing abortion to slavery and the Nazi genocide to Protestant congregations and youth groups to urge them into the anti-abortion movement. While the "prolife" movement was previously overwhelmingly Catholic, evangelicals' embrace of anti-abortion ideology and Buckley's ideas shows how the nativist acceptance of Catholics laid the foundation for future collaboration.

The same year, LaHaye joined a group of emerging New Right leaders to plan a way to mobilize evangelicals into becoming Republican voters, leading to Jerry Falwell's founding of the Moral Majority. On January 1, 1980, LaHaye built on

Schaeffer's theories in *The Battle for the Mind*, a story of a vast secular humanist conspiracy that had seized control of the US government. LaHaye told Premillennialists that they needed to become politically active because there were pre-tribulation tribulations—in other words, true Christians had an obligation to confront sinful society during a crisis of moral values that would come as a test before the Rapture.

Therefore if Christians did not want to be "Left Behind" they had to "regain" control of the political sphere in the United States—which like Postmillennialists they believe was founded as a "Christian Nation." The mobilization and recruitment efforts of the New Right and New Christian Right coalitions with which LaHaye was involved helped elect Ronald Reagan President.

Americans continue to be enthralled by the prospect of an impending apocalypse, including those who do not subscribe to any form of conservative evangelicalism. This influence can be seen in popular culture, from the massively popular *Left Behind* series co-authored by LaHaye, to secular science fiction and zombie shows such as *The Walking Dead*. Sociologist Philip S. Gorski refers to this as a "a secular form of religious nationalism," which he argues also explains why the evangelicals supporting Trump in the primaries were those who tended to attend church less frequently (2016).

Apocalyptic preparations and purchases trend upwards when millennial fears are heightened. Events such as the rise of ISIS and its path of terror are chronicled online in millennialist frames in a "Rapture Index." In 2012, Americans bought up survival shelters in anticipation of the predicted Mayan apocalypse (Allen et al 2012).

The result of LaHaye's writing was theological and eschatological turmoil in evangelical and fundamentalist communities. This launched the tendency called by critics "dominionism;" based on the concept that Christians—no matter what their views on the End Times millennialist schedule—need to take dominion over the earth. There is some confusion and controversy over the difference between the religious movements of "Dominion Theology" and the broader Dominionist tendency within the US Christian Right to pursue control of the secular and political institutions as a mandate from God.

Rushdooney, the "father" of Reconstructionism, also promoted Christian homeschooling movement to remove children from the ungodly secular state and train them for the Christian nation. This ideology underlies another growing conservative Christian movement, Biblical or Christian patriarchy. Christian Patriarchy supports a hierarchal family structure and strict gender roles, which the man at the head of a subservient wife, who is expected to remain at home and bear children. Part of the emphasis on childbearing involves the desire to shift the demographics of America in their favor and bring about a Christian nation through electoral power (Joyce 2010).

Trump's apocalyptic language regarding ISIS, Mexican, and Muslim immigrants, and America's imminent doom trades on this lengthy preoccupation with the End Times.

Heteropatriarchy, male supremacism, and misogyny

In the initial drafting of this article we used the term Heteropatriachy as the heading for this section. Now we see the need to shift to using the terms "male supremacism" and "misogyny" to "highlight the conceptual congruity with White supremacism and racism and a distinction from traditional patriarchalism (DiBranco 2017b). This alteration also recognizes a complex relationship between gender and sexuality, as Right-wing gay men (such as Alt-Right personality Milo Yiannopolous) have used anti-woman sentiment to gain acceptance in typically homophobic White and male supremacist movements (DiBranco 2017b).

Other fundamentalist Christian movements, such as the Promise Keepers, have promoted similar ideologies about appropriate gender roles and male authority, but heteropatriarchy is not the exclusive province of religious ideology (Hardisty 1999).

Familiar comments from Christian Right spokespeople about abortion as baby-killing or homosexuality as equivalent to pedophilia and bestiality have readied conservatives to accept extreme and hateful rhetoric. However, Trump's landslide of sexist, misogynistic, and just plain disturbing rhetoric about women—a mix of sexualization and insults—stands out as unique amongst the Republican presidential candidates.

At a debate in August 2015, moderator Megyn Kelley, a prominent Fox News anchor, took the unusual step of asking Trump how he would respond to charges of being part of the "war on women" as he calls women "fat pigs, dogs, slobs and disgusting animals." Trump responded, to audience cheers, that "the big problem this country has is being politically correct," a demonstration that this phrase operates as coded language for misogyny alongside racism and xenophobia. Trump followed up with degrading criticism of Kelly as a "bimbo," menstruating, and not "pure" (Zimmerman 2015; Richter 2015).

These insults seemed poised to hurt his showing among women, but a poll the following month showed him leading the Republican pack among female voters (Henderson 2015). Historian Catherine Rymph (2006) explains that the exodus of feminism and women's rights advocacy from the GOP means that, among those who are left in the party, "voters, including women, who don't like Democratic feminism or so-called 'political correctness' in general may very well find refreshing Trump's delight in using language about women that many find offensive." Fox News hastened to make peace with this language in light of breaking ratings records.

The Independent Women's Forum (IWF), which promotes a form of libertarian or equity "feminism" that subverts the meaning of the term feminism" by denying the existence of structural inequality against women in the US, understands Trump's appeal among "the people who are most likely to be disgusted with political correctness and a culture of victimhood."

However, IWF, along with Concerned Women for America (CWA), the largest conservative women's organization and one of the biggest Christian Right players, nonetheless voiced significant concerns with Trump and their preference for Carly Fiorina, the only female Republican candidate in 2016.

To the dismay of many Republican women, Trump's popularity demonstrates that the ideology seeded by conservative women's groups no longer remains fully under their control. Equity feminists, informed by a libertarian and in many cases secular ideology, view inequality between men and women as due to women's own choices and differences, also denying the prevalence of sexual and domestic violence against women, while CWA adheres to conservative Christian doctrines on gender and patriarchy.

Conservative women leaders are used as mouthpieces to defend controversial misogynistic policies, resulting in harsh rhetoric that refers to sexual and domestic assault survivors as liars, supporters of rape exemptions for abortion bans as traitors, and disparagement of feminists as seeking unfair advantages in their false claims of victimhood (DiBranco 2017b).

These organizations should not be surprised when women from the Christian and Libertarian Right ignore the female candidate, in favor of a successful man whose spouts familiar misogynistic rhetoric. And many women are willing to ignore this vitriol because they give their support to Trump based on White and Christian nationalist ideologies, or the neoliberal and producerist sentiments the next section will discuss. The late Phyllis Schlafly, a traditional antifeminist infamous for blocking the Equal Rights Amendment in the 1970s, favored Trump's immigration and foreign policy stances, seeing him as America's "last hope" (Hayward 2015).

Though heteropatriarchy often stems from Christian Right ideology, many of the movement's spokespeople have over the years turned to "kinder, gentler"-sounding gendered rhetoric, for instance presenting women as victims and reserving their worst slurs for abortion doctors, as a pragmatic choice for winning over a wider section of the American population. That the rank and file may not follow or recognize this change (especially when screaming at women outside a Planned Parenthood office) They may still benefit Trump's language choices. Direct mail, intended only for supporters, continues to use extremely emotional and fear-mongering rhetoric that motivates donations and actions (Shields, 2009; Godwin and Mitchell 1984).

Yet given that Trump's misogynist rhetoric is largely divorced from traditional moral "family values" issues of abortion and homosexuality (targeting women because he doesn't like their appearance or attitude, or objectifying them in other way) we should also look at the growth of the Men's Rights Movement (MRM) and associated ideologies.

The MRM has been a largely online movement of misogynistic blogs and messaging boards joined by a shared and explicit hatred of feminism and demonstrably of women. The mostly White "manosphere" has Christian members, but seems to be particularly comprised of atheist and secular men (who may be former conservative Christians). Most are influenced by atheist Ayn Rand and the fantasy of "going Galt" (described in the next section on producerism and neoliberalism) (Anderson 2012; Zvan 2014). Men's Rights Activists (MRAs) share a striking resemblance with equity feminist ideology in claiming that not women but men are victim. Some equity feminist women explicitly support the MRA ideology.

However, the Men's Rights Movement has been distinguished by the virulence of its rhetoric. Paul Elam, founder of the most popular MRM site, "A Voice for Men," accuses women who go clubbing of "begging" to be raped. Men's Rights Activists often condemn women's sexual choices and view themselves as entitled to sex, a key tenet of the associated "pick-up artist" community, where men share tips on how to manipulate women into sex.

Trump's apparent belief that all women desire him, and simultaneously are gold diggers who want his money, fits right in. Pick-up artists and MRAs have touted Trump as an example of an "alpha" male, given how "he insults and dominates women, preys on their insecurities and refuses to ever apologize for it" (Clark-Fiory and Cuen 2015). The Red Pill, a prominent MRM community, promoted a video of Trump disparaging a female reporter that opens with their definition of "misogynist": "a person who tells a woman the truth." Like many Trump supporters, MRAs deify the idea of speaking your mind and countering what they call "political correctness."

Trump's online supporters have also popularized the term "cuckservative" in insulting his opponents. A "cuckservative" is "a Republican and/or conservative who is too cowardly to do anything about his country being taken away from him, akin to a man being cuckolded by his wife" (Rozsa 2015). This term is wielded against conservatives who take allegedly "politically correct" stances by criticizing other conservatives for particularly sexist, racist, or otherwise prejudiced remarks. This is an example of how men also use sexism against one another. Trump's bullying appeals to the American heteropatriarchal ideal of masculinity, regularly reinforced by a variety of movements and institutions including anticommunism, warmongering, and antifeminism (Storrs 2015; Critchlow 2005).

Producerism and neoliberalism

The New Right of the 1970s and 1980s not only recruited evangelicals and fundamentalists, but also sought to strengthen the bridge built in the 1950s between traditional moral values Protestant Calvinists and conservative Catholics and the neoliberal laissez-faire "Free Market" advocates in the Republican Party, which included both anti-tax economic conservatives and anti-government libertarians (Himmelstein 1990).

Typical "Old Right" economic theories can be found in the sermons and other writings of the Rev. Henry Ward Beecher. The massive railway strike of 1877 prompted the well-known preacher to warn of alien ideas from Europe being imported into the US by labor unions. Beecher "thought 'un-American' the idea that government should provide for the welfare of its citizens, described collectivist theories as destructive of that 'individuality of the person' that alone preserved liberty, and unabashedly insisted that 'God has intended the great to be great and the little to be little'" (Heale 1990, 28). A network of Old Right industrial and business interests built a national network of cooperating institutions between the late 1800s and Roosevelt's 1930s New Deal. In 1934, the National Association of

Manufacturers (NAM), one of the major collaborative organizations, responded to the New Deal by launching a 13-year, $15 million public relations campaign "for the dissemination of sound American doctrines to the public." Reaching millions of Americans, this propaganda included denouncing labor unions while calling for reductions in the size of government and the number of government regulations (NAM).

Three economists restored the tarnished reputation of Old Right elitist economic theories in a way that could be peddled to the middle class and working class masses: Ludwig von Mises, Friedrich Hayek, and Milton Friedman. Along with old-timer libertarian ideologues including former presidents Herbert Hoover and Robert Taft, and a few "iconoclastic individualists and objectivists like Albert Jay Nock and Ayn Rand," they would lay the foundation for contemporary neoliberal concepts of political economy (Himmelstein 1990, 46).

This provided one of the three major pillars of the 1950s Fusionist coalition. According to Himmelstein, "The core assumption that binds these three elements is the belief that American society on all levels has an organic order—harmonious, beneficent, and self-regulating—disturbed only by misguided ideas and policies, especially those propagated by a liberal elite in the government, the media, and the universities" (Himmelstein 1990, 43–60).

While Rand was an atheist and strongly anti-religion, putting her personally at odds with Buckley and on the fringes of the Right-wing political coalition of the time, her ideology as transmitted by the novels *The Fountainhead* (1943) and *Atlas Shrugged* (1957) achieved massive popularity including within the contemporary Christian Right. Rand's ideology of money as virtue meshes with the emergence of a capitalist Jesus in the suburbs, and her glorification of America and "the highest type of human being—the self-made man—the American industrialist" (Rand 1957). This fits into the Christian and White nationalist images of America. Rand buys deeply into the mythic American Dream; her heroes are successful entrepreneurs, inventors, and businessmen who create value and reject altruism, glorifying money as the foundation of morality and virtue. This form of "Objectivism" tells the privileged that they deserve all they have, and moreover, they are the true victims of a society that tries to leech off their success.

Populist producerism

Objectivist philosophy of the "producers" versus the "looters" and "moochers" looks similar to populist producerism. Populism plays different chords in each sector of the Right—conservative, dissident, and fascist—but the recurring melody is producerism. The producerist frame portrays a noble middle class of hard-working producers being squeezed by a conspiracy involving secret elites above and lazy, sinful, subversive parasites below (Kazin 1995, 35–36, 52–54, 143–44; Berlet and Lyons 2000, 4–6; Canovan 1981, 54). Stock (1996, ix) writes that the two key themes in historic U.S. populist movements are "the politics of rural producer radicalism and the culture of vigilante violence." This idea of "producers" battling "parasites" for the soul of the nation is at the root of fascist ideology (Sternhell, Sznajder, and Asheri 1995[1989]). Producerism is the conspiracist melody that masks the malady of class exploitation. Producerist antisemitism was central to the success of German Nazi ideology in attracting an alienated audience from which to build a mass base. Postone (1986) argues that Nazi scapegoating of Jews centered on the idea that Jews represented parasitic financial capitalism in a battle with productive (and concrete) labor, industry, and technology.

Producerism in other countries and historic periods often links a conspiracy theory of history with xenophobia, racism, and religious bigotry. People can develop different narratives and pick different scapegoats, but the basic paradigm leads to an attack on the evil "parasites" by the noble "producers." The dynamic starts with conspiratorial allegations about parasitic elites (seen as manipulating society) and this leads to anger being directed upwards.

The list of scapegoats among the alleged elite "parasites" can include international bankers, Jews, globalists, socialists, liberal secular humanists, and government bureaucrats. These mythic elite parasites above are described as working in a subversive conspiracy with the parasites below. These "underclass" parasites are often stereotyped as lazy (and thus draining the economic resources of the productive middle), or poisoning the culture with their lack of moral standards or their sinful sexuality (Herman 1997; Berlet and Lyons 2000).

For example Republican Presidential Candidate Mitt Romney referred to the "Makers" versus the "Takers," estimating that the "Takers" comprised 47 percent of the US population—a contention that when it leaked probably helped submerge his candidacy.

Politico's Michael Lind (2015) argued that Trump's Tea Party popularity demonstrated that the movement had been mischaracterized as libertarian when it is Rightwing—reflecting William Jennings Bryan and Huey Long of populist fame, but not Rand—given Trump's support for government services like Medicare.

This is accurate yet misses the actual intertwining of these ideologies by expecting followers to demonstrate too much pure political consistency. Remember the logically inconsistent Tea Party signs to "Keep Government Out of Medicare"? Even Rand accepted Social Security and Medicare when it came to her personal use, and Tea Partiers have also favored paraphernalia referring *Atlas Shrugged* hero John Galt (Heller 2009; Weiss 2012). Political and social movements often do not fit easily into soundbites. Trump benefits also from White Tea Partiers who interpret Rand's novels through a racist lens in seeing a learned "attitude of victimization" among people of color (Weiss 2012).

Trump's lack of empathy for undocumented immigrants and other vulnerable populations, and his pride in his exorbitant wealth, resonates with Americans who buy about half-a-million copies of Rand's books each year. Almost three decades ago, *New York Magazine* began a profile in its list of the top 20 New Yorkers, "If he smoked, Donald Trump would have cigarettes monogrammed with a dollar sign—the symbol of Ayn Rand's hero in *Atlas Shrugged*.

Trump is the quintessential late-eighties realization of the conservative novelist's forties and fifties capitalist supermen" (Smith 1988, 113). Rand herself liked to wear a broach in the shape of a dollar sign (Burns 2009, 259), while until recently the Trump collection at Macy's offered dollar sign cufflinks, which complement that dollar sign charm on his book, *A Pocket Guide to Trump: How to Get Rich*.

It sounds like the story of a Randian hero when the senior editor of the Independent Women's Forum (an "equity feminist" organization supported by the libertarian Koch brothers), writes, "Trump's supporters aren't urban sophisticates ready to weep over the latest tale of victimhood. Like their hero, a real estate guy from Queens, they adhere to the ethos of an older, less sensitive moral culture, and they long for somebody who is focused on winning rather than placating the offended (and may, even more thrillingly, make politically incorrect jabs at his opponents)" (Hays 2015).

Conclusions

Democracy and human rights in the United States face a combined threat. Yet this may also bring more dissenters into a more holistic response. Loretta Ross, a longtime reproductive justice and women's human rights leader, is optimistic about the power vested in intersectional feminist organizing. "Now with the Women's March on Washington using the 'Women's Rights Are Human Rights' call for mobilizations in used in 616 simultaneous marches worldwide, Ross wrote at Rewire in 2017:

> I believe feminists in the United States have finally caught up to the rest of the global women's movement. I feel like celebrating our inevitable progress toward victory for equality, dignity, and justice, despite the reasons we are marching in the first place: to unite to challenge the immoral and probably illegitimate presidency of Donald Trump...
>
> *(2017)*

We end where we began, by insisting that race, gender, and class are inextricably linked in the construction of systems of oppression. All over the world there are people devoted to ending all systems of oppression and building equality, democracy, and human rights for all.

17

FROM FASCIST RATLINES TO REPUBLICAN PARTY POLITICS[1]

How Nazi collaborators came to America

Chip Berlet

Some supporters of the Trump Administration in the United States believe in a vast conspiracy of Democrats, liberals, Leftists, socialists, communists, "homosexuals," (and those nasty non-monogamous heterosexuals) to destroy America from within.

Many of them believe that collectivism, labor unions, all forms of socialism, and environmentalism threaten the very survival of Western Christian Culture. These claims are not new (Johnson 1983, Barkun 2003). Nor is linking these exotic paranoid fantasies to a claim of a global and age-old Jewish or Muslim conspiracy. (Just for the record—these credulous conspiracy theories have no basis in discernable facts.) These conspiracy theories have a long lineage, with false claims about devious Jewish perfidy stretching back generations, as do claims of Muslim savagery.

For most Americans it sounds absurd to claim that "ratlines" brought collaborationist fascist and Nazi emigres to the United States. A "ratline" is a derogatory term for the smuggling of enemy or criminal individuals into a country where most decent citizens would be horrified if the process was made public. Organized crime and government intelligence agencies are the chief practitioners. Let us start with a contemporary example and then jump back to the end of WWII.

President Trump took office in 2017. Trump quickly appointed a man named Sebastian Gorka to be his deputy assistant. Gorka is a militant anti-socialist who has supported far-Right groups in Hungary—that some critics labelled as harbouring

1   This chapter is based in part on research and writing by Russ Bellant, Chip Berlet, Margaret Quigley, and Holly Sklar, some of which was published in different forms in *The Boston Phoenix, CovertAction Quarterly*, and *The Nation Magazine*. In addition, over many years, the following authors sometimes shared information that made our collective ongoing research possible: Frederick Clarkson, Sara Diamond, Jean V. Hardisty, Martin A. Lee, Ruby Sales, James Scaminaci III, Christopher Simpson, Paul Valentine, and several others who prefer to remain off this public list. Some of their work is listed in the references.

antisemitic conspiracy theories. These theories were popularized by the Nazi-collaborationist Hungarian Arrow Cross movement during World War II. Gorka denied all of this. He resigned his post in August 2017.

White racist nationalism, antisemitism, and the Republican Party

The ideological and narrative connection to President Trump in this story is the idea widespread in the Republican Right that socialism is part of a vast conspiracy that threatens the very survival of the "West." And by "the West" many of these folks mean the proper White Christian heterosexual masculinist West (DiBranco and Berlet 2016; DiBranco 2019; Institute for Research on Male Supremacism 2019)

In 2019 similar claims were part of the rhetorical package used by some supporters of President Trump. Jews and Muslims have been demonized by apocalyptic Christians since the First Crusade which began in August 1066 (Cartright 2018). Some Trump supporters stepped over the line into the cesspools of historic racist White supremacy, anti-Islamic myths, and antisemitic conspiracy theories.

The resurrected myth of an age-old Jewish conspiracy bubbled and festered during the Trump candidacy. By 2019 it was an open and overflowing sewer. In the past the chief villains in this fantasy conspiracy were the Rothschild family. In 2018 the named villain was international financier and philanthropist George Soros.

Now we jump to the German Nazi invasion of Hungary in March 1944 and the subsequent mass murder of Hungarian Jews. After World War II, antisemitism remained widespread in Hungary according to the late expert on the Hungarian genocide Randolph Braham (1963: vol. 1-2; interview with author); and the scholar Mary N. Taylor who studies contemporary Hungarian politics and citizenship at the CUNY Graduate Center (interview with author). According to journalist Paul Blumenthal (2017), when Gorka was active in Hungarian Politics, he was:

> closely associated with far-right, antisemitic political parties, including founding his own party with two former members of the openly antisemitic Jobbik party. In 2007, he defended his party's support for the Hungarian Guard, or Magyar Gárda, an antisemitic militia that uses the dress and symbols of the Arrow Cross Party. The Hungarian Guard was later banned by the country's government for its violent and antisemitic actions.

Blumenthal explained the "new far-right European groups and parties that Gorka has participated in are perhaps best known for their bigotry against Muslims. But they also include antisemitic elements and venerate past symbols of native fascist movements that supported the Nazis in World War II."

We have been here before

Back in 1989 journalist Holly Sklar and I attended a showing of the Costa-Gavras film "Music Box" in which a fictional character from Hungary (suggestively named

"Michael Laszlo") is exposed as a World War II war criminal who became a US citizen by masking his activities Nazi collaborationist Hungarian Arrow Cross Party. The movie was fictional but there were plenty of facts to back it up. This is what we wrote in 1989 about a fascist collaborator brought to the United States by one of our own intelligence agency ratlines. This Nazi collaborator was named Laszlo Pastor:

> Arriving in the United States in the 1950s Pasztor eventually joined the Republican Party's "ethnic" campaign outreach unit and proceeded to recruit racists, neofascists, antisemites, and at least one former member of the SS. Pasztor's political career flourished, and by 1987 he, was boasting of his frequent visits to the White House, State Department and Helsinki Commission. Laszlo Pasztor and other former Nazi collaborators were eager to assist U.S. efforts to shape the post-Cold War world, especially in Eastern Europe (Berlet and Sklar 1991).

Pasztor's office in Washington DC was the "Coalitions for America," a project of New Right leader Paul Weyrich's Washington-based Free Congress Foundation (now defunct). The Pasztor-Weyrich-White House relationship was explored in a report on Coors family funding of Right-wing groups, in which author Bellant revealed the close ties between Weyrich and Bush administration officials such as White House Chief of Staff John Sununu (Bellant 1991a, 1991b; Berlet and Sklar 1991).

Pasztor considered himself to be a patriot defending Hungary–and later the United States–from what he saw as the pernicious plague of Marxism. Pasztor died in 2015 at the age of 93. To his death he denied our evidence and claimed innocence.

False conspiracy claims linking Jews and Leftists have a long lineage that traces back not just to Hitler's conspiracy theories about Jews, but similar antisemitic conspiracy theories that mobilized the murders of Jews in a number of European countries going back centuries (Bronner 2003; Cohn 1957; Gow 1997, 1999; Oberman 1984; Smith 1996).

Nazi-collaborationist death squads in World War II Europe

While many Americans are aware of some of the genocidal activities of Hitler's Nazi Germany, less known is the number of European countries where Nazi collaborators murdered Jews.

This is a short list of some of the White nationalist and antisemitic movements with the most sadistic and brutal record of murderers for faith and nation that slaughtered not only Jews but also a wide range of perceived enemies of mythic "pure" racial ethno-religious bloodlines. These were the nation's names during WWII and their murderous Nazi collaborationist squads:

- Belarus: (Belarus Brigade and Byelorussian Auxiliary Police)
- Estonia: (Estonian Security Police)

- Hungary: (Arrow Cross)
- Latvia: (Latvian Auxiliary Police, especially the *Arajs Kommando*)
- Lithuania: (Lithuanian Security Police and Iron Wolf organization)
- Romania: (Iron Guard)
- Ukraine: (Organization of Ukrainian Nationalists (OUN)), especially a specific branch of it known as the Banderas (OUN-B). Also the Ukrainian Auxiliary Police and collaborators with Germany's Nazi Ukrainian Auxiliary *Einsatzgruppe*.
- Yugoslavia: (In what was once Yugoslavia the murders were carried out by the Serbian and Croatian nationalists who, when they weren't busy killing Jews, were killing each other and the Roma.)
- Croatian Nationalists (*Ustaša*)
- Serbian Nationalists (Serbian State Guard)

The United States Holocaust Museum maintains a useful online Holocaust Encyclopaedia at https://encyclopedia.ushmm.org/content/en/article/collaboration. My concern about the term "Holocaust" is that it can tend to mystify and exceptionalize what are more accurately called "Genocidal White Nationalist Mass Killings." These were mass terrorist murders of Jews, Muslims, Roma, dark-skinned peoples, communists, socialists, people in the LGBTQ communities, the infirm and the disabled, among other groups seen as undesirable for the task of creating a White "Master Race." All genocides are grotesque. This is why many progressive researchers refer to the "Nazi Genocides" during World War II.

In Bulgaria there were some notable exceptions during World War II. Otherwise "ordinary" neighbors of some Jews in Bulgaria engaged in passive and active resistance to Nazi collaborationist attempts to send Jews to slave work camps or the death camps. This story is told in an in an extraordinary documentary "The Optimists: The Story of the Rescue of the Bulgarian Jews from the Holocaust" (Comforty 2003). There are many other examples of resistance in countries across Europe. Some people stood up and resisted. We can learn from them. Resistance in *not* futile.

The Nazi-collaborationist ratline after World War II

After World War II the US government decided that to defend itself from what it perceived as a growing threat of global communism led by the Soviet Union. Therefore, they reasoned, it was acceptable (even necessary) to allow thousands of Nazis and Nazi collaborators into the United States.

The story of the recruitment of Nazi collaborationist rocket scientists became known first. It was called "Operation Paperclip" (Jacobsen 2014) Less known was the wholesale recruitment of Nazi collaborators–and even Nazi spies–into the US to assist the CIA and other US intelligence agencies (Lasby 1975; Simpson 1988; Hunt 1985, 1991; Jacobsen 2014, Krim 2018). According to *The New York Times*, "In Cold War, U.S. Spy Agencies Used 1,000 Nazis" (Lichtblau 2014).

Charges of Republican Party official cooperation with antisemites and former Nazi collaborators first started circulating in serious research in the 1960s. One of the first clues was a *Washington Post* article titled "The Fascist Specter Behind the World Anti-Red League" (Valentine 1978).

Almost a decade later a book detailed the scandal: *Inside the League: The Shocking Expose of How Terrorists, Nazis and Latin American Death Squads Have Infiltrated the World Anti-Communist League* (Anderson and Anderson 1986) The book traced connections to contemporary US intelligence agencies and Right-wing Cold War organizations. Despite the diligent research—there was little outcry.

Members of the World Anti-Communist League helped organize "Death Squads." These were mobile killing teams like those the Nazis used during World War II. Similar teams had the "unofficial" backing of the governments in Chile and Argentina and were coordinated in part by agents of and collaborators with US intelligence agencies (Dinges 2005; Kornbluh 2013).

The issue of the former fascist collaborators inside the Republican Party finally surfaced on a national scale during the 1988 presidential campaign, with coverage in *Washington Jewish Week*, the *Philadelphia Inquirer*, and a detailed Political Research Associates report by Russ Bellant: "Old Nazis, The New Right, and the Republican Party (1991b)." Bellant later expanded his research into two 1991 books for South End Press which he has now posted online.

The potentially explosive campaign scandal was quickly short-circuited by the supposed removal of a few overexposed individuals, including Laszlo Pasztor, from the Bush Campaign's National Coalition of American Nationalities. Yet on January 27, 1989, just a few days after Bush's inauguration, Pasztor was among the Hungarian-American leaders invited to a State Department briefing by Mark Palmer, the US Ambassador to Budapest, Hungary. This incident was reported months later in an article by professor Braham … but it was far off the national front pages.

Pasztor helped the Bush White House staff stage an April 1989 briefing on Hungary (Bellant 1991b). Members of the National Security Council reportedly attended the event held at the Old Executive Office Building next to the White House. The White House confirmed the meeting took place (noting that Bush himself didn't attend). The White House stonewalled reporters asking for further information. Pasztor apparently was on the original invitation list but was cut after warnings from other government agencies that Bellant and I (and other researchers and journalists) were tracking Pasztor's invitations and subsequent travels inside Washington, DC.

Following the 1988 campaign exposures numerous Jewish and human rights groups demanded a full investigation. The Republican Heritage Groups Council asked Chiang Kai-Shek booster Anna Chennault, a virulent anti-communist, to oversee a report. Its facile dismissal of allegations was found unacceptable by Republican National Committee Chief Counsel Benjamin L. Ginsberg who warned Chennault that the Heritage Group's continued tie to the Republican Party was "in severe jeopardy."

Meanwhile the former director of the Office of Special Investigations of the US Department of Justice called Bellant's book "well documented and reliable."

The *Harvard Educational Review* wrote that Bellant exposes:

> ...the roots and growth of domestic fascist networks, which include Nazi collaborators, within the Republican Party. He reveals how such members, during the Reagan era, held positions of power on the Republican Ethnic Heritage Groups Council, an ethnic outreach division of the GOP. Bellant also scrutinizes the American Security Council for its participation in anti-semitic and racist practices under the guise of anticommunism.

The Anti-Defamation League's national office in New York City, however, refused to confirm Bellant's research and told some reporters to ignore Bellant's meticulously researched and footnoted book. Several senior ADL staff outside of the New York offices later privately apologized to me and distanced themselves from the increasingly anti-Left histrionics of ADL fact-finding director Irwin Suall. One Midwest senior ADL official told me that it seemed that the New York National Office was more interested in helping Mossad track Leftists than pursuing ADL's original mandate.

Spying on the Left

In 1993 the Anti-Defamation League became ensnared in a national scandal when news broke that the organization was involved in illicitly sharing spy files on Left-wing activists with a secret network of police and Right-wing groups (Ames 2014; Crew 1993; Friedman 1993a, 1993b). Kim Malcheski (n.d.) wrote an extensive research memo for the litigation against the spy ring titled: "Summary of the 700+ pages released by the San Francisco District Attorney's office regarding spying activities of R. Bullock, Fact Finder for the Anti-Defamation League and Tom Gerard, retired police officer from the San Francisco Police Department." Writing in the *Village Voice*, Robert L. Friedman (1993) warned that "The Anti-Defamation League is Spying on You." *The New York Times* solicited an Op-Ed by Dennis King and me condemning ADL's rampant spying on Leftists and pro Palestinian groups.

We submitted the piece, which they headlined "The A.D.L. Under Fire: It's Shift to Right Has Led to Scandal." Unbeknownst to us, the *Times* had held the bottom of the page for a denunciation of King and me from ADL leadership in New York City suggesting we were aiding antisemitism. It bore headline "It's a Big Lie, Hailed by antisemites." King and I went on to write a longer study of ADL's failures published in *Tikkun magazine* (1993).

To this day, the ADL does not adequately hold the Republican Party accountable for its long flirtation with fascists. And ADL fails to hold President Trump to the same standard by which the ADL national office judges some Democratic Party elected officials and candidates. Despite this there are still many ADL employees inside of and outside of the national office who remain loyal to the organization's original mandate: "To stop the defamation of the Jewish people, and to secure justice and fair treatment to all."

Trump's venomous speech causes scripted violence

When a well-known person denounces a specific group of people as not deserving full citizenship and threatening the nation, the result can be a violent act against any person seen as being in the targeted group. How do we know this?

Sadly, the answers emerge from the horrific mass murders in Europe in the 20th century and the role of mass media in speeding information to a large audience. The awful outcome of this process was made manifest in late October 2018 when 11 Jews at a religious service at a historic synagogue in Pittsburgh, Pennsylvania were killed by a gunman who believed Internet conspiracy theories falsely claiming they were part of a plot against American interests. There were many injuries and our nation grieved. Yet not enough attention was paid to the process of demonization and scapegoating in mass media that painted targets on the back of the victims.

As consumers of mass media, we as a society take time to adjust to new forms of information dissemination and how to judge it.

The classic example came from outer space! In 1938 Orson Welles produced a radio program based on the early science fiction book *War of the Worlds*, by British author H. G. Wells, which first was serialized in magazines 1897. Some people hearing the "radio play" thought it was a live news broadcast and began calling police and other emergency forces asking how to escape for battling the attack from outer space. Yes, we laugh now, but don't be smug. There are a lot of us on this planet who have yet to adjust to the Internet as an information source.

Scholars theorizing about how mass media information can lead to violence sometimes start with the genocide of the Armenian people begun during the First World War in what is now Turkey. The scope of the murders during that genocide was enabled by the mass media network of the telegraph. This communication medium not only allowed false, derogatory, and inflammatory information to be spread throughout a vast geographic area by rumor, and being mentioned in newspaper articles, but also directed the killing machinery of the military seeking the expulsion or elimination of the targeted Armenian population.

In Germany in the 1920s it was radio reports and newsreel films that joined newspapers as mass media spreading lies about Jews, Leftists of all stripes, and other targets of Adolph Hitler's venom.

The year 1933 saw Hitler's mass media propaganda coordinator, Joseph Goebbels, turning radio into the tool of the Nazi Party for broadening its political base and its targets. According to Goebbels, "What the press has been in the Nineteenth Century, radio will be for the Twentieth Century." Radio broadcasts fuelled the genocidal murders in Germany and more than a dozen other countries in Europe.

Television was the new media platform in the early 1960s when an egomaniacal and histrionic Senator Joseph McCarthy of Wisconsin was broadcast on the new media called television. McCarty was holding hearing on persons and organizations alleged to be a threat to the United States because of their participation in a range of political and cultural groups in which socialists and communists were said to be active—and sometimes held leadership position. Persons protesting these hearings were physically attacked. In one famous incident in May of 1960, police used fire hoses to sweep angry students down the steps of City Hall in San Francisco where a hearing was being held by the House Committee on Un-American Activates (dubbed HUAC in popular prose).

Today the new mass media platform is the Internet. These days, any high profile and popular figure can reach tens of millions of people. The technology is new, but the process of blaming scapegoats for societal problems remains the same. Some people with targets painted on their backs by malicious verbal falsehoods end up injured or killed.

The ringleaders of these sorts of attacks are called "demagogues" (Roberts-Miller 2017). Demagogues can be engaged in politics, religion, or entertainment as long as they are known by a large segment of a population through mass media. Before World War II the basis for this analysis emerged from what is called the "Frankfurt School" of social science research. This explains the December 5, 2016 headline in the *New Yorker Magazine*: "The Frankfurt School Knew Trump Was Coming" by Alex Ross.

As Ross explains, several "frankfurters" (as graduate students gleefully call them over beers), moved to the United States. In 1950 two of them, Max Horkheimer and Theodor W. Adorno, wrote a study on *The Authoritarian Personality*.

Ross explains how the authors:

> …constructed a psychological and sociological profile of the "potentially fascistic … individual." The work was based on interviews with American subjects, and the steady accumulation of racist, antidemocratic, paranoid, and irrational sentiments.

Timothy Snyder is a professor at Yale University who was moved by the ascent of Donald Trump to write a booklet titled *On Tyranny: Twenty Lessons from the Twentieth Century*. Snyder explains these processes are not new. "Aristotle warned that inequality brought instability, while Plato believed that demagogues exploited free speech to install themselves as tyrants."

In the United States today there are White Nationalist demagogues who defend racial inequality by claiming White people are the real "producers" of the wealth of the nation but are being dragged down by a heavy anchor of the "parasitic" non-White, or immigrant "undeserving poor." This caricature of political economy is called "producerism" by scholars. The "producerist" narrative is a form of rhetoric found in exclusionary racial and religious nationalist movements taking over governments around the world. This frame is also used by top Republican activists and candidates.

When authoritarianism is mixed with Right-wing populist rhetoric promoting racial nationalism by a demagogic leader it can be a core building block for the crafting of fascist social movements. Fascism is the most militant and aggressive form of Right-wing populism. There are already too many victims of this failure by the major US media outlets to hold Trump accountable for fanning the flames of fear, abuse, and violence.

18

THE PATRIOT MOVEMENT, ARMED INSURGENTS, AND TRUMPISM[1]

Spencer Sunshine and Chip Berlet

Kazin (1995) supplies the backstory to "Patriot" movements in his book *The Populist Persuasion*, which identifies populism as a rhetorical style. Diamond (1995) notes their rootedness in "Americanist" motifs. Stock calls these activists "Rural Radicals," and suggests that this form of "righteous rage" is "in the American grain." According to Stock, the two key aspects of such movements are "the politics of rural producer radicalism and the culture of vigilante violence" (Stock 1996). Both Kazin and Stock highlight the concept of "producerism," as does the book *Right-Wing Populism in America* (Berlet and Lyons 2000). These concepts have appeared previously in this volume.

Republican Presidential candidates Mitt Romney in 2008 and Donald Trump in 2016 both used producerist frames during their campaigns (Gupta and Fawcett 2012).

We draw distinctions among different sectors and activities of the US Right, as suggested by Durham (2000) and other scholars. This not only helps to analyze these diverse movements, but also allows for strategic and tactical plans to counteract their bigotry and aggression. Contemporary US Right-wing populist movements in the United States are clustered into two models of activism.

---

1   This chapter is adapted from a major study published by the Journal of Peasant Studies in 2019.

Extracted from "Rural rage: The roots of right-wing populism in the United States," in the Journal of Peasant Studies, Volume 46, 2019, Issue 3; as part of the global Forum on Authoritarian Populism and the Rural World series. Online at https://www.ta ndfonline.com/doi/full/10.1080/03066150.2019.1572603.

Both authors have attended numerous events of the Patriot and Militia movements over many years and reported on them as journalists.

Partisan political activism in support of Right-wing politicians in the Republican Party and some smaller Right-wing political parties and groups.

Insurgent political and social movements, which are suspicious of both the Republican and Democratic parties, and believe the current government might be controlled by subversive and treacherous elites.

In this latter insurgent group, many social movement activists may either vote for the most militant Right-wing politicians in the Republican Party, vote for third party candidates, or abstain from voting. Most of their political activism is tied to their participation in Right-wing social movements. The term "insurgent" means people or groups that vigorously challenge the status quo in ways ranging from peaceful protests to disruptive actions. They can be militant reformists or revolutionaries in terms of ideology; some, but not all, are armed. When we refer to a broad "Patriot" movement in the United States, it should be noted that many, but not all, of the participants are armed insurgents.

Militant armed vigilantism by White insurgents has been a recurring reality in the United States, starting with the colonial Bacon Rebellion in 1676, and continuing after independence with the 1791 Whisky Rebellion during George Washington's presidency. In our view, the United States was founded on White nationalism, and remains mired in that modality. Organized "White supremacist" groups are the most violent example of this fact. Openly "White supremacist" groups such as the Ku Klux Klan and neonazi units continue to exist. Historically, armed White insurgents have held White supremacist or White nationalist views that varied in intensity. From a social movement perspective, we find it useful to draw a distinction between organized White Supremacist organizations and the Patriot movement.

Patriot movement groups in the United States are united by a common political fixation: a radical, Right-wing interpretation of the Constitution that derides federal power and is hostile to "Big Government"—especially environmental regulations and progressive taxation. This is framed in a way that enflames pre-existing White Christian nationalism including anti-immigrant xenophobia; as well as gender panics promoted within the Christian Right with its obsession with Godly patriarchy and opposition to gay men and lesbians, as well as others who step outside the norms of Right-wing Christian evangelicalism and fundamentalism.

William Potter Gale in California developed the theory of the US government was controlled by a secret cabal operating outside the "real" constitutional laws of the United States (Levitas 2002; Zeskind 2009). Gale's complex conspiracy theory forged an armed insurgent Right-wing movement known as the "Posse Comitatus." This concept—which in Latin means "power of the county"—is derived from the ability of a county sheriff to assemble a unit of armed citizens to track down and arrest law breakers. Thus, the cliché in Hollywood movie "Westerns" of the sheriff and the "posse" chasing down the "varmints." (This latter term is a variant of the word for "vermin" (Online Etymology Dictionary 2017). Gale's proposal went further, however; he claimed that county sheriffs could decide what laws were Constitutional. And if the sheriff did not agree with the Posse

Comitatus's creative reading of the Constitution, group members could take the law into their own hands.

Reasons for the revitalization of the Patriot movement in 2016–2017 included:

- The continuing downward mobility of many Americans that followed the 2008 economic collapse.
- The federal bank bailouts and economic stimulus package, which favored investors and the wealthiest in the nation.
- Growing anger and alienation focused on an alleged parasitic underclass which Republican Presidential Candidate Mitt Romney in described as a "majority of takers versus makers in society."
- The rise of the Tea Party and Sarah Palin's candidacy for vice president in 2013, which knocked a substantial part of the Republican Party off its regular political moorings.
- A more general climate of anti-Black racism, Islamophobia, and anti-immigrant xenophobia.

Other grievances included the alienation of Right-wing populists from the neoconservative wing of the Republican Party. Issues included the neoconservatives' aggressive foreign policies (as exemplified by the Afghanistan and Iraq wars and occupations), commitments to transnational free trade agreements, and increasing acceptance of LGBTQ rights and legal abortion.

Today's Patriot movement has distanced itself from Christian Identity and other openly racist groups. Correspondingly overt anti-Black racism and antisemitism are largely discarded buried deep underneath; instead have been supplanted by the more socially acceptable Islamophobia. Because of this change, the Patriot movement is more easily able to dodge accusations of White supremacy and antisemitism that damaged the reputations of the 1990s militias.

The idea that the United States is heading for an economic or political collapse due to Left-wing conspiracies is widespread in the Patriot Right, Christian Right, and white supremacist movements. The result is a "subversion panic" which impels countersubversion movements. This fear-based conspiracist narrative, which spreads through both rural and urban areas, is enhanced and exploited by survivalist supplies vendors, Right-wing investment firms, and vendors of bulk gold and silver. Right-wing AM radio and internet demagogues push these themes and frequently feature advertisers selling survivalist items (Hodai 2011). In some Christian Right congregations, the pastor's sermon warns of the coming prophetic religious apocalypse and the need to prepare. This feeds into discussions of liberal treachery and the need for survival stockpiles that flavors the post-sermon coffee hour.

Obama nation

The most obvious spark that started the prairie fire of the Patriot's wrath was the election of a Black man, Barack Obama, as President of the United States in 2008.

This generated a maelstrom of conspiracy theories on the Right about collectivist treason and fears of impending totalitarian "Big Government" totalitarianism. They, in turn, merged with existing White nationalism and prejudice against Muslims, Mexicans and other Latin American immigrants, and other groups identified by white racist groups as "not really belonging" in America. In addition, conspiracy theories linking Obama to Satan's plans in the Millennial "End Times" spread across US Christian evangelical movements. One pollster was startled to find that 15 percent of voting Republicans in New Jersey were "unsure" whether or not President Obama might be the prophetic "Antichrist" who attempts to establish global Satanic rule—but another 14 percent were sure of it (Public Policy Polling 2009).

Patriot movement revives

The revived Patriot movement at first focused on recruiting returning veterans, as well as from the increasingly aggressive gun culture. This was fostered by the histrionic propaganda claiming that the Obama administration was planning to ban private firearm ownership. The Patriot movement had long a political outlier on a national level, although in the western US states its ideas had gained some traction in local and state governments. But under the Obama administration, the Patriot movement spread like poisonous mushrooms.

A widely publicized example of an armed anti-government Patriot Movement confrontation involved the Patriot movement activists who in 2014 rallied to the defense of rancher Cliven Bundy near the aptly named town of Bunkerville, Nevada (Egan 2014).

> The confrontation pitted heavily armed federal agents at the gates of corrals where several hundred Bundy cattle had been rounded up, against men with assault rifles on an Interstate 15 overpass and hundreds of protesters in a dry riverbed below.
>
> *(Egan 2014)*

The cattle were being removed from public lands, the use of which required Bundy to pay a grazing fee; which Bundy had refused to do for years (Egan 2014). The relaxed law enforcement demeanor in Nevada stood in marked contrast to the aggressive and sometime brutal treatment of unarmed black people protesting police shootings after an incident in Ferguson, Missouri, and other cities.

The 2016 presidential election

A sense of unease over the future of the United States was prevalent during the 2016 presidential election. As a Presidential candidate, Donald Trump was a major purveyor of the "Birther" allegations that Obama was not born in the United States and/or was not a citizen; as well as a continuing irritation from the Right with having a liberal Black president.

On January 2, 2017, an armed band—led by Cliven Bundy's sons Ammon and Ryan Bundy, alongside Arizona rancher LaVoy Finicum, a family friend—seized the Malheur National Wildlife Refuge headquarters outside of remote Burns, Oregon. While the initial occupiers were almost entirely from out-of-state, they had been drawn to Oregon partly by the state's vibrant, armed Patriot movement. The occupation lasted 41 days. The initial issue involved two local ranchers who had received unusually stiff sentences under a terrorism act for arsons that burned federal land. Soon, however, the occupiers started to demand that the federal government relinquish the refuge lands entirely (Sunshine 2016).

With Donald Trump's immigrant bashing, rabid Islamophobia, misogyny, bellicose ultra-nationalism, authoritarianism, and embrace of conspiracy theories, the mainstream of the Republican Party—and its base—has shifted dramatically to the Right (Altemeyer 2016; DiBranco and Berlet 2016). This has popularized and spread the views of the Patriot Movement and created a fertile organizing climate both for the movement and many other Right-wing populists. And while the Patriot movement's tactics are still fringe, its ideas are steadily inching toward center stage in the political drama in the United States.

19

TRUMP, SADO-POPULISM, ALT-RIGHT, AND APOCALYPTIC NEOFASCISM

Chip Berlet

Donald Trump went to high school with my brother at New York Military Academy in the 1960s. A few years ago, the original school closed and was sold to new owners. Today NYMA has changed dramatically into a more well-rounded educational facility that admits both young men and young women.

Back in the 60s, however, NYMA was an "old-school" all-male military academy. On the baseball team Donald Trump was a pitcher (NYMA class of 1964), and my brother a catcher. According to my brother's assessment Trump was "really good at baseball … but not very smart … and also a jerk and a bully."

Before he died my brother would regale friends and family with stories of the hijinks carried out by the NYMA cadets. Such as claiming cadets built a radio transmitter device to make the metal plate surgically implanted in one teacher's head buzz like a swarm of bees—or stuffing the barrel of the ceremonial cannon with junk so that when it was fired at the weekly full-uniform parade the garbage rained down on the local town. Even if these stories are apocryphal, it says something that resonates with us today.

We expect some high-school students would think that sadistic tricks are funny. We also hope they eventually mature into adults. NWMA (like some other all-male boarding schools in the 1950s and 1960s), was a safe space for ultra-masculinist manoeuvres. My brother confirmed that some cadets, like the proud boys-to-men they were, kept written lists of the names of the women with whom they had sex. Some of the more sadistic older cadets coerced younger boys into performing sexual acts on them.

According to Yale professor Timothy Snyder, President Trump functions as a "sado-populist … whose policies were designed to hurt the most vulnerable part of his own electorate." Trump voters feel real pain with Trump as President of the United States, explains Snyder, but based on Trump's demeaning rhetoric toward despised "Others" Trump supporters can "fantasize" that their "leader of choice" will hurt their "enemies" even more than they themselves (2018, 272).

Who are the real enemies of the United States of America? That's the main question being debated in the US political right. We know their enemies list from Internet posts, AM talk radio, and Fox News (Neiwert 2008, 2017). And we know these themes have deep roots in developing "The American Character and its Discontents" which feature "God, Guns, Gold, and Glory" (Langman and Lundskow 2016). We also know "How Democracies Die" (Levitsky and Ziblatt 2018).

Analyzing Donald Trump therefore requires enumerating the various ideological, political, and social factions in the remarkable coalition Trump commanded as their free-floating signifier in the Presidential election of 2016. Trump's supporters do not ignore what Trump says in his speeches and tweets, they reframe the content on-the-fly to meet their pre-conceived expectations. Trump is an online militarist "prefigurative space" cadet.

In our 2016 study, doctoral candidate Alex DiBranco and I discussed the nature of Trump's four core ideological constituencies:

- White nationalism,
- Christian nationalism,
- heteropatriarchy and masculinism, and
- neoliberal "Free Market" enthusiasm.

DiBranco and I chose not to discuss militarism and several other electoral constituencies common in US elections because they span both major parties. The leaders of Trumps four core ideological tendencies were convinced they would outmaneuver the Trump Administration into blessing their specific political and religious wish list above all others. The four core constituencies continued to expand their manoeuvres at least until late 2019 when this book went to press. Outlier groups supportive of Trump still include the diverse Alt-Right movement, which interacted openly with White supremacists, antisemites, neofascists, and neonazis.

Donald Trump is the product of a childhood immersed in White racist nationalism, and the sneering smug elitism of the wealthiest 1 percent. His years as a teenager at New York Military Academy honed his militarism, masculinism, and misogyny – the three M's of male antisocial authoritarian aggression. This is very similar to the core ethos of the contemporary Alt-Right movements and groups.

Trump and Alt-Right

Emerging as a loose amalgam of online self-impressed bullies, Alt-Right grew into an organic and eclectic media environment that transformed into a street-fighting force and eventually an actual social movement. Alt-Right is the home for men and boys longing for their lost hegemony over all other people in American society—even if this desire is re-created in a fantastic reality drawn from comic book characters an film heroes.

Alt-Right mushroomed into a poisonous cloud spewing anti-Left propaganda (Neiwert 2017). Its basic thrust is aimed at collapsing democracy and human rights in the United States on behalf of Right-wing economic and political elites. Its voice is that of macho male gasbags polluting the public sphere with self-aggrandizing masturbatory messages. Alt-Right is an amorphous online network of primarily-unaffiliated news and messaging outlets using both traditional internet platforms, but especially emphasizing social media such as Twitter and more obscure and hidden posting sites. Persons who consider themselves activists in the extended Alt-Right communities, which include like-minded women, are the new Brownshirts.

In the *pot au feu* ingredients simmering in the Alt-Right toxic stewpot, critics have tasted the influence of Oswald Spengler, Julius Evola, Willis Carto, Alain de Benoist, Richard Spencer, and even a deadly nightshade herbal sprig of Hitlerian rhetoric. These influences have been sanitized and served up by a range of right-wing institutions considered mainstream by many in the corporate media. Let's be clear: Alt-Right is an example of the morphing into public respectability of neo-fascist ideologies in the United States since Trump took office.

One highly concise and accurate definition of Alt-Right comes from a main-stream weekly news magazine specializing in digesting the news:

> It's a weird mix of old-school neo-Nazis, conspiracy theorists, anti-globalists, and young right-wing internet trolls — all united in the belief that white male identity is under attack by multicultural, "politically correct" forces.
>
> *(The Week 2017)*

A key figure behind the creation of Alt-Right was Steve Bannon who gained fame as a pit bull at the rabidly right-wing Breitbart News website. Bannon became a top advisor to Republican Presidential candidate Donald Trump (Wilson 2017). A Bannon-affiliated stealth propaganda-generating media company had been hired by Trump aides to surreptitiously suppress voter turnout for Democratic Presidential nominee Hillary Clinton as part of a strategy funded by a snake pit of billionaire donors (Morris 2016; Gold 2016; Cadwalladr 2017; Grassegger and Krogerus 2017). Russian intelligence agencies also gave Trump a helping hand.

While Alt-Right's technology is new, its ideological baggage has been carried by right-wing political and social movements for many decades. The trail we are following eventually traces back to the founding of the new nation by patriarchal Christian men who built White nationalist capitalism over the mass graves of the indigenous peoples and enslaved Black Africans.

A key innovation of Alt-Right is that being a gay man is acceptable if he is willing to verbally brutalize women—especially feminists, lesbians, and non-binary gender identified persons (DiBranco 2017). Physically harming women is celebrated within Alt-Right, whose followers stoop to issuing threats of violence (DiBranco 2017). Critics of Alt-Right are also threatened. One Alt-Right supporter was arrested for assault after intentionally sending Alt-Right critic Kurt Eichenwald (a well-known journalist with epilepsy), an online message that, when opened, displayed flashing strobe lights that caused Eichenwald to suffer a seizure (Weil 2017).

This sadistic viciousness was modelled by candidate Trump when he publicly and on-camera made fun of a senior *New York Times* investigative reporter, Serge F. Kovaleski, by making supposedly-funny crippled-hand gestures mimicking the congenital joint condition of the highly-respected journalist who is disabled physically and works from a wheelchair (Arkin 2017). One 2016 poll of likely voters found Trump's mocking gestures were his worst offense as a potential Republican candidate (Carmon 2017) Trump's core supporters cheered Trump on.

In terms of sociological frames and narratives, Alt-Right gives voice to the rhetoric of right-wing populism that is fuelling Trumpian phenomenon (Berlet 2016, 15:2–3) Revisiting the core elements of right-wing populism, we see that they are congruent the main Alt-Right playlist (Canovan 1981, 46–51, 179–190; Kazin, 1995; Berlet and Lyons 2000; Lyons 2018). Alt-Right is a fascistic social and political movement.

The building blocks of fascist movements

Historic fascist social and political movements are composed of a constellation of interlocking elements of which the following are the main components:

- authoritarian political and/or religious leaders;
- exclusionary racial, religious, ethnic, or gender nationalisms;
- use of populist rhetoric by respected leaders turned demagogues;
- framing the named scapegoats as despised "Others";
- demonizing designated "Others" as "Outsiders" that are unfit for citizenship;
- conspiracy theories of subversion and treason from above and below;
- apocalyptic or millenarian claims of threats to the "real" nation;
- narratives prompting "scripted violence" against the scapegoats.

How Alt-Right uses the above components to build a mass movement

To understand how provocateurs in the Alt-Right conglomeration reach a mass popular audience, one needs to understand how the above elements are weaponized in cyberspace spread reactionary messages and ideas. The social science here was clearly established after the Nazi genocides but are today seldom reported in the corporate media.

Here is a list of some of the specific processes used in cyberspace. It was first published in the journal *Logos* in early 2019:

> **Tropes:** Rhetorical devices used in a figurative manner such as in metaphors or puns or even illustrations to convey a mental image that conveys a meaning—often with considerable baggage—especially within a biased target audience online.
>
> **Memes:** A repeated phrase or image—usually with a clear message such as in a trope—that is shared across cyberspace in a self-replicating manner by online

users who distribute the message without encouragement so that it spreads like an atomic reaction.

Dog Whistles: Phrases that can be interpreted differently by different audiences, with some people not hearing any content at all. When a person hears a phrase in the form of a trope they may insert into the message the identity of their favorite loathed enemy target group. For example, when Trump talked about the "international banks," farmers and ranchers in Oregon probably thought "Wall Street," while antisemites heard "Jews," and other conspiracists might have detected a reference to the Freemasons or reptilian aliens. Tropes and memes assist the use of "dog whistles" by political candidates and organizers. Pat Buchanan is a master of the rhetorical form by which he masks his quasi-fascist ideas.

Astroturf Movement: A fake grass-roots movement funded by political elites but without an actual mass base. The term is borrowed from the commercial brand of artificial grass. The Tea Party Movement started as an *Astroturf Movement* but eventually emerged as an actual mass-based social and political movement (Barsamian 2010; Scher and Berlet 2014).

Manosphere: Websites and other sectors and sections of online media targeting "manly" men who complain about women, often in crude and violent language, that makes the term "misogynist" seem inadequate to capture the viciousness of the tropes and memes (DiBranco and Berlet 2017).

Trolling: Posting text and messages intentionally worded and designed to antagonize opponents in such a way that they will overreact, and then can be further antagonized and mocked for their intemperate response. Based on the fishing term for dragging a hooked line through a school of fish in the hope that at least one will be attracted to "bite" on the live bait or artificial lure.

Gamergate: The term used by pro-feminist critics to describe the online *Krystalnacht*, launched by misogynist manospheric men to bully and attack women programmers to force them out of the computer game programming industry—especially women who developed alternatives to splashing blood and guts across computer screens.

The masculinist core of the right-wing backlash is too often understated. DiBranco (2017, 2019) explains that Trump's sexist comments about women in general "energized members of a secular misogynist Right" including the so-called men's rights movement which rose in the 1990s, as well as the more recent Gamergate and the rise of Alt-Right. She notes there was "no pushback against Trump's rhetoric and policy plans from "a brand of conservative, libertarian" feminist groups which emerged in the 1990s which DiBranco says "provides a dangerously legitimizing female face for misogynist ideology centered on overt hostility to women and the promulgation of rape culture" According to DiBranco's research, it is through highly provocative cyberspace posts that:

> ...misogynist personalities such as Mike Cernovich, associated with the pick-up artist community, and Milo Yiannopoulos, a Brietbart writer, expanded

their online following, to be leveraged in future attacks on feminism and women. Yiannopoulos had over 300,000 Twitter followers at the time the social media platform finally banned him for offensive content in 2016.

In March of 2017 Yiannopoulos, who identifies as a gay man, had more than "1.9 million Facebook likes and 568,000 subscribers on YouTube" (DiBranco 2017). Meanwhile, Christian masculinist White Nationalism is being exported around the world in campaigns to block abortion rights and deny rights for those who identify as part of the LGBTQ communities (Hardisty and Berlet 2011; Berlet 2011).

Bannon, Yiannopoulos, Ann Coulter appeared to be among the many stars in a fictitious remake of Leni Reifenstahl's propaganda documentary for the German Nazis "Triumph of Will" featuring Trump's apparently inadvertent parodies of Hitler. It is unclear if Alt-Right will ever transform into an actual mass-based political or social movement, but it draws from deep roots. The claims that Alt-Right is a new phenomenon within Republican Party politics, however, ignores a clear pattern of flirting with White supremacy, antisemitism, and theocratic Christian nationalism with its baggage of Islamophobia, patriarchal and masculinist anti-feminism, and vicious misogyny.

What is crucial to understand for the future of democracy is that the media environment has shifted into a new dimension in which the very concept of a "fact" is being challenged, and this is being exploited by Trump's handlers who smash conventional media traditions with ease. The tactic of using right-wing populist rhetoric as a tool for serving up greed globally is gutting democracies like a bloody basket of Russian sturgeon. Writing in the *Chronicle of Higher Education* in September 2018, Jason Stanley observed that:

> …in recent years, several countries across the world have been overtaken by a certain kind of far-right nationalism; the list includes Russia, Hungary, Poland, India, Turkey, and the United States.

In addition, there is emerging internationally some sort of traditionalist religious coalition backed by organizations in the United States and Russia that may also involve an expansive view of racial or cultural Whiteness. Ruby Sales (2019) has studied how conservative Christian dominionists in the United States are building close ties with conservative Russian Orthodox activists around the issues of opposing abortion and gay rights. The actual leadership and attendance at its meetings is remarkably White.

This global network promoting theocratic nationalism was forged in the United States as the "World Congress of Families." It has now been renamed as the "International Organization for the Family" (Hardisty and Berlet 2012; Berlet 2018). This effort was first field-tested by White right-wing Christians exporting their homophobia to Uganda in Africa (Kaoma 2014; 2018).

Christian dominionism, apocalyptic expectations, and conspiracy theories

Global "Christian dominionism" is a religious-political movement that not only seeks to make America a "Christian nation" but wants to convert millions around the world before Jesus returns in triumph to Jerusalem's Temple Mount (and then in the dominionist script an angry God wipes out all non-believers).

Matt Rothschild (2003), then editor of the *Progressive* magazine, looked at how President George W. Bush mixed religious and secular apocalyptic and millennial themes, and pronounced them a form of "messianic" militarism:

> Bush, a Methodist, but also a born-again evangelical, probably does not believe in the Rapture or the idea that the End Times are close at hand, but he and his handlers know how to speak to that audience…
>
> *(Rothschild 2003).*

The "dominionist" Christian Right in the United States is a closed information system whose leadership believes in a literal struggle against satanic powers. This has prompted some Republican political candidates to drop hints in Biblical code. For example, when devout Christian evangelicals and fundamentalists say that their struggle is against "principalities and powers" they are saying that Democrats are "agents of Satan."

Dualistic apocalyptic narratives long ago slipped away from American Christian religious theology and began to influence religious and secular belief systems and ideologies in Europe and the United States. Christian dominionism is explained later in this edited collection which follows several increasingly brutal and murderous trends in a chronological order and written at the time when the authors were studying the trend.

According to Lahr (2007) the Cold War spawned the rise of a form of "political evangelicalism" rooted in Bible-based prophetic "Millennial Dreams and Apocalyptic Nightmares" of a battle between good and evil. Now some of Trump's handlers craft language that is familiar to the religious and secular alike, but is interpreted very differently by each group.

Apocalyptic millenarianism (admittedly a mouthful) is embraced in the United States today by far more people than identify themselves as born-again Christian evangelicals and fundamentalists. It has morphed into a secular version peculiar to the United States represented by books such as "Moby Dick", the movies "High Noon" and "Apocalypse Now," television series such as "Buffy the Vampire Slayer" and many more.

This version of the Christian apocalypse seeps into our brains as schoolchildren studying American classics. Through this process, we as a nation absorb phrases and images from the Christian Bible.

As the millennial "End Times" wrap up, there appear "the four horsemen of the apocalypse," and some people "behold a pale horse" representing death. God punishes the sinful and unbelievers with his "terrible swift sword," while some 144,000 Jews convert to Christianity at the last minute. Then the rest of the Jews (and everyone else who are not "real" Christians) have their bodies crushed as in "stamping out a vintage" like the "grapes of wrath" with their blood flowing as a river down past Mount Megiddo in Israel (aka Armageddon). Then their souls are cast into the sulphurous fires of Hell while the righteous "inherit the Earth" as the wind blows over the bones of the dead. You do not need to be an English scholar to know which way this wind blows. These ideas have sunk deep hooks into the hearts and minds of many Americans whether they are religious or not (Berlet 2008, 221–257; 2011).

Many Christians do not buy into this precise scenario—but millions—perhaps tens of millions in the United States alone—take seriously the possibility that the prophetic End Times are near. May think that the battles that rage in the Middle East might be part of the war between good and evil prophesied in the book of Revelation. And for that brand of Christianity, for Jesus Christ to return, Jews in Israel first must smash the Islamic sacred shrines atop a large hill in Jerusalem and rebuild the Temple of Solomon. Later chapters discuss this in detail.

Millennial expectation helps explain Trump's announcement that the United States was moving its embassy in Israel to Jerusalem. It is payback to the approximately 80 percent of White Christian Evangelicals who voted for Trump in the election (Lovett 2016). This courtship included the selection of Christian Right icon Mike Pence as Trump's Vice President running mate. Trump now plays simultaneously ping-pong with the brains of the leaders of the nation of Israel, American Jews who support that leadership, and apocalyptic Christians who think they get the last bloody laugh as a reward from God.

Pause here and consider that despite all of this, many Christians are allied with the struggle against the rhetoric of right-wing populism and neofascism in the United States. This is based on their readings of Biblical text (see for example Isaiah 10:1–2, Matthew 5:9). As Civil Rights Movement organizer and human rights activist Ruby Sales explains, there is a struggle within Christianity between those of us who pursue liberation and those that want to build empires (Sales 2004).

This struggle is not only going on in America. Now we see the formation of a global pan-Aryan alliance of religious nationalists who spread their exclusionary messages around the world on the internet. Their texts have influenced the perpetrators of mass killings from Norway to New Zealand. This is documented in an online collection featuring the older and current work of Berlet, Clarkson, Hardisty, Sales, and Scaminaci (2019).

Neofascism, tyranny, and Trump

Many of the earliest print articles and television reports calling Trump a "fascist" were rhetorical froth fed to an audience of Democrats and leftists who deserved better. Some pundits used outdated definitions, or even resuscitated the hoax quote attributed to Mussolini equating fascism with modern business corporations. MSNBC cable TV broadcasts especially pandered to stereotypes and myths on the Left.

Fascism is the most militant and violent form of right-wing populism. Most right-wing populist movements never develop into full-blown fascist movements. And most fascist movements fail in their bid to seize state power. Yet right-wing populist movements can terrorize whole sectors of a nation's population who have been scapegoated and labelled a threat to the "real people" of an imaginary nation Berlet and Lyons 2000).

"Imagined communities" is what Benedict Anderson called the development of the nation-state. All nations, then, are not only an "imagined political community" but the nation is seen as "both inherently limited and sovereign" (Benedict Anderson 1991, 5–7). That nationhood is not a fixed identify but a malleable process opens the door to the construction of exclusionary forms of national identity demanded not only by Right-wing populism in the United States, but also around the world (Mudde and Kaltwasser 2014; Kaltwasser, Taggart, Ochoa Espejo, Ostiguy, and Mudde 2017; Vatsov 2017 a, b.)

Fascism as a project launches a campaign to restore the "real people" of the nation to power; and the subjugation, expulsion, or murder of the people who do not belong. When this happens on a mass scale, we call it genocide. Roger Griffin is a British scholar who has written and edited numerous books and essays about fascism, terrorism, and apocalyptic beliefs. Griffin's compact definition of fascism has become one of the standards:

> [F]ascism is best defined as a revolutionary form of nationalism, one that sets out to be a political, social and ethical revolution, welding the "people" into a dynamic national community under new elites infused with heroic values. The core myth that inspires this project is that only a populist, trans-class movement of purifying, cathartic national rebirth (palingenesis) can stem the tide of decadence.
>
> *(Griffin 1991, xi)*

This catharsis comes after a period of decadence and moral decay. Fascism is a form of right-wing apocalypticism, which Vogelin noted as early as 1938.

Griffin adds that to "generate a populist mass movement" fascists use a "liturgical style of politics." the word "liturgical" in this sense means a public display of beliefs usually related to religious practices; but it also can be rooted in some existing cultural tradition of piety and seriousness. This form of a "political religion" is sometimes referred to as the "sacralisation of politics" Gentile 2008, 326–375; (Vondung 2008, 110–111; Berlet 2008: 221–257). This process was discussed by Vogelin as early as 1938.

Debunking popular myths about fascism

Fascism is not corporate power. As far as experts on fascism have been able to determine after decades of searching, the Italian fascist dictator Benito Mussolini never said or wrote that "Fascism should more properly be called corporatism, since it is the merger of state and corporate power." It is a fake quote (Skeptical Libertarian blog 2013, Snopes 2019)

Another example is a famous speech by the Soviet leader Georgi Dimitrov, who said "Comrades, fascism in power was correctly described by the Thirteenth Plenum of the Executive Committee of the Communist International *as the open terrorist dictatorship of the most reactionary, most chauvinistic and most imperialist elements of finance capital.* Many will quibble with that definition, but note that too many hyperbolic leftists in the United States leave out the phrase "**Fascism in power**."

As this book heads to the printing press, fascism is not yet in power in the United States is not a fascist nation. Furthermore, at the beginning of the speech Dimitrov credits the concept to Clara Fraser, a leading communist intellectual who wrote the original study of fascism for the communist leadership in 1933. Fraser described fascism as beginning as a mass movement. Many sociologists today would agree.

Canadian scholar Henry Giroux (2018) and American essayist Frank Rich meticulously chronicled where Trump's was leading us as a nation. Both thought the term "fascist was appropriate." Is Trump a full-blown fascist? Writing in late 2019 I think that fascism is being forged, but the project is as yet not complete. It would be a serious mistake, however, to *not* read the work of Rich, Giroux, and other scholars and activists analysing the current crisis of democracy in the United States. The potential for neofascism is real, and these and other analysts need to be consulted when forming an opinion. There are already too many murders being carried out—usually by right-wing male fanatics wound up by the conspiracy theory rhetoric of the US Right.

Trump is an authoritarian tyrant. These and other enemies of democracy have been studied over many years by professor Robert Altemeyer (he prefers just Dr. Bob). His research in the book *The Authoritarian Spector* (1996) forms the basis of his online series of analyses of Donald Trump as a quintessential authoritarian (2016-2019).

Trump is an authoritarian, but he is also building a mass base for fascism in the United States and encouraging bigots (including neofascists and neonazis) with his inflammatory rhetoric. There is little doubt that Trump is not conscious that he is doing that—but he is surrounded by people for whom preserving democracy is not their primary goal.

The issue for most of us in the United States is preserving democracy itself with resistance to tyranny and systems of oppression in their many forms. Ehrenreich in (1990) explained why the US middle class has a "Fear of Falling." This mirrors the anxiety of those in the middle classes in Germany who voted for Hitler (Fritzsche 1990, 1999). Hochschchild (2016) has written about the anger and sense of betrayal due to the fading American Dream among many who supported Trump. Judis (2016) covers the fear and anxiety of people facing economic stress. Kellner (2016) writes of the "American Nightmare: Donald Trump, Media Spectacle, and Authoritarian Populism." In 2017 van der Linden reviewed several of these books in an essay titled "Trump, Populism, Fascism, and the Road Ahead." In 2018

Stanley noted that higher education in the United States, which had historically been "a bulwark against authoritarianism," sometimes became its "pawn." How about a nice game of chess?

The future belongs to whom?

The collection of studies in this book is an effort to document how the Republican Party over several decades has been eviscerating constitutional freedoms and basic human rights in the United States of America: from Reagan to Alt-Right. It is based on the right-wing conspiracy theory that collectivism in *any* form leads to tyranny and fascism. The result is the undermining of a government's role in weaving a social safety net, common in other industrialized nations. Elements of neofascism have slipped through the holes in that net and into the heartland fields and office towers of the United States.

The election of Trump as President of the United States was prefaced in part by Republican Party alliances since World War II—both overt and covert—with immigrant European Fascist and Nazi collaborators with their theories of White supremacy (Bellant 1991a, 1991b; Berlet and Sklar 1990); neo-Nazis and Klansmen during the Civil Rights era (Mason 2009, Berlet and Mason 2015); and White nationalists and antisemites during the Reagan years (Bellant 1991a, 1991b).

Under President Reagan, and in the name of anticommunism, some Republicans spawned death squads and the "Dirty Wars" in Central and South America to crush collectivism and restore "Free Markets" These forms of US anticommunism were justified in part by the theories of Reagan's favorite economic theorists: Ludwig von Mises, Friedrich August von Hayek, and University of Chicago icon Milton Fried-man. These economists are generously described as reactionaries. As an advisor to the Pinochet Regime in Chile, Friedman looked the other way as thousands of suspected leftists were imprisoned or killed—which even drew a rebuke from British Prime Minister Margaret Thatcher (Berlet 2017).

Trump's alliance with Alt-Right was not an aberration but a reverberation. There is still today a wing of the Republican Party that believes straight, White, Christian men should rule America with an iron hand and a closed fist.

Some of the key architects of this regressive restorationist project (William F. Buckley, Jr., Patrick Buchanan, Paul Weyrich, Connie Marshner, William Marshner) have all celebrated the authoritarian regime of Spain's Francisco Franco—a Catholic integralist who built a right-wing coalition that included not just authoritarians but also fascists and supporters of Hitler.

In the 1970s Weyrich and the Marshners sent young Catholic conservatives from the United States to a training center in Spain where they sat in classrooms with portraits of Spain's notorious Nazi collaborator General Francisco Franco on the wall. Part of the studies included learning about alleged leftist-socialist-communist conspiracies. (Author Berlet interview in 2018 with a source who attended the training over 20 years ago). Alt-Right icon Steve Bannon was influenced by Francoist Catholics such as Christian Right ideologs Paul Weyrich and Connie and

William Marshner. Now Steve Bannon is planning a new international study center to train right-wing Christian cadre and their allies.

The rise of Christian Right evangelical movements of the 1970s created a need to sanitize the White supremacist and antisemitic conspiracy theories of the Christian evangelical movements of the early 1900s. Christian fundamentalists also needed to reframe their anti-science histrionics exposed in the Scopes Monkey Trial. This was the task of the New Christian Right which was built in the 1970s. The White nationalism and antisemitism of some leaders of the New Christian Right was hardly a secret, but building a broad coalition necessitated keeping these views in the closet, even after they were repeatedly exposed.

Conspiracy theories, toxic rhetoric, and violence

President Trump denounces a nebulous conspiracy of a "Deep State" against core American values. The alleged conspirators are named daily on AM talk radio, and Fox News. Millions of evangelicals in certain churches across America know the enemies of America: abortionists, homosexuals, and other gender traitors. Far too many Trump acolytes defame and attack Muslims, Mexicans, socialists, liberals, and the Democratic Party as part of a vast conspiracy. This creates more targets for abuse and violence.

The social science linking Trump's vicious conspiracist rhetoric to actual assaults and murderous attacks was first developed in the period following the Nazi genocide of Jews as well as many other targets of lethal scapegoating—not just in Germany but across Europe (Allport 1954). Today we know the process involves three steps:

1. Publicly circulated the destabilizing **"Narratives of Insecurity"** (Affendi 2015)
2. Which public leaders exploit using the rhetoric of **"Scripted Violence"** (Berlet 2014)
3. Producing Unpredictable Acts of violent **"Stochastic Terrorism"** (Hamm & Spaaij 2017)

Fantastic and false anticommunist conspiracy theories about US liberals and the Democratic Party are circulated by Trump supporters individually and in their mass media. Anti-Communist movements trace back to attempts to crush labor unions in the late 1800s and early 1900s. We should not forget that the Ku Klux Klan—an organization built by White Christian men—experienced a substantial growth spurt during the Civil Right Era in the 1960s (Cunnigham 2013) This period saw a reign of terror and murder, primarily aimed at Black people, but also a few White allies.

Aho (2016) in a study of the sociology of "American Religion and Politics" refers to the resurgence of right-wing "patriot" and "militia" groups as pursuing a "Far Right Fantasy." Robert P. Jones, who runs the Public Religion Research Institute, is one of many folks who respect religious beliefs and who welcome

"The End of White Christian America" (2016) as our nation becomes more diverse and unfair power is equalized.

Step back with me to the year 1965. A Black civil rights activist Ruby Sales was with an integrated group doing voter registrations of Black citizens in the South when a man with a shotgun pointed it at her. A brief moment before the gunman pulled the trigger a White northern Episcopal seminarian stepped in front of the 17-year-old Sales, took the blast, and fell dead at her feet. Jonathan Daniels is recognized as a hero in his home state of New Hampshire. It took months for Sales to recover from the shock, but when she did, she enrolled at the same Episcopal Divinity School in Cambridge, Massachusetts attended by Daniels. I met Sales there when speaking to a class. For over a decade have worked together trying to heal the wounds caused by right-wing bigots. Sales has spent her life helping to heal what hurts people in our divided nation (On Being 2017). Do not dare to falsely assume I think religion—any religion—is the cause of our decaying democracy in the United States of America.

Many of the contemporary conspiracy theories are adaptations of scurrilous lies utilized by Fascist and Nazi movements in Europe drawing from the historic poisoned wells of ancient antisemitic conspiracy theories. Millions of Jews died. The modern prototype of these lies trace back to the antisemitic hoax manuscript *The Protocols of the Elders of Zion* concocted in the early 1900s. Now the text of the Protocols and a plethora of fake antisemitic claims scurry across the internet in electronic packets of lethal vitriol.

Neofascism remains woefully undertheorized, even by scholars. Too many celebrated pundits still skip the last thirty years of social science in their glib outdated sketches of right-wing populism and fascism. Too many influential public intellectuals and journalists still rely on flawed and outdated language blaming "extremists" and "hate groups" instead of focusing on structural inequalities in a nation based on unfair hierarchies of power in which we are all complicit. We need a new vocabulary that holds *all of us* accountable for systems of oppression.

Author Matthew Lyons argues that the concept of fascism as a right-wing revolutionary force means we are facing in the United States a "three-way fight" in which progressive forces need to challenge both fascist movements and rapacious forms of greedster capitalism (2018, 260–261). But Lyons explains that this "theoretical model ... only approximates reality. There are more than three sides in the struggle, and to understand the different forces and their interrelationships, we have a lot more work to do."

Defending democracy and human rights

As the first chapter in this book explains, the current process of deconstructing democracy in the United States began with William F. Buckley, Jr. in the 1950s (Himmelstein 1990; Diamond 1995). It wasn't until the election of Ronald Reagan as President in 1980 that this goal scored its first real national success. To achieve this, long-range political strategist worked with savvy and patient grassroots organizations.

In recent years Republican elected officials and political activists have replaced the American Bar Association with the right-wing Federalist Society in vetting judges for the federal court systems (Avery and McLaughlin 2013). The packed judicial system in an alliance with conservatives in the US Congress now oversee the dismantling of the progressive reforms most industrialized nations regard as providing for the necessities of life—considered to be basic human rights by the United Nations (United Nations: Human Rights 2018). As this is happening our environment is being plundered to enrich a handful of elites in a way that will soon render our planet toxic to our continued survival—assuming we can outrace the rising seas. Greed is *not* good.

Monocausal explanations of the rise of Trump that do not factor in hierarchies of race and gender and class are incomplete. We must dig deeper, we must look back to the worst ideas and actions of those in our land who support—even unconsciously—the myriad systems of oppression in the United States since its founding—social, cultural, political, economic. There is no fixed "political center." Forces championing liberation or empire constantly struggle to move the normative values and goals of society in their direction (Sales 2004). Those favoring democracy and human rights appear in leadership roles throughout US history: Douglass 1857; Hamer 1964; Reagon 1983).

In the ostensible millenarian year 2000, Matthew N. Lyons and I saw our book *Right-Wing Populism in America: Too Close for Comfort* published. The subtitle showed that we were worried that democracy in the Unites States was being destabilized by right-wing social and political movements. Now their sock puppet is in the White House. Justice and democracy itself continue to erode. Resistance is *not* futile.

In 1853, Theodore Parker, a Unitarian minister in the United States, called for the abolition of slavery, claiming this pulled history in an ark toward freedom, human rights, and democracy for all. Parker said "I cannot calculate the curve and complete the figure by the experience of sight; I can divine it by conscience. But from what I see I am sure it bends towards justice."

Parker had great foresight. Slavery in the United States was abolished in 1865, but only after a bloody Civil War. The Rev Dr Martin Luther King, Jr picked up this theme in several speeches when he said, "the arc of the moral universe is long, but it bends toward justice" (1965, 1967).

"Power concedes nothing without a demand," Frederick Douglass told us in 1857. As this book is published, the arc of history in the United States is being yanked backwards away from justice and toward the restoration of unfair hierarchies of privilege and power based on race, gender, class, and more.

All of us who value democracy and human rights must demand the fulfilment of the many promises made in the name of America as a nation that seeks to be great.

The time to settle unpaid debts is at hand.

AFTERWORD

Defending democracy itself

Chip Berlet and Bill Fletcher, Jr.

We first worked together over a decade ago when planning a presentation on the rise of the Right in the United States for a national meeting of a labor union of government employees. We realized that over several decades we had ended up on the same page of ideological, and historical analysis. Well, we were not *exactly* on the same page... More like in the same chapter. This was true because we come from different political backgrounds and affiliations, as well as different experiences growing up in a nation where the promises of democracy have never been fulfilled.

We also shared a sense of foreboding. We knew we were not alone in this growing fear of falling into an abyss. This metaphoric abyss was swallowing democracy itself and replacing it with authoritarian rule protecting an enriched elite in both political parties. These smug elites were stuffing their wallets with cash as they picked the pockets of most residents in the United States.

In late 2017 we made a major presentation near Washington, DC to progressive labor activists. The subject was Right-wing populism, White nationalism, authoritarianism, and the harbingers of fascism circling the Trump Administration like vultures as our nation was sickening into a fever of chaos we could not predict. And we were scared. While we had studied the past, we could not predict the future. All of us in the room were scared and frustrated by our realization that even at this late date, far too many powerful leaders in the union and workers' rights movements shared neither our analysis nor our fears.

Prior to the Presidential election of 2016, we met in Brooklyn, New York at a venue where the owner considered herself progressive and that housed progressive and radical Left groups. We warned that the election of a preening megalomaniac named Donald Trump might become President (Fletcher and Berlet 2016). A few months later we were dismayed when the "progressive" owner of the venue invited a notorious antisemite to speak on the same political crisis we had addressed.

"Things Fall Apart" wrote Yeats in 1919 from the perspective of a reactionary Christian in the chaotic period in Europe after World War One. Yeats was longing to restore unfair power and privilege and warned that "the centre cannot hold:"

> the best lack all conviction, while the worst
> Are full of passionate intensity.
> Surely some revelation is at hand;

We do not know what will be revealed next. We rejoin a struggle as part of a united front to defend democracy. We do so with a sense of hope and a fierce commitment to justice, democracy, and human rights that perish without each other. In 1964 the Reverend Martin Luther King, Jr. reframed a message first spread by the movement to abolish slavery in the United States in the mid-1800s. King told us that "the arc of the moral universe is long, but it bends toward justice" (King 1964; Parker 1853).

Reverend King, Rosa Parks, and many other activists in the Civil Rights Movement were trained at the Highlander Education and Research Center. Founded in 1932 in the segregated South, the Highlander campus is now located in the southern state of Tennessee. Highlander teaches activists theories of radical liberation from cultural, political, and economic systems of oppression. In September 2017 the Center celebrated its 85th anniversary at its rural campus. In March 2019 Highlander's library and archive building was firebombed and burnt to the ground by White supremacists, who left their symbols behind as a warning (Kelley and Themba 2019).

What the authors in this collection know is that while "the arc of the moral universe...bends toward justice," it is because millions of hands over many centuries have struggled together in united efforts to grab that damn arc and bend it unceasingly toward a better future, because we know that without justice there can be no peace.

POSTSCRIPT[1]

Those who profess to favor freedom and yet depreciate agitation, are people who want crops without ploughing the ground; they want rain without thunder and lightning; they want the ocean without the roar of its many waters. The struggle may be a moral one, or it may be a physical one, or it may be both. But it must be a struggle. Power concedes nothing without a demand. It never did and it never will.

> Frederick Douglass, "An address on West India Emancipation."
> August 3, 1857, Canandaigua, New York

---

1 Editor's note: several versions of this text are in circulation. This version was transcribed by the editor of this collection from the original pamphlet edited and published by Douglass in Rochester, New York. Note several versions in books and websites have a minor error; the original word used by Douglass is "depreciate" not "deprecate." A facsimile of the typed speech is available at the Library of Congress; https://www.loc.gov/resource/mfd.21023/?st=gallery/.

    See a useful overview at https://freedomcenter.org/voice/civil–rights–america/. Also note the speech was delivered in Canandaigua, New York, a popular spot for large gatherings to hear speakers a few miles south of Rochester, NY.

SELECTED ORGANIZATIONS WITH RESOURCES

Anti-Defamation League is one of the oldest US organizations collecting and publishing information on the denigration of and attacks on individuals and institutions targeted by bigots.

- https://www.adl.org/—Their "Hate Symbol Database" is extremely useful.
- https://www.adl.org/education-and-resources/resource-knowledge-base

Center for Media and Democracy hosts a collection of related websites from the perspective of activists working for democracy and human rights. These resources are filled with information useful to researchers.

- https://www.prwatch.org/
- https://www.exposedbycmd.org/
- https://www.alecexposed.org/wiki/ALEC_Exposed
- https://www.sourcewatch.org/index.php?title=SourceWatch

Center for the Study of Hate and Extremism is based at the University of California at Santa Barbara. The director is professor Brian Levin who has decades of experience and is frequently a consultant to various government agencies and committees of the US Congress.
https://csbs.csusb.edu/hate-and-extremism-center/

Facing History and Ourselves was founded as a resource center for teachers using a curriculum on the history and nature of genocide. This organization has created an amazing array of materials that cross many topical issues and current events:

- Main website: https://www.facinghistory.org/

- For teachers and researchers: https://www.facinghistory.org/educator-resources/.

People for the American Way publishes a plethora of information about the US Christian Right and other right-wing movements.

- Main Website: http://www.pfaw.org/
- PFAW also has a lively blogsite at: http://www.pfaw.org/blog/.

Political Research Associates is a social justice think tank that since 1981 has produced investigative research and analysis on the U.S. Right to support social justice advocates and defend human rights. PRA has a long history of studying the Christian Right, White Nationalism, Heteropatriarchy and the Patriot and Militia movements. Their expertise helps journalists, advocates, educators, scholars, and the public to understand and challenge the Right-wing. PRA produces investigative reports, articles, and activist resource kits; publishes the quarterly magazine *The Public Eye*; advises policy makers and social justice advocates; and offers expert commentary for media outlets.

PRA's core issue areas over many decades include:

- Civil liberties: https://www.politicalresearch.org/search/node?keys=civil+liberties
- Economic justice: https://www.politicalresearch.org/research/economic-justice
- Gender and reproductive justice: https://www.politicalresearch.org/research/gender-and-reproductive-justice
- LGBTQ Rights: https://www.politicalresearch.org/research/lgbtqi-justice
- Racial and Immigrant justice: https://www.politicalresearch.org/research/racial-and-immigrant-justice
- A full alphabetical list of current PRA research areas is here: https://www.politicalresearch.org/research
- Much of PRA's huge collection of older printed matter is available to researchers at the Tufts University Special Collections:
- https://dl.tufts.edu/concern/eads/r207v060m

Note that there is an additional cache of Right-wing periodicals from the former **Institute for First Amendment Studies** at this library archive:
https://dl.tufts.edu/concern/eads/k0698j74x

Public Eye Magazine: Vol. 1, No. 1 through Vol. 6. Published by The Public Eye Network
https://www.publiceyenetwork.us/
Public Eye Magazine: Vol. 7 No.1 and forward. Published by Political Research Associates
https://www.politicalresearch.org/public-eye-magazine/

Southern Poverty Law Center publishes study guides, and a multitude of other research resources for defending human rights.
https://www.splcenter.org/

Specializing in scholarly research

Selected groups studying right-wing movements

Bard Center for the Study of Hate. Run by Kenneth Stern, author of *A Force upon the Plain: The American Militia Movement and the Politics of Hate*. Stern has been studying and opposing Right-wing movements for decades.

Berkeley Center for Right-Wing Studies at the University of California is run by professor Lawrence Rosenthal. The Center holds conferences, schedules speakers, and is developing a new field of scholarship. https://crws.berkeley.edu/. The Center also has access to the research archive of the ground-breaking author Sara Diamond.

Center for Radical Right Analysis is an international group of reliable scholars that collect and disseminate information on racist and other anti-democratic Right-wing groups around the world.
https://www.radicalrightanalysis.com/

Hate Studies – An International Network
https://internationalhatestudies.com/category/extremism/
In the United States: The Gonzaga Institute for Hate Studies
https://www.gonzaga.edu/academics/centers-institutes/institute-for-hate-studies

Note that Political Research Associates (listed above) frequently runs original studies by scholars in its *Public Eye Magazine*.
https://www.politicalresearch.org/public-eye-magazine

Additional research resources can be found in a number of archives around the United States, especially:

Historical Society of Wisconsin is located on the campus of the University of Wisconsin. Now retired, librarian Jim Danky collected numerous right-wing periodicals:
https://www.wisconsinhistory.org/Records/Article/CS4082

Wilcox Collection of Contemporary Political Movements
University of Kansas:
https://kuscholarworks.ku.edu/handle/1808/21350

Studying male supremacism

Center for the Study of Men and Masculinities, Stony Brook University
https://www.stonybrook.edu/commcms/csmm/

Institute for Research on Male Supremacism
https://www.malesupremacism.org/

Model Campus-based Center, University of Massachusetts
https://www.umass.edu/masculinities/about/workshops-events

INDEX